The
Happiness
Trap

ALSO BY RUSS HARRIS

ACT with Love: Stop Struggling, Reconcile Differences, and Strengthen Your Relationship with Acceptance and Commitment Therapy

The Confidence Gap: The Guide to Overcoming Fear and Self-Doubt

The Illustrated Happiness Trap: How to Stop Struggling and Start Living

When Life Hits Hard: How to Transcend Grief, Crisis, and Loss with Acceptance and Commitment Therapy

The Happiness Trap

How to Stop Struggling
and Start Living

Second Edition

RUSS HARRIS

SHAMBHALA

Shambhala Publications, Inc.
2129 13th Street
Boulder, Colorado 80302
www.shambhala.com

Published by arrangement with Exisle Publishing Pty Ltd,
Chatswood, NSW, Australia.

Disclaimer: This book is a general guide only and should never
be a substitute for the skill, knowledge, and experience of a qualified
medical or mental health professional. The author, publisher, and their
distributors are not responsible for any adverse effects or consequences
resulting from the use of the information in this book.

Cover design: Daniel Urban-Brown and Kate Huber-Parker
Interior design: Kate Huber-Parker

9 8 7 6 5 4 3 2 1
Second Edition

Printed in the United States of America

Shambhala Publications makes every effort
to print on acid-free, recycled paper.

Shambhala Publications is distributed worldwide by
Penguin Random House, Inc., and its subsidiaries.

Library of Congress Cataloging-in-Publication Data
Names: Harris, Russ, 1962– author.
Title: The happiness trap: how to stop struggling and start living /
Russ Harris.
Description: [Second edition]. | Boulder, Colorado: Shambhala, 2022. |
Includes bibliographical references and index.
Identifiers: LCCN 2021050378 | ISBN 9781645471165 (trade paperback)
Subjects: LCSH: Happiness.
Classification: LCC BF575.H27 H375 2022 | DDC 152.4/2—dc23/eng/20211109
LC record available at https://lccn.loc.gov/2021050378

DEDICATION

To my sibs: Adrian, Darrell, Yulanie, and Quentin. There's an old saying: "Families are like branches on a tree. We grow in different directions, yet our roots remain as one." Thank you for all the love and joy and kindness and laughter you bring into my life.

Contents

PART THREE

HOW TO MAKE LIFE MEANINGFUL

What's New in Edition Two?

When I set out to write the second edition of this book (sixteen years after the first one), I was expecting it to be a quick job; just a few minor changes here and there. But I quickly realized the book needed a major overhaul from start to end. When I eventually finished the task, I was surprised to find over 50 percent of the book was new material! I guess that reflects just how much has changed over the years in the way I think about, talk about, and practice this stuff.

Among many other changes, I've added in a lot of new tools, techniques, and exercises; new information about the nature and purpose of emotions (and how to overcome emotional numbness); many new topics and chapters, including how to break bad habits, push through procrastination, stop panic attacks, disrupt worrying and obsessing, deal with values conflicts and difficult dilemmas, overcome "people-pleasing" and perfectionism; practical tips for those experiencing the effects of trauma; and last but definitely not least, a stack of new material on self-compassion.

On top of all that, I've chopped out a whole lot of waffle, repetition, and technical jargon. So if you liked the first edition, I hope and trust you'll get a whole lot more out of this one.

Happy reading,
All the best,

Russ Harris

PART ONE

WHY IS IT HARD TO BE HAPPY?

[1]

Life Is Difficult

Being human hurts. In our short time on this planet, we'll have many moments of marvel, wonder, and joy—but also many of angst, dread, and despair. We'll know the highs of love, connection, and friendship—but also the lows of loneliness, rejection, and loss. We'll experience the delights of success, victory, and achievement—but also the miseries of failure, defeat, and disappointment.

In other words: life is difficult. And if we live long enough, we're all going to experience pain, stress, and suffering in many different forms. The problem is most of us don't know how to deal effectively with this reality. We work hard to find happiness—but all too often, we fail; and even when we succeed, it's usually short-lived, leaving us dissatisfied and wanting more.

So why is it so hard to be happy? I'm glad you asked. This book is based on a huge body of scientific research that shows we all easily get caught in a powerful psychological trap. We go through life holding on tightly to many unhelpful beliefs about happiness—ideas widely accepted because "everyone knows they are true." And these beliefs seem to make good sense— which is why you encounter them in so many self-help books and articles. But unfortunately, these misleading ideas tend to create a vicious cycle in which the more we pursue happiness, the more we suffer. And this psychological trap is so well hidden, we don't even realize we're caught in it.

That's the bad news.

The good news is there's hope. We can learn how to quickly recognize we're stuck in "the happiness trap"—and, more importantly, how to escape it. This book will give you the skills and knowledge to do so. It's based on a powerful psychological model known as Acceptance and

Commitment Therapy (ACT), a science-based approach with over 3000 published studies that show its effectiveness.

ACT (pronounced as the word *act*) was developed in the United States in the mid-1980s by psychologist Steven C. Hayes and his colleagues Kelly Wilson and Kirk Strosahl. Since that time, it has spread around the globe. Today there are hundreds of thousands of psychologists, therapists, counselors, coaches, and doctors practicing ACT in dozens of different countries—from the United States, United Kingdom, and Uganda to India, Indonesia, and Iran.

One reason for the growing popularity of ACT is that it's astoundingly effective in helping people with a wide range of problems. Those three thousand scientific studies I mentioned earlier cover everything from depression, addiction, and anxiety disorders to psychosis, chronic pain, and trauma. However, ACT is not just a treatment for psychological disorders; it is also used to help people adjust well to chronic illness and disability, and build meaningful, rewarding lives even in the face of serious ongoing health issues. And on top of all that, it's widely used by the armed forces, emergency services, government departments, professional sports teams and Olympic athletes, businesses, hospitals, and schools—to enhance health and well-being, reduce stress, improve performance, and increase resilience.

Last but not least, we all know about the importance of eating healthy food, exercising regularly, and cultivating good relationships with others; these are foundational building blocks for health, happiness, and well-being. But how hard is it to *actually do* these things on an ongoing basis? Easy in theory, hard in practice, for most of us. Fortunately, ACT gives us all the tools and strategies we need to break bad habits, overcome procrastination, motivate ourselves to start and maintain healthy new behaviors, and build better relationships with the people in our life. Shortly we'll look at how ACT achieves this, but first let's consider . . .

Is Happiness Normal?

Life is not fair. Some people have horrific childhoods where they've been abused, neglected, or abandoned by their caregivers, whereas others grow up in loving, supportive families. Some live in extreme poverty or areas rife with violent crime, or in war zones, prisons, or refugee camps. Others live in good housing conditions with excellent amenities. Some have serious illnesses, injuries, or disabilities, whereas others have glowing health. Some have access to good quality food, education, justice, medical treatment, welfare, travel, entertainment, and career opportunities, whereas others are deprived of most or all of these things. And some people—because of their skin color, religion, gender, politics, or sexual orientation—are continually subjected to prejudice, discrimination, or victimization. In any country in the world, there's a vast gulf between the least and most privileged members of society. And yet . . . people on both sides of that gulf are human and therefore have many things in common, including the fact that no matter how privileged or disadvantaged we may be, we are all naturally predisposed to psychological suffering.

Perhaps you've noticed how the self-help sections of bookstores keep growing larger. Depression, anxiety, anger, divorce, relationship issues, addictions, trauma, low self-esteem, loneliness, grief, stress, lack of confidence—if you can name it, there's a book on it. And with every passing year, psychologists, coaches, counselors, and therapists steadily increase in number—as do prescriptions for medication. Meanwhile, on the television and radio, in magazines and newspapers, in podcasts and social media, the "experts" bombard us with nonstop advice on how to improve our lives. And yet—even with all this support and advice, human misery is growing, not declining!

The statistics are staggering. The World Health Organization (WHO) identifies depression as one of the biggest, most costly, and most debilitating diseases in the world. In any given year, one-tenth of the adult population lives with clinical depression, and one in five will suffer from it at some point in their life. And more than one-third of the adult population will, at some point in their life, suffer from an anxiety disorder. Furthermore, one in four adults will at some stage suffer from drug or alcohol addiction. (In the United States alone, there are currently over fourteen million people with alcoholism!)

But here's the most shocking statistic of all: almost one in two people will at some point seriously consider suicide—and struggle with it for two weeks or more. Scarier still, one in ten people will at some point actually attempt to kill themselves. (Fortunately, very few succeed.)

Think about those numbers for a moment. Think of your friends, family, and coworkers. Almost half of them will at some point be so overwhelmed by misery that they seriously contemplate suicide—and one in ten will try it!

Now think about all those common forms of suffering that are not considered to be "psychological disorders" but nonetheless make us miserable: work stress, performance anxiety, loneliness, relationship conflicts, sickness, divorce, bereavement, injury, aging, poverty, racism, sexism, bullying, existential angst, self-doubt, insecurity, fear of failure, perfectionism, low self-esteem, "midlife crisis," "impostor syndrome," jealousy, fear of missing out, a lack of direction in life . . . and the list goes on.

Clearly, lasting happiness is not normal! Which naturally begs the question . . .

Why Is It So Hard to Be Happy?

To answer this question, let's journey back in time, three hundred thousand years. Life was pretty dangerous for our Stone Age ancestors: huge wolves, saber-toothed tigers, woolly mammoths, rival clans, harsh weather, food shortages, and cave bears, to name but a few of the perils. So if a Stone Age person wanted to survive, their mind had to be constantly on the lookout for things that might hurt or harm them! And if their mind wasn't good at this job, they died young. Therefore, the better our ancestors became at anticipating and avoiding danger, the longer they lived and the more children they had.

With each passing generation, the human mind became increasingly skilled at noticing, predicting, and avoiding danger. So now, three hundred thousand years later, our modern minds are constantly on the lookout, assessing and judging everything we encounter: Is this good or bad? Safe or dangerous? Harmful or helpful? These days, though, it's not tigers, bears, and wolves that our mind warns us about—it's losing our job, being rejected, getting a speeding ticket, embarrassing ourselves in public, getting cancer, or a million and one other common worries. As a result, we all spend a lot of time worrying about things that, more often than not, never happen.

Another essential for survival is belonging to a group. Our ancient ancestors knew this all too well. If your tribe boots you out, it won't be long before the wolves find you. So how does the mind protect you from rejection by the group? By comparing you with other members: Am I fitting in? Am I doing the right thing? Am I contributing enough? Am I as good as the others? Am I doing anything that might get me rejected?

Sound familiar? Our minds are continually warning us of rejection and comparing us to the rest of society. No wonder we spend so much energy worrying whether people will like us! No wonder we're always looking for ways to improve ourselves or putting ourselves down because we don't "measure up." We only need to glance at a magazine, television, or social media to instantly find a whole host of people who appear to be smarter, richer, slimmer, sexier, more famous, more powerful, or more successful than us. We then compare ourselves to these glamorous media creations and feel inferior or disappointed with our lives. To make matters worse, our minds can conjure up a fantasy image of the person we'd ideally like to be—and then compare us to that! What chance have we got? We will always end up feeling not good enough.

Now, in pretty much any society throughout the world in any period of history, the general rule for success is get more and get better. The better your weapons, the more food you can kill. The larger your food stores, the greater your chances for survival in times of scarcity. The better your shelter, the safer you are from danger. The more children you have, the greater the chance that some will survive into adulthood. No surprise, then, that our minds continually look for "more and better": more money, a better job, more status, a better body, more love, a better partner. And if we succeed, if we do get more money or a better car or a better-looking body, then we're satisfied—for a while. But sooner or later (and usually sooner), we end up wanting more.

In summary then, we are all hardwired to suffer psychologically: to compare, evaluate, and criticize ourselves; to focus on what we're lacking; to rapidly become dissatisfied with what we have; and to imagine all sorts of frightening scenarios, most of which will never happen. No wonder humans find it hard to be happy!

But to make matters worse, many popular beliefs about happiness are inaccurate, misleading, or false and will actually make you miserable if you buy into them. Let's look at two of the most common ones.

Myth 1: Happiness Is Our Natural State

Many people believe happiness is "our natural state." But the statistics above show very clearly, this is not the case. What *is* natural for human beings is to experience an ever-changing flow of emotions—both pleasant and painful—varying throughout the day depending on where we are, what we're doing, and what is happening. Our emotions, feelings, and sensations are like the weather: continually changing from moment to moment. We don't expect it to be warm and sunny all day long, all year round. Nor should we expect to be happy and joyful all day long. If we live a full human life, we will feel the full range of human emotions: the pleasant ones, like love and joy and curiosity, and the painful ones, like sadness, anger, and fear. All these feelings are a normal, natural part of being human.

Myth 2: If You're Not Happy, You're Defective

Following logically from myth 1, Western society assumes that psychological suffering is abnormal. It is seen as a weakness or illness, a product of a mind that is somehow faulty or defective. This means that when we do inevitably experience painful thoughts and feelings, we are often ashamed or embarrassed about it, or we criticize ourselves for being weak, silly, or immature.

ACT is based on a radically different assumption: if you're not happy, you're normal. Let's face it: life is tough and full of challenges; it would be weird if we felt happy all the time. The things that make life meaningful come with a whole range of feelings—both pleasant and painful. For example, consider a close relationship. When it's going well, we will experience wonderful feelings such as love and joy. But sooner or later, in even the best relationships, we will experience conflict, disappointment, and frustration. (There is no such thing as the perfect relationship.)

The same holds true for every meaningful project we embark on—from building a career or raising a family, to looking after our physical health and fitness. Although meaningful projects often bring feelings of excitement and enthusiasm, they also inevitably bring stress and anxiety. So if you believe myth 2, you're in big trouble, because it's virtually impossible to create a better life if you're not prepared to have some uncomfortable feelings. (The good news is, you will soon learn how to handle such feelings differently, to respond to them in a radically different way, so they have much less impact and influence over you.)

What Exactly Is "Happiness"?

Happiness. We want it. We crave it. We strive for it. But what exactly is it?

If you ask most people this question, they're likely to describe happiness as a "good feeling": a pleasurable feeling of joy, gladness, or contentment. The ancient Greeks had a special word for a life based on the pursuit of happy feelings: *hedemonia*, from which we get the word *hedonism* (seeking pleasure). We all enjoy pleasurable feelings, so it's hardly surprising that we chase them. However, like all human emotions, feelings of happiness are fleeting; they come and they go. No matter how hard we try to hold on to them, they never hang around for long. And as we shall see, a life spent in pursuit of "feeling good" is, in the long term, deeply unsatisfying. Indeed, research shows that the harder we chase after pleasurable feelings and try to avoid the uncomfortable ones, the more likely we are to suffer from depression and anxiety.

But there's another meaning of happiness that's radically different: the experience of living a rich and meaningful life. When we clarify what we stand for in life and start acting accordingly—behaving like the sort of person we really want to be, doing the things that matter deep in our hearts, moving in life directions we consider worthy—then our lives become infused with meaning and purpose, and we experience a profound sense of vitality. This is not some fleeting feeling—it is a powerful sense of a life well lived. The ancient Greek word for this type of happiness is *eudemonia*, these days often translated as "flourishing." When we live our lives in this way, we will, for sure, have many pleasurable feelings; and we'll also have many difficult ones, like sorrow, anxiety, and guilt. (As I said before, if we live a full human life, we will feel the full range of human emotions.)

This book, as you've no doubt guessed, focuses on this second meaning of happiness rather than the first. Of course, we all like to feel good, and it makes sense to appreciate and enjoy pleasant feelings when they appear. But if we try to have them all the time, we're doomed to failure.

The reality is: life is difficult. There's no escaping this fact. Sooner or later, we will all grow infirm, get sick, and die. Sooner or later, we will all lose important relationships through rejection, separation, or death. Sooner or later, we will all come face-to-face with crisis, disappointment, and failure. This means that in one form or another, we are all going to experience plenty of painful thoughts and feelings.

But the good news is that, although we can't avoid such pain, we can learn to handle it much better—to "unhook" from it, rise above it, and create a life worth living. This book will teach you some simple but effective skills to rapidly take the impact out of painful thoughts, feelings, emotions, sensations, and memories. You'll learn how to drain away their power, so they no longer hold you back or bring you down; how to let them come and go, without getting swept away by them. And you'll also learn how to build yourself a rich and meaningful life—no matter what you've been through in the past, or what you're facing right now—which will give rise to a deep sense of vitality and fulfillment.

Now pause for a moment and notice how your mind is reacting to this.

Is it positive, enthusiastic, excited, hopeful, optimistic? If so, enjoy that while it lasts—but please don't cling to it; because as we'll see later, trying to hold on tightly to pleasant thoughts and feelings creates all sorts of problems.

On the other hand, perhaps your mind is doubtful or pessimistic, saying things like, "This won't work for me" or "I don't believe this; it's bullshit." If so, recognize such thoughts are completely natural; this is your mind doing its job, trying to save you from something that might be unpleasant or painful. How so? Well, suppose you invest lots of time, effort, and energy in reading this book and applying it in your life; suppose you do all that and *it doesn't work*! That would be pretty painful, right? So your mind is trying to save you from that painful possibility. And throughout this book, you can expect your mind to do this in many ways. So each time that happens, I hope you'll remember two things:

1. This is completely normal; all minds do this.
2. Your mind isn't trying to make your life harder; it's just trying to keep you safe, protect you from pain.

The Journey Ahead

This book is like a trip through a foreign country: much will seem strange and new. Other things will seem familiar yet somehow subtly different. At times you may feel challenged or confronted, at other times excited or amused. Take your time on this journey. Instead of rushing ahead, savor it fully. Pause when you find something stimulating, curious, or unusual. Explore it in depth and learn as much as you can. To create a life worth living is a major undertaking, so please take the time to appreciate it.

[2]

The Choice Point

Have you ever wondered why we're called "human beings"? I think a better name would be "human doings," because whether it's eating, drinking, cooking, cleaning, talking, walking, playing, or reading, we're always doing something (even if it's just sleeping).

At times, we do things that help us move toward the sort of life we want; let's call these behaviors "toward moves." And at other times, we do things that take us *away* from the sort of life we want; let's call these behaviors "away moves."

The diagram below illustrates this.

Away

Things I do that take me away from the life I want to build

Toward

Things I do that take me toward the life I want to build

Toward Moves

When we're behaving like the sort of person we want to be, responding effectively to our challenges, and doing things that make life better in the long term, we're doing "toward moves." For many people, toward moves include spending quality time with loved ones, keeping fit and looking after their physical health, being caring and kind toward others, pursuing hobbies or interests, having fun, playing sports, relaxing, being creative, getting out into nature, contributing actively to their group or community, or doing personal growth activities (such as reading this book).

There is no list of "right," "correct," or "best" toward moves; we each decide for ourselves which of our behaviors come under this umbrella. Basically, toward moves are things you say and do—no matter how small they may be—that enhance your life; that make it richer, fuller, and more meaningful. And one of the main aims of this book is to help you do a whole lot more of them.

Away Moves

When we're behaving *unlike* the sort of person we want to be, doing things that keep us stuck or make life worse in the long term, we're doing "away moves." For example, for many people, away moves include withdrawing from or fighting with loved ones, avoiding physical exercise, putting unhealthy substances into their body, losing their temper, being aggressive or unkind, procrastinating on really important tasks, and so on. Away moves can also include things we do inside our heads (technically known as "cognitive processes") such as worrying, ruminating, obsessing, and overanalyzing. (*Ruminating* means "dwelling on, brooding on, or stewing over things.")

In other words, away moves are things we say and do that make our lives worse, keep us stuck, exacerbate our problems, inhibit our growth, negatively impact our relationships, or impair our health and well-being in the long term. They are things we ideally want to reduce or stop doing—and another big aim of this book is to help you do a whole lot less of them.

As with toward moves, there's no "official list" of away moves; we all decide for ourselves which of our behaviors fit this category. For example, if someone has strong religious beliefs that prohibit alcohol, then *that individual* might see drinking alcohol as an away move. But if someone is a professional wine taster, then *that individual* might see drinking alcohol as a toward move. *For myself*, drinking wine in moderation (two or three glasses a week) is a toward move, but drinking an entire bottle in one night is an away move; however, *for you*, those amounts might be very different.

A Very Important Point

The point I am about to make is so important, I am considering getting it tattooed on my forehead (in bold red capitals). Here it is:

Any activity can be a toward move or an away move, depending on the situation.

Let's unpack that. Suppose I stay in bed and keep hitting the snooze button primarily to avoid dealing with some really important tasks—*for me,* that would be an away move. (It might not be an away move for someone else; but it would be for me.) However, on vacation, when I hit the snooze to enjoy the well-earned pleasure of a long sleep-in—*for me,* that's a toward move. Yet for someone else, that might *not* be a toward move. Some people like to get up at the crack of dawn on vacation and go for a run or do a yoga workout, and they see sleeping in as wasting the day. (I'm not entirely sure which planet these people come from. They claim to be from Earth, but I find that hard to believe.)

Likewise, if I'm mentally rehearsing a talk while sitting in my office during work hours, as part of my preparation for a workshop or webinar—I consider that a toward move. But suppose I'm mentally rehearsing that talk when I'm at home while someone I love is trying to tell me something very important—and as a result, I'm disengaged and not really paying attention to them, and they're getting upset about it. In this situation, I'd consider mental rehearsal to be an away move. (Confession: the above example is not purely hypothetical; I have been guilty of doing this on, well, let's say, "more than one" occasion. And trust me: it's always an away move!)

For one last example, imagine canceling a social event at the last minute. Suppose you were doing this in order to cope with a medical emergency (e.g., taking a sick friend to the hospital); in that situation, I'm guessing you'd consider it a toward move. Now suppose you're very lonely and socially isolated, and you've gotten into the habit of canceling whenever you feel anxious, and each time you do that, it increases your sense of loneliness. In that particular situation, if you cancel yet again because you're feeling anxious, I'm guessing you'd call it an away move.

It's essential to understand this principal because it underpins everything in this book; the technical name for it is *workability*. If what you're doing in a particular situation is helping you move closer toward the life you want to build, we say it's "workable" (a toward move); but if it's having the opposite effect, we say it's "unworkable" (an away move). And only *you* can ever decide whether something is workable for *you*.

What Triggers Away Moves?

When life isn't too difficult, when things are going reasonably well and we're feeling pretty good, it's often quite easy to choose toward moves. But how often is your life like that? The reality, for most of us, is that life is frequently hard. And all too often, we *don't* get what we want. We continually run up against unexpected problems and challenging situations. We repeatedly experience painful emotions, such as anxiety, sadness, anger, loneliness, or guilt. We have countless unhelpful thoughts: "I'm not good enough," "I can't cope," "It's not fair," "I'm a loser," "It's all too hard," "Life sucks!" (and zillions of variants on these themes). And on top of all that, we often have to contend with strong urges or cravings, painful memories, and a myriad of unpleasant physical sensations. Throughout this book I will use the phrase "difficult thoughts and feelings" as an umbrella term for all these unpleasant inner experiences.

When these difficult situations, thoughts, and feelings show up in our life, we may respond to them either with toward moves or away moves, as illustrated below.

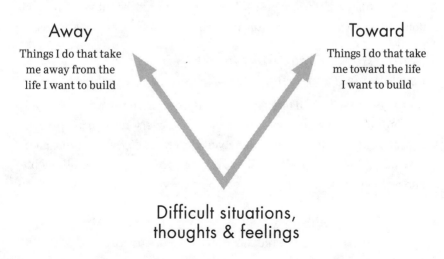

Away

Things I do that take
me away from the
life I want to build

Toward

Things I do that take
me toward the life
I want to build

Difficult situations,
thoughts & feelings

Now unfortunately, when difficult thoughts and feelings arise, we easily get "hooked" by them—much like a fish on the end of a line. We get hooked in two main ways that usually overlap with each other. Let's call these "OBEY mode" and "STRUGGLE mode."

OBEY Mode

In OBEY mode, our thoughts and feelings dominate us; they command our full attention or dictate our actions. When we OBEY our thoughts and feelings, we either give them so much attention that we can't usefully focus on anything else, or we allow them to tell us what to do. The thought "It's hopeless" hooks us and we OBEY: we give up, we stop trying. A painful memory shows up and we OBEY: we give it so much of our attention we get dragged back into the past and lose touch with what's happening here and now. A feeling of anger hooks us, and we OBEY: we shout or say mean things or become aggressive. An urge or craving hooks us and we OBEY: we indulge whatever the habit or addiction may be.[*]

STRUGGLE Mode

In STRUGGLE mode, we actively try to stop our thoughts and feelings from dominating us. We STRUGGLE against them; we do whatever we can to avoid them, escape from them, suppress them, or get rid of them. In STRUGGLE mode we may turn to drugs or alcohol or junk food or procrastination or withdrawing from the world or basically anything that gives us momentary relief from those painful thoughts and feelings—even when doing so has negative impacts on our health, well-being, and happiness.[†]

Getting Hooked and Away Moves = Psychological Suffering

When our thoughts and feelings "hook" us, they reel us in, jerk us around, and pull us into away moves. Indeed, almost every recognized psychological disorder—depression, anxiety disorders, addiction, chronic pain, trauma, OCD, you name it—is due to this basic process: difficult thoughts and feelings hook us and pull us into away moves.

---

* In ACT, the technical term for OBEY mode is *fusion*.
† In ACT, the technical term for STRUGGLE mode is *experiential avoidance*.

Said slightly differently, when we respond to our thoughts and feelings in OBEY mode or STRUGGLE mode (or often both), we behave in self-defeating ways. And this very same pattern also underpins bad habits, unhealthy routines, relationship problems, poor performance, unhealthy perfectionism, excessive people-pleasing, procrastination, and all the other self-defeating or life-draining things we do when under pressure. The diagram below illustrates this.

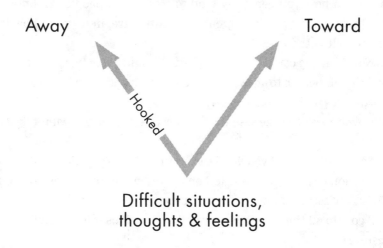

Away

Toward

Hooked

Difficult situations,
thoughts & feelings

Unhook, and Move toward the Life You Want

Fortunately, there are times when we manage to *unhook* ourselves from difficult thoughts and feelings—and do toward moves instead. And the greater our ability to do this, the better life gets: our suffering lessens, and our well-being increases. In a nutshell, that's what this book is all about.

A big part of the work in this book is getting in touch with your "values": your heart's deepest desires for how you want to behave as a human being; how you want to treat yourself and others and the world around you. For example, think of someone you love very much. When you're being who you really want to be in this relationship, how do you treat your loved one? I'd guess (and I could be wrong, of course) that you want to be loving, kind, supportive, honest, reliable, caring, and considerate. If I guessed right, if those *are* qualities of behavior you desire, then we'd call them "values."

To make this clearer, pick an important role you play regularly that involves interacting with other people (e.g., friend, partner, parent, neighbor, employee, student, or team member). Now imagine I interview one of the people you interact with when you're in that role. And imagine I start asking this person *about you.* I begin by asking about how you generally tend to treat them, and what you say and do when they're distressed or struggling or going through a tough patch. Next, I ask them how you generally tend to treat other people. And finally, I ask them what your three greatest qualities are, in terms of how you interact with others.

Now if magic could happen, if dreams could come true, what would you love this person to answer (and genuinely mean)? Please take at least two minutes to think about this . . .

Now, repeat the exercise for another role you play. Again, take two minutes . . .

So how did it go? If you did the exercise, you probably identified some values, some ways you want to behave when you're in those roles. (If you're confused or found the exercise too difficult, no need for concern; we'll go into all this in depth later in the book. This is just a preliminary "taste.")

The simple fact that you are reading this book suggests you are living by your values right now. You are reading it because you care about reducing your suffering and improving your life. You may also be reading it because you want to be a better friend, partner, parent, relative, or neighbor. This points to a value of "being caring": being caring toward yourself or others or both.

It's important for us to clarify our values because once we know what they are, we can make good use of them. We can use them as an "inner compass" to guide us through life and help us make wise choices and also as a source of energy and motivation to help us do more toward moves.

Another big part of this approach is to learn "unhooking skills" so that when difficult thoughts, feelings, memories, or urges show up, we can rapidly unhook from them before they can pull us into away moves. The better we get at unhooking and choosing toward moves, the better our quality of life and the greater our health, well-being, and happiness. This is illustrated below.

Away   Toward

Difficult situations,
thoughts & feelings

Choice Points

The diagram above is officially called the "choice point," because in any
moment when life is difficult, and painful thoughts and feelings show up,
we *potentially* have a choice. We can respond to what is happening with
effective, life-enhancing behaviors (toward moves) or with ineffective,
life-diminishing behaviors (away moves). But note the word *potentially*.
We only have this choice *if* we have developed good unhooking skills.
Without them, we have little choice; without them, our "default setting"
is to get hooked and pulled into away moves (and often, we won't even
realize that's happened until it's too late). Basically, the less our ability to
unhook, the less choice we have; instead, our thoughts and feelings tend
to dominate us, run our lives, dictate what we can and can't do.

I originally cocreated the choice point with two colleagues, Joe Ciarrochi and Ann Bailey, in order to simplify the ACT model, and we'll be using this concept throughout the book. Indeed, shortly I'll ask you to fill in
a blank choice point diagram, based on your life as it is today, so you can
use it as a road map for the journey ahead. But first, let's quickly consider
three strategies for success as you work through this book:

Strategy 1: Treat Everything as an Experiment

Throughout these pages I will ask you to play around with many different tools, techniques, and strategies that I expect to be helpful. However,
nothing works for everyone. Everything you do will be an experiment;

you never know for sure what's going to happen. So, please bring an attitude of openness and curiosity to each experiment in the book and really notice your experience. If it turns out to be helpful, as intended, that's all well and good. But if it's not helpful, please either modify it to suit your purposes or drop it and move on to the next part of the book.

In other words, don't take anything on board just because I say it's helpful; trust your own experience. Take as little or as much from this book as you like and leave anything that's not right for you.

Strategy 2: Expect Your Mind to Interfere

Whenever I ask you to do something that pulls you out of your comfort zone, your mind is likely to protest. It's as if we have a "reason-giving machine" inside our head, and as soon as we're faced with doing something uncomfortable, it starts cranking out all the reasons why we can't do it, shouldn't do it, or shouldn't even have to do it: "That won't work for me," "That's silly," "I can't do it," "I don't have the time," "I don't have the energy," "I'm not in the mood," "I'll do it later," "I'm too anxious," "I'm too depressed," "I can't be bothered," and so on.

Sometimes the reasons our mind comes up with are based on harsh judgments: "I'm too stupid/weak/lazy to do it," "I'll only screw it up," "I don't deserve a better life." At other times, they are based on anxiety: "What if it goes wrong?" "What if other people get upset?" "What if I make a fool of myself?" At yet other times, they are based on past experience: "I've tried that before and failed." And sometimes they're based on our feelings: "I'm not in the mood," "I can't be bothered," "I don't feel like it."

Whatever your reason-giving machine comes up with, please remember what I said in the last chapter: this is basically your mind trying to protect you from uncomfortable thoughts and feelings. So when those reasons to skip an experiment arise, there's a "choice point" for you.

Option 1: allow your mind to dominate you, to talk you out of doing the exercise in question.

Option 2: allow your mind to say whatever it wants, but don't buy into it; let it chatter away like a radio playing in the background while you get on with the experiment.

(If you've read a lot of self-help, you may be surprised that I didn't suggest a third option: get into a debate with your mind and start challenging those "negative thoughts"; push them away and replace them with more "positive thoughts." We don't do that in ACT because, as we'll explore in later chapters, a lot of the time it simply doesn't work.)

Strategy 3: Practice Is Essential

A new client walked into my room clutching the first edition of this book. She sat on the couch, threw the book on the coffee table, and snapped, "I've read your book! It didn't work."

"I see," I said, a bit taken aback. "And while you were reading it, did you practice all the exercises?"

She looked at me, sheepishly. "No."

"Well then," I said, "I'm not really surprised it didn't work."

If we want to become competent at any new skill—playing a guitar, driving a car, cooking Japanese food—we need to practice. We can't learn new skills simply by reading books about them. For sure, reading books can *give us ideas* about new skills, help us to understand what's involved, and provide us with insights into how we can develop them, but it won't actually give us the skills. Even if we read ten thousand books about playing guitar, driving, or cooking, we won't develop the skills to do those things. We need to actually pick up that guitar and strum away or get behind the wheel and hit the road or get in that kitchen and rattle those pots and pans. And the same is true for psychological skills, like the ones we cover in this book. Simply reading about *how* to unhook will not give you unhooking skills; you need to *actually do* the experiments and practice the exercises repeatedly.

Time to Complete a Choice Point

Okay, so now it's time to complete a choice point diagram. I strongly encourage you to either (a) draw one on a sheet of paper (it's easy: just draw two straight arrows diverging from one central point) or (b) print one from my free eBook, *The Happiness Trap: Extra Bits*. As the name suggests, this eBook contains additional materials to support the main book, including audio recordings and printable worksheets. You can download a copy from the "Free Resources" page on my website, www.thehappinesstrap.com.

Once you've drawn or printed it, please fill in the choice point diagram, guided by my prompts below. (If you're not currently able to write, then at least spend a few minutes imagining what you *would* write if you could.) There's an example of a completed version near the end of the chapter, so if you get stuck at any point, skip ahead and use it for guidance.

Part A: What Are Your Hooks?

1. At the bottom of your choice point, write down four or five of the most difficult situations you are dealing with in your life today (e.g., work problems, medical problems, relationship issues, bullying or rejection, prejudice or discrimination, financial problems, lack of friends, bereavement).

2. Underneath those, write down difficult emotions that tend to recur (e.g., sadness, anxiety, guilt, loneliness, anger) and/or difficult sensations (e.g., a tight chest, knots in the stomach, racing heart, feelings of numbness or emptiness).

3. Next, write down any urges you struggle with (e.g., urges to smoke, drink, gamble, or yell).

4. Finally, write down unhelpful thoughts that tend to frequently occur, especially self-judgments (e.g., "I'm stupid," "I can't cope," "I keep screwing up," "I'm a loser"), beliefs (e.g., "I have to do things perfectly," "I must always please other people," "My life will never get better"), and negative predictions (e.g., "I'll fail," "I'll get sick," "They'll reject me"). If relevant, also include recurrent painful memories.

As you work through this book, you'll learn a wide range of unhooking skills to take the impact out of those difficult thoughts and feelings, so they can't jerk you around, hold you back, or bring you down; how to let them flow through you, without sweeping you away. You'll also learn how to take effective action, guided by your values, to improve those difficult situations (or leave them, if that's a better option).

Part B: What Are Your Away Moves?

Alongside the left arrow, write down common away moves you make, when you go into OBEY or STRUGGLE mode (in response to the thoughts and feelings you've written at the bottom). Away moves are mostly things you do physically (e.g., eating too much junk food, shouting at your loved ones, watching too much TV, hiding away in your bedroom, drinking excessively). However, they might include things you do inside your head, such as worrying, obsessing, and ruminating (cognitive processes).

So an individual thought, like "I'm going to fail," would go at the bottom of the choice point; it just pops up, and there's nothing you can do about that. But if, in response to that thought, you start worrying, ruminating, or obsessing, then those cognitive processes would go on the away arrow.

Remember, away moves are behaviors that you personally consider to be unworkable: taking you away from the life *you want* to build; away from the person *you want* to be. This is your own personal viewpoint you're mapping out, nobody else's.

Also remember, away moves are things you *do*, not things you *feel*. So emotions, feelings, sensations, and urges are not away moves; they always go at the bottom of the choice point, never on the away arrow. Away moves are unworkable things you do *in response to* all that stuff at the bottom.

Part C: What Are Your Toward Moves?

No matter how difficult your life is, no matter how badly you've been hooked by your thoughts and feelings, no matter how extensive your away moves . . . one thing's for sure: at times, you do some toward moves (such as reading this book). So, alongside the right arrow, begin by writing toward moves you're already doing (e.g., "reading *The Happiness Trap*").

After that, write down toward moves you'd like to start doing (make sure to include "learning unhooking skills"). This could include goals you want to pursue, actions you want to take, and values you want to live by. Note: toward moves are about what you *do*, not how you *feel*. So you wouldn't write "feeling relaxed" or "feeling happy" on the toward arrow; you'd write down what you'd *do differently* if you felt that way.

If you have trouble with this, try the following:

- Look at an away move and ask yourself, "What would I like to do instead of this?"
- Think back to the two roles you picked in the exercise above. What did your answers suggest you'd like to start or keep doing in those roles?
- Think about those three fundamentals of health and well-being I mentioned in the last chapter: exercising, healthy eating, and building strong relationships. What would you like to start or keep doing in these arenas?

Away

Excessive drinking

Zoning out for hours
in front of TV

Avoiding socializing

Avoiding exercise

Eating crap

Spending much of the day
in bed on weekends

Snapping at people

Avoiding best friend

Buying things I don't
really need

Excessive worrying

Excessive social media

Neglecting the dog

Toward

Reading *The Happiness Trap*

Learning unhooking skills

Living values of self-caring,
loving, forgiveness

Moderate/sensible drinking

Riding bike, going to gym

Seeing friends

Healthy eating

Making up with best friend

Seeing a career counselor

Budgeting

Getting out into nature

Reading great books

Discovering cool new music

Playing with the dog

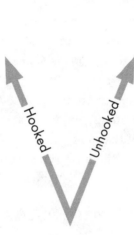

Situations

conflict with best friend, tedious high-stress job, big
financial debts, no partner, long and lonely weekends

Feelings

anger, anxiety, sadness, loneliness

Thoughts

"I'm boring, weak, unlovable, stupid. No wonder I have no friends. Life
sucks! Will I ever find a partner or a decent job? There's no hope."

EXAMPLE OF A COMPLETED CHOICE POINT DIAGRAM

If you find it easy to fill in the toward arrow, all well and good. But if you find it hard or impossible, rest assured that's completely normal. Most people initially find it quite challenging, and sometimes even anxiety provoking. So if your toward arrow is empty or sparse, that's not a problem; simply acknowledge that right now, at this point in time, you don't have much idea of what you can do to make life meaningful. This will soon change! In later chapters, I'll take you through some exercises that will help you to fill in all the blanks.

Where to from Here?

So now that you have a sense of what this book is about, take a moment to notice what your mind is saying. Is it enthusiastic ("Let's get cracking!") or skeptical ("This guy's full of it") or anxious ("This sounds like hard work!") or doubtful ("I don't think this will work for me.")? Or is it just staying quiet?

Whatever your mind is saying, simply acknowledge it.

If it's saying something that makes you want to persist, that's great news; at times, our minds are helpful and encouraging, so let's appreciate that when it happens.

On the other hand, if it's saying something that makes you want to give up, there's a choice point for you: Do you give up because your mind says something negative? Or do you let your mind say whatever it wants, acknowledge that it's trying to protect you from discomfort, and carry on reading?

I hope you choose the latter, because in the next chapter we're going to explore a topic of vital importance. . . .

[3]

The Black Hole of Control

Michelle has tears streaming down from her eyes. "What's wrong with me?" she asks. "I have a great husband, great kids, great job, a lovely home. I'm fit, healthy, well off. So why aren't I happy?"

It's a good question. Michelle seems to have everything she wants in life, so what's going wrong? This is actually a common scenario in the Western world, and later in this chapter we'll explore why. But first, let's take a look at another popular happiness myth.

Myth 3: It's Easy to Control What You Think and Feel

Many self-help books and programs subscribe wholeheartedly to this myth. One of the most popular claims you'll encounter is this: if you repeatedly challenge your negative thoughts and, instead, fill your head with positive ones, you will be happy, confident, and successful. If only life were that simple!

The fact is, we have much less control over our thoughts and feelings than we would like. I'm sure you don't need me to tell you this. I'm willing to bet you've already tried countless times to think more positively about things—but those negative thoughts keep coming back, don't they? As we saw in chapter 1, our minds have evolved over three hundred thousand years to think the way they do, so it's unlikely a few positive thoughts will make much difference! (It's not that positive thinking has *no effect at all*; such techniques *do* often make us feel better—at least, temporarily. But they don't get rid of negative thoughts in the long term.)

The same holds true for uncomfortable emotions such as anger, fear, sadness, guilt, and shame. There are multitudes of psychological strategies to "get rid of" such feelings. But you've undoubtedly discovered that even if you can make them go away temporarily, after a while they're back. And then they go away again. And then they come back again. And so on and so on.

I'm guessing you've already spent a lot of time and effort trying to have "good" feelings and "positive" thoughts instead of those "bad" or "negative" ones (I know I have!), and you've probably found that as long as you're not too stressed or your situation isn't too challenging, you can often pull it off. However, I'm sure you've discovered that the more stressed you are, the more difficult the situation you're in, the less ability you have to control your thoughts and feelings. In really difficult situations, when life hits you hard, when you're tackling major challenges or stepping out of your comfort zone to face your fears—you simply can't expect to feel happy!

Sadly, this myth is so deeply entrenched in our culture that we tend to feel stupid, weak, or inadequate when our attempts to control our thoughts and feelings fail. This raises the question: given that it so obviously contradicts our direct experience, how did this myth get established in the first place?

The Illusion of Control

The human mind is a wonderful thing. It enables us to make plans, invent new things, coordinate actions, analyze problems, share knowledge, learn from our experiences, and imagine new futures. The clothes on your body, the chair beneath you, the roof over your head, the book in your hands—none of these things would exist but for the ingenuity of the human mind. The mind enables us to shape the world around us and conform it to our wishes, to provide ourselves with warmth, shelter, food, water, protection, sanitation, and medicine. Not surprisingly, this amazing ability to control our external environment gives us high expectations of control in other arenas as well.

Now, in the material world, control strategies generally work well. If we don't like something, we figure out how to avoid it or get rid of it, and then we do so. A wolf outside your door? Get rid of it! Throw rocks at it, or spears, or shoot it. Snow, rain, or hail? Well, you can't get rid of those things, but you can avoid them by hiding in a cave or building a shelter.

Dry, arid soil? You can get rid of it by irrigation and fertilization, or you can avoid it by moving to fertile ground.

But how much control do we have over our inner world: over our thoughts, memories, emotions, urges, and sensations? Can we simply avoid or get rid of the ones we don't like? Well, let's see . . .

Here's a little experiment. As you keep reading this paragraph, try not to think about ice cream. Don't think about the color or the texture. Don't think about how it tastes on a hot summer's day. Don't think about how good it feels as it melts inside your mouth.

Stare at the floor and try not to think about ice cream for one minute. How'd you do?

Exactly! You couldn't stop thinking about ice cream.*

Now here's another little experiment. Remember the last meal you ate—whatever it was, breakfast, lunch, or dinner. Remember it as vividly as you can: what you ate, how it was cooked, how it tasted. Done that? Good. Now delete it. Totally obliterate that memory so it can never come back to you, ever again.

How did you fare? (If you think you succeeded, check again; see if you can still remember it.)

Next, tune in to your left leg and notice how it feels. Feeling it? Good. Now make it go completely numb—so numb that we could cut it off with a hacksaw and you wouldn't feel a thing.

Did you succeed?

Okay, now here's a little thought experiment. Suppose I'm a mad scientist (if you know me, that's not a huge stretch) and I've kidnapped you for an evil experiment. I've wired you up to the world's most sensitive "lie detector" (technically known as a polygraph). This machine measures your heart rate, breath rate, blood pressure, brain waves, and adrenaline levels. And if it detects even the tiniest hint of fear or anxiety, a red light will flash and a loud alarm will ring.

So you're strapped in a chair, wired to this thing, and I place my hand

---

* A tiny number of people manage briefly to suppress thoughts about ice cream by thinking about something else. This is *not* good! A huge amount of research on thought suppression shows that, in the long term, such methods not only fail but have a rebound effect, leading to an increase in frequency and intensity of the very thoughts you're trying to avoid. We explore this in later chapters.

on a big red lever attached to a massive electrical generator. And with a mad cackle, I inform you, "In this experiment I'm about to do on you, you must not feel any anxiety whatsoever—because if you do, I will pull this lever, which will electrocute you with one million volts!"

What would happen?

You'd be fried, right? Even though your life depends on it, you could not stop yourself from feeling anxious. Indeed, even the tiniest hint of anxiety that shows up in that situation would itself be a trigger for massive anxiety.

Now, one last experiment. Stare at the star below, then see if you can stop yourself from thinking for two whole minutes. That's all you have to do. For two minutes, prevent any thoughts whatsoever from coming into your mind—especially any thoughts about the star or the task I've just asked you to do!

Hopefully by now you're getting the point that thoughts, feelings, sensations, and memories are just not that easy to control. As I said before, we do have *some* control over these things, but it's so much less than we want. I mean, let's face it: if these things were that easy to control, wouldn't we all just live in perpetual bliss?

How We Learn about Emotional Control

From a young age, we are taught that we should be able to control how we feel. When you were growing up, you probably heard a number of expressions like, "Don't cry or I'll give you something to cry about,"

"Don't be so gloomy; look on the bright side," "Big boys don't cry," "Stop feeling sorry for yourself," "There's no need to be frightened," "Think positive," "Don't be scared," "Cheer up; it may never happen," "No use crying over spilled milk," "Plenty more fish in the sea," and so on.

With words such as these, the adults around us sent out the message, again and again, that we ought to be able to control our feelings. And certainly it appeared to us as if they controlled theirs. But what was going on behind closed doors? In all likelihood, many of those adults weren't coping too well with their own painful feelings. They may have been drinking too much, taking tranquilizers, crying themselves to sleep every night, having affairs, throwing themselves into their work or suffering in silence while slowly developing stomach ulcers. However they were coping, they probably didn't share those experiences with you.

And on those (hopefully) rare occasions when you did get to witness their loss of control, I'll bet they never said anything like, "You see these tears rolling down my face? This is because I'm feeling something called 'sadness.' It's a normal emotion that we all feel at times, and I'm going to teach you some psychological skills so you can handle it effectively."

The idea that we should be able to control our feelings is strongly reinforced in our school years. For example, kids who cried at your school were probably teased for being "cry-babies" or "sissies"—especially if they were boys. Then, as you grew older, you probably heard phrases (or even used them yourself) such as, "Get over it!," "Shit happens!," "Move on!," "Chill out!," "Don't be a chicken!," "Snap out of it!," "Toughen up," "Build a bridge," "Deal with it," "Take it on the chin," "Suck it up," "Don't have a pity party," "Don't worry about it," "Relax," "Don't think about it," and so on.

These phrases imply that we should be able to turn our feelings on and off at will, like flicking a switch. And this myth is compelling because many people around us *seem*, on the surface, to be happy. They *seem* to be in control of their thoughts and feelings. But "seem" is the key word here. The fact is that most people are not open or honest about the struggle they go through with their own thoughts and feelings. They "put on a brave face" and "keep a stiff upper lip." They are like the proverbial clown crying on the inside; the bright face paint and chirpy antics are all we see. I commonly hear my clients say things like, "If my friends/family/

colleagues could hear me now, they'd never believe it. Everyone thinks I'm so strong/confident/happy."

Penny, a thirty-year-old receptionist, came to see me six months after the birth of her first child. She was feeling tired, anxious, and full of self-doubt about her mothering skills. At times she felt incompetent or inadequate and just wanted to run away from all the responsibility. At other times she felt exhausted and miserable and wondered if having a child had been a huge mistake. On top of that, she felt guilty for even having such thoughts!

Although Penny attended regular mothers' group meetings, she kept her problems a secret. The other mothers all seemed so confident, she feared that if she told them how she was feeling, they would look down on her. When Penny eventually plucked up the courage to share her experiences with the other women, her admission broke a conspiracy of silence. They had all been feeling the same way to one degree or another, but they'd all been putting on the same act of bravado, hiding their true feelings for fear of disapproval or rejection. There was a huge sense of relief and bonding as these women opened up and got honest with one another.

As we grow up, many of us are taught to bottle up painful feelings and hide them from others; that having such feelings means we are weak, silly, or defective. As a result, most of us are reluctant to tell our friends and family when we are feeling sad or anxious or not coping in some way—for fear of being judged. Our silence about what we are really feeling, and the false front we put on for others, simply adds to the powerful illusion of emotional control.

So why is it so important to dispel this myth? To answer that, let's consider . . .

What's Your Problem?

Presumably, if you're reading this book, there's room for your life to improve. Maybe your relationship is in trouble, or you're lonely or heartbroken. Maybe you hate your job or perhaps you've lost it. Maybe your health is deteriorating. Maybe someone you love has died or rejected you or moved far away. Maybe you have low self-esteem or self-confidence.

Maybe you have an addiction or financial problems or legal difficulties. Maybe you're experiencing depression, anxiety, trauma, or burnout. Or maybe you just feel stuck or disillusioned.

Whatever the problem is, it undoubtedly gives rise to unpleasant thoughts and feelings—and you've probably spent a lot of time and effort in STRUGGLE mode, trying to escape them or blot them out. But suppose that STRUGGLE against your "bad" thoughts and feelings is actually making your life worse? In ACT we have a saying for this: "The solution is the problem!"

How Does a Solution Become a Problem?

What do you do when you have an itch? You scratch it, right? And usually this works so well you don't even think about it: scratch the itch and it goes away. Problem solved.

But suppose one day you develop a patch of eczema. The skin is very itchy, so naturally you scratch it. However, with this condition, the skin cells are highly sensitive, so when you scratch them, they release chemicals called histamines, which are highly irritating. And these chemicals inflame the skin even further. So after a while, the itch returns—but more intensely than before. And, of course, if you scratch it again, the same thing happens. In the short term, there's relief; but in the long term, it gets even worse! The more you scratch, the worse the eczema, the greater the itchiness.

Scratching is a good solution for a fleeting itch in normal, healthy skin. But for a persistent itch in abnormal skin, scratching is harmful: the "solution" becomes part of the problem. This is commonly known as a "vicious cycle." And in the world of human emotions, vicious cycles are common. Here are a few examples:

- Joe fears rejection, so he feels overly anxious in social situations. He doesn't want those feelings of anxiety, so he avoids socializing whenever possible. He doesn't accept invitations to parties or pursue friendships. He lives alone and stays home every night. This means that on the rare occasion when he does socialize, he's more anxious than ever because he's so out of practice. Furthermore, living alone with no friends or social life just serves to make him feel completely rejected, which is the very thing he fears!

- Maria also feels anxious in social situations. She copes with this by drinking heavily. In the short term, alcohol reduces her anxiety. But the next day she feels hungover and tired, and she often regrets the money she spent on alcohol or worries about the embarrassing things she did while under the influence. Sure, she escapes anxiety for a little while, but the price she pays is a lot of other unpleasant feelings over the long term. And if she ever finds herself in a social situation where she can't drink, her anxiety is greater than ever because she doesn't have alcohol to rely on.

- Prisha is overweight and hates it, so she eats some chocolate to cheer herself up. For a few moments, she feels better. But then she thinks about all the calories she's just consumed and how that will add to her weight—and ends up feeling more miserable than ever.

- There's a lot of built-up tension between Alexei and his wife, Sylvana. Sylvana is angry at Alexei because he works long hours and doesn't spend enough time with her. Alexei doesn't like those feelings of tension in the house, so to avoid them he starts working longer hours. But the more hours he works, the more dissatisfied Sylvana gets—and the tension in their relationship steadily increases.

You can see that these are all examples of STRUGGLE: trying hard to avoid, get rid of, or escape from unwanted thoughts and feelings.

Below I've organized some of our most common "struggle strategies" into two main categories: fight and flight. Fight strategies involve fighting with or trying to dominate your unwanted thoughts and feelings; flight strategies involve escaping or avoiding them.

Fight Strategies

SUPPRESSION: You try to directly suppress unwanted thoughts and feelings. You forcefully push unwanted thoughts from your mind, or you push your feelings "deep down inside."

ARGUING: You argue with your own thoughts. For example, if your mind says, "You're a failure," you may argue back, "Oh, no, I'm not—just look at everything I've achieved in my work."

TAKING CHARGE: You try to take charge of your thoughts and feelings. You may tell yourself things like, "Snap out of it!" "Stay calm!" or "Cheer up!" Or you try forcing yourself to be happy when you're not, or try to replace negative thoughts with positive ones.

SELF-JUDGMENT: You use harsh self-judgment to try to bully yourself into feeling differently. You call yourself names like "loser" or "idiot." Or you criticize and blame yourself: "Don't be so pathetic!"

Flight Strategies

OPTING OUT: You opt out of situations, events, or activities that tend to trigger uncomfortable thoughts or feelings. For example, you drop out of a course, avoid going to a social function, procrastinate on an important task, or avoid a challenge, to escape feelings of anxiety.

DISTRACTION: You distract yourself from your thoughts and feelings by focusing on something else: you smoke a cigarette, eat some ice cream, go shopping, or play computer games.

SUBSTANCES: You try to avoid or get rid of unwanted thoughts and feelings using substances such as drugs, alcohol, sugar, chocolate, junk food, tobacco, and so on.

The Problem with Struggle Strategies

What's the problem with using methods like these to try to control our thoughts and feelings? The answer is nothing, if

- we use them sensibly, appropriately, and in moderation;
- we use them in situations where they can realistically work; and
- using them doesn't stop us from behaving like the sort of person we want to be, doing the things that matter to us.

So if we're not too distressed or upset—if we're just dealing with run-of-the-mill, everyday stress—then deliberate attempts to control our thoughts and feelings aren't likely to be a problem. Indeed, in some situations, distraction can be a good way of dealing with unpleasant emotions. If you've just had a row with a loved one and you're feeling hurt and angry, it could be helpful to distract yourself by going for a walk or burying your head in a book until you calm down. Similarly, if you're stressed and drained after a grueling day's work, then having a glass of wine to "unwind" may be just the ticket.

However, struggle strategies become problematic when

- we use them excessively;
- we use them in situations where they can't work; or
- using them stops us from doing things that matter to us.

When Struggle Is Excessive

To varying degrees, every one of us uses struggle strategies to avoid unwanted thoughts and feelings. And in moderation this is no big deal. For instance, when I'm feeling particularly anxious, I sometimes eat chocolate. This is basically a form of distraction: an attempt to avoid some unpleasant feeling by focusing on something else. But because I only do this in moderation, it's not a major problem in my life—I maintain a healthy weight, and I don't give myself diabetes.

However, back in my early twenties it was a different story. Back then I was a junior doctor, and I found my work incredibly stressful. So I ate a truckload of cakes, cookies, and chocolates to try to avoid my anxiety. (On a bad day I could go through five whole packets of double-coated chocolate Tim Tams, a popular Australian cookie.) As a result, I became seriously overweight and developed high blood pressure. (Not exactly a great role model for my patients!) Because I used it *excessively*, this struggle strategy had serious consequences.

If you're worried about upcoming exams, you might try to distract yourself from your anxiety by watching television. Now, that's fine if you're only doing it every now and then. But if you do it too much, you'll spend all your evenings watching television and you won't get any studying done. This, in turn, will create more anxiety as your studies lag further and further behind. Therefore, as a method for anxiety control, distraction simply can't work in the long run. And then there's the obvious: dealing with your anxiety in this way prevents you from doing the one thing that would be genuinely helpful—studying.

The same goes for zoning out with alcohol or drugs. Moderate drinking or taking the occasional tranquilizer isn't likely to have serious long-term consequences. But if we use these struggle strategies excessively, this easily leads to addiction—which then usually leads to many complications, which in turn give rise to even more painful feelings.

Using Struggle Strategies in Situations Where They Can't Work

If we love somebody deeply and we lose that relationship—whether through death, rejection, or separation—we will feel a whole range of painful emotions. What we feel varies enormously from person to person and may include many different emotions including anger, sadness, anxiety, guilt, loneliness, despair, or fear. Such feelings are normal reactions to any significant loss, whether a loved one, a job, or a limb; we expect to feel them as part of a normal grieving process.

Unfortunately, rather than allowing ourselves to feel all those perfectly normal emotions, many of us do what we can to push them away. We might bury ourselves in work, drink heavily, throw ourselves into a new relationship "on the rebound," or numb ourselves with drugs. But no matter how hard we try to push those feelings away, deep down inside they are still there. And sooner or later, like a muscle-bound, time-traveling, humanoid killer robot with an Austrian accent . . . *they'll be back.*

It's a bit like holding a ball under the water. As long as you keep pushing it down, it stays beneath the surface. But eventually your arm gets tired and the moment you release your grip, the ball leaps straight up out of the water.

Donna was twenty years of age when her husband and child died in a tragic car crash. Naturally, she felt an explosion of sadness, fear, loneliness, and despair. But Donna didn't know how to effectively handle those painful feelings, so she turned to alcohol to push them away. Getting drunk would temporarily soothe her pain, but once she sobered up, her pain returned with a vengeance—and then she'd drink even more to push it away again.

By the time Donna came to see me six months later, she was knocking back almost two bottles of wine a day, as well as taking Valium and sleeping tablets. The single biggest factor in her recovery was her willingness to stop running away from her pain. Only when she learned how to open up and make room for her feelings, to take the impact out of them and allow them to freely come and stay and go in their own good time, was she able to come to terms with her terrible loss. Once she could do this, it enabled her to grieve effectively for her loved ones and channel her energy into building a new life. (Later in the book, we'll look at how she accomplished that.)

When Struggle Strategies Prevent Us from Doing What Matters

What domains of life are most important to you? Health? Work? Family? Friends? Religion? Sport? Nature? It's no surprise that life is richer and more fulfilling when we actively invest our time and energy in the aspects of life that are most important or meaningful to us. Yet all too often our attempts to avoid unpleasant feelings get in the way of doing what truly matters to us.

For example, suppose you're a professional actor and you love your work. Then one day, quite out of the blue, you develop an intense fear of failure just as you are due to appear onstage. So you refuse to go on (a malady commonly known as stage fright). Refusing to go onstage may well temporarily reduce your fear, but it also stops you from doing something that truly matters to you.

Or suppose you've just gone through a divorce. Sadness, fear, and anger are all natural reactions, but you don't want to have these unpleasant feelings. So you try to lift your mood by eating junk food, getting drunk, or chain-smoking. But what does this do to your health? I've never met anyone who didn't care about their health—and yet many of us use emotion control strategies that actively damage our physical bodies.

How Much Control Do We Actually Have?

The degree of control we have over our thoughts and feelings depends largely on how intense they are and what situation we are in—the less intense the emotions and the less stressful the situation, the more control we have.

For instance, if we're dealing with typical everyday stress and we're in a safe, comfortable environment such as our bedroom or a yoga class, or the office of a coach or therapist, then a simple relaxation technique can often make us feel calmer right away.

However, the more intense our thoughts and feelings are, and the more stressful the environment we are in, the less effective our attempts at control will be. Just try feeling totally relaxed when you're going for an interview or arguing with your partner or asking someone out on a date, and you'll soon see what I mean. While you can *act* calmly in those situations, you will not *feel* relaxed (no matter how hard you practice your relaxation techniques).

We also have more control over our thoughts and feelings when the things we're avoiding aren't too important. For example, if you're avoiding cleaning your messy garage or your car, then it's probably fairly easy to take your mind off it. Why? Because in the larger scheme of things it's simply not that important. If you don't do it, the sun will still rise tomorrow, you will continue to draw breath, and nothing bad will happen to your job, your health, or your loved ones. All that will happen is that your garage or car will remain messy.

But suppose you suddenly develop a large, suspicious-looking black mole on your arm and you avoid going to the doctor. Would it be easy to take your mind off it? Sure, you could go to a movie, watch television, or surf the internet and maybe, for a little while, you could stop thinking about it. But in the long term, you will inevitably start thinking about that mole, because the consequences of avoiding action are potentially serious.

So, because many of the things we avoid are not that important, and because many of our negative thoughts and feelings are not that intense, we find that our struggle strategies can often make us feel better—at least for a little while. Unfortunately, though, this leads us to believe we have much more emotional control than we actually do.

What Is "Experiential Avoidance"?

No one likes feeling bad, so, naturally, we all try to avoid or get rid of unpleasant thoughts and feelings. Psychologists call this "experiential avoidance": the ongoing attempt to avoid or get rid of unwanted inner experiences.

Experiential avoidance is normal, and in low levels it is not a problem. But a high level of experiential avoidance leads to excessive use of struggle strategies, which comes with three big costs:

1. When used excessively, these strategies eat up a lot of time and energy that could be invested in more meaningful, life-enhancing activities (toward moves).
2. We may feel hopeless, frustrated, or inadequate because although we're trying very hard to get rid of them, those unwanted thoughts and feelings keep coming back (often with greater intensity than before).
3. When used excessively or inappropriately, many struggle strategies lower our quality of life over the long term. (In other words, they become away moves).

These unwanted outcomes lead to even more unpleasant feelings, which then lead to even more struggle. It's a vicious cycle. And I do mean "vicious"; there's a wealth of research showing that a high level of experiential avoidance is a major factor in depression, anxiety disorders, addiction, impaired performance, low self-esteem, relationship conflicts, eating disorders, disengagement and demotivation at work, OCD, trauma, chronic pain syndrome, and many other psychological problems.

It's worth noting that sometimes struggle strategies are automatic and unconscious. For example, you may have heard of the vagus nerve, the second-longest nerve in the body after the spinal cord. Sometimes when we experience intense pain—physical, emotional, or psychological—our vagus nerve *literally* numbs us: it actually "cuts off" our feelings to spare us from the pain. This isn't a conscious choice; this is simply our nervous system looking after us. Unfortunately, this gives rise to other unpleasant feelings, such as numbness, emptiness, hollowness, or a sense of being "dead inside": a fairly common experience in depression or trauma.

In a Nutshell

So here is "the happiness trap" in a nutshell: to increase our happiness, we try hard to avoid or get rid of unwanted thoughts and feelings—but paradoxically, the more effort we put into this STRUGGLE, the more difficult thoughts and feelings we create.

It's important to get a sense of this for yourself, to trust your own experience rather than simply believing what you read. So please complete the following exercise. (If you don't wish to write in the book, you can print out a worksheet from my free eBook, *The Happiness Trap: Extra Bits*, downloadable from the "Free Resources" page on www.thehappinesstrap.com.) There are three parts to the exercise, and I highly recommend you write down your answers; however, if you're currently unable or unwilling to do so, please spend at least ten to fifteen minutes seriously thinking about this.

Part A: What Have You Tried?

Begin by completing this sentence: The inner experiences (thoughts, feelings, emotions, memories, urges, images, sensations) I most want to avoid or get rid of are . . . *obsessive thinking about past relationships, loneliness, feelings of inadequacy*

Next, take a few minutes to write a list of every single thing you've ever tried doing to avoid or get rid of these unwanted inner experiences. Try to remember every single struggle strategy you have ever used (whether deliberately or by default).

Note: Please do this nonjudgmentally—with genuine curiosity! Please do not start judging these methods as "good" or "bad," "right" or "wrong," "positive" or "negative." We don't want to get caught up in judgments or righteousness about what we should or shouldn't be doing. The aim is simply to find out if these methods are "workable"—i.e., do they work *in the long term* to give you the life you want? (And obviously, if any of these methods do improve your life in the long term, they count as toward moves—so keep doing them!)

Come up with as many examples as possible, including the following:

DISTRACTION: What do you do to distract yourself from or "take your mind off" painful thoughts and feelings (e.g., movies, TV, internet, books, computer games, exercise, gardening, gambling, food, drugs, alcohol, etc.)?

OPTING OUT: What important, meaningful, or life-enhancing activities, events, tasks, challenges, or people do you avoid, quit, escape, procrastinate on, or withdraw from? (Of course, if they're not important, meaningful, or life-enhancing, then opting out is no problem!)

THINKING STRATEGIES: How do you try (consciously or not) to think your pain away? Tick any of the following that you have ever done, and write in any others that aren't included:

- Worrying
- Fantasizing about a better future
- Imagining escape scenarios (e.g., leaving your job or your partner) or revenge scenarios
- Thinking to yourself "It's not fair . . ." or "If only . . ."
- Blaming yourself, others, or the world
- Talking logically and rationally to yourself
- Positive thinking; positive affirmations
- Judging or criticizing yourself
- Giving yourself a hard time
- Analyzing yourself or others (trying to figure out "Why am I/others like this?")
- Analyzing the situation, life, or the world (trying to figure out why this happened or why life/the world is like this)
- Planning; strategizing; constructive problem-solving
- Making to-do lists
- Repeating inspirational sayings or proverbs
- Challenging or disputing negative thoughts
- Telling yourself "This too shall pass" or "It may never happen"

Other thinking strategies: _____

_____

_____.

SUBSTANCES: What substances do you put into your body primarily to avoid or get rid of pain: foods, drinks, cigarettes, recreational drugs, naturopathic or herbal remedies, tea, coffee, chocolate, aspirin, over-the-counter or prescription medications?

ANY OTHER STRATEGIES? What other strategies have you used at times to escape, avoid, or distract yourself from unwanted thoughts and feelings? For example, have you tried meditation, having affairs, aggressiveness, Tai Chi, massage, exercise, picking fights, dancing, music, suicide attempts, self-harming, "tolerating it," "putting up with it," "sucking it up and getting on with it," prayer, smashing things, staying in bed, reading self-help books, seeing a therapist or doctor or other health professional, getting angry at life or other people?

Part B: How Has This Worked in the Long Term?

Many of these struggle strategies give you short-term relief from painful thoughts and feelings. But consider: do they permanently get rid of those unwanted thoughts and feelings, so they never come back? Most of the time, with most of these strategies, for how long does your pain go away before it returns?

Part C: What Has This Cost You?

Now clearly, some of these methods, if used moderately and wisely, will improve life in the long term—in which case, they are toward moves, and it makes sense to keep doing them. However, when we overuse or overrely on these methods—when we use them excessively, rigidly, or inappropriately—they have significant long-term costs. So consider: When you have *excessively* or *inappropriately* used them, what have these methods cost you in terms of health, money, wasted time, relationships, missed opportunities, work, increased pain, tiredness, wasted energy, frustration, disappointment, and so on? Really take your time; think this through.

Finally consider this: How many of these methods give you relief from pain in the short term but keep you stuck or make your life worse or have significant costs in the long term? On the line below, put an X in the place that best represents your answer:

none_____ a few_____ about half_____ most__X____ all_____

(The higher your level of experiential avoidance, the closer your X is likely to be toward the far-right end of the line.)

Please complete all three parts of the exercise above, before reading on.

If you did this exercise thoroughly and were truly honest with yourself, you probably discovered three things:

1. You've invested a lot of time, effort, energy (and money) in STRUGGLE: trying to avoid or get rid of unwanted thoughts and feelings.
2. Many of these strategies did, at times, give you short-term relief from unwanted thoughts and feelings—but *in the long term,* they returned.
3. Many of these strategies, when *used excessively or inappropriately,* have significant costs in terms of wasted money, wasted time, wasted energy, and negative effects upon your health, vitality, and relationships. In other words, they made you feel better in the short term, but in the long term they lowered your quality of life.

How Are You Feeling? What Are You Thinking?

Pause for a moment and notice how you are feeling. Are you curious or intrigued? Or are you perhaps a bit dazed, confused, or disturbed? Maybe even anxious, guilty, or angry? If uncomfortable feelings are showing up for you, rest assured, that's normal! This is a whole new perspective that challenges many deeply entrenched beliefs. Strong reactions are common.

Also notice what your mind is saying right now. Is it saying something helpful or encouraging? Or is it perhaps judging and criticizing you—calling you foolish or stupid? For many readers, it's likely to be doing the latter. If so, rest assured: you're not foolish or stupid (even if your mind disagrees with me). These strategies you've used are universal; every person on the planet uses them to avoid or get rid of pain. We all try to distract ourselves; we all opt out of things that are difficult; we all try to think our way out of our pain; and we all put substances of one form or another into our bodies. Indeed, our friends, family, and health professionals often actively encourage us to do these things!

The point is . . . no matter how hard we try to avoid or get rid of these thoughts and feelings, in the long term, they keep coming back! And unfortunately, often what we do to get short-term relief makes our life worse in the long term. It's a vicious cycle, which we all get stuck in at times.

Not So Fast!

"Wait a moment," I hear you say. "Why haven't you talked about things like giving to charity or working diligently or caring for your friends? Isn't giving to others supposed to make people happy?"

Good point. It's not just the things you do that matter; it's also your motivation for doing them. If you're giving to charity primarily to get rid of thoughts that you're selfish, or you're throwing yourself into work mainly to avoid feelings of inadequacy, or you're looking after your friends primarily to counteract the fear of rejection, then chances are you won't get much satisfaction out of those activities. Why not? Because when your primary motivation is the avoidance of unpleasant thoughts and feelings, this drains the joy and vitality from what you are doing. For example, recall the last time you ate something rich and tasty to get rid of feelings of stress, boredom, or anxiety. I'm guessing it wasn't that satisfying. However, did you ever eat that very same food, not to get rid of bad feelings but purely and simply to enjoy it and appreciate its taste? I bet you found that much more fulfilling.

Great advice about how to improve our lives comes at us from all directions: find a meaningful job, do this great workout, get out in nature, take up a hobby, join a club, contribute to charity, learn new skills, have fun with your friends, and so on. And all these activities *can* be deeply satisfying *if* we do them because they are genuinely important and meaningful to us. But if we do these activities primarily to escape from unpleasant thoughts and feelings, chances are, they won't be very rewarding. Why not? Because it's hard to enjoy what you're doing while you're trying hard to escape from something you find threatening.

So, when you do things because they are truly meaningful to you—because deep in your heart, they truly matter to you—then we would *not* classify them as struggle strategies. We would call them "values-guided actions" (I'll explain this term in chapter 10), and we would expect them to *improve* your life in the long term.

But if those very same actions are mainly motivated by experiential avoidance—if their primary purpose is to avoid or get rid of unwanted thoughts and feelings—then we *would* call them struggle strategies (and it would be most surprising if you found them fulfilling).

Remember Michelle, who seems to have everything she wants in life and yet she's not happy? Michelle's life is driven by avoiding feelings of inadequacy and unworthiness. She is plagued by thoughts like, "I'm unlovable," "Why am I so inadequate?" and "Nobody likes me," along with all the accompanying feelings of shame and anxiety.

Michelle works hard to make those thoughts and feelings go away. She pushes herself to excel at her job, frequently working late to accommodate others; she dotes on her husband and kids and caters to their every whim; she tries to please everyone in her life, always putting their needs in front of her own. She's afraid to say no to anyone in case she offends them, and she spends large parts of everyday people-pleasing.

Michelle learned this behavior in early childhood. Growing up with abusive, domineering parents, she learned from a young age to do everything possible to keep them pleased or the consequences would be terrible. As a child, people-pleasing protected her. But as she continues to do this in her adult life, the toll it takes on her is enormous. And does it get rid of those upsetting thoughts and feelings? You guessed it. By continually putting herself last and working so hard to win others' approval, she merely reinforces her sense of unworthiness. She is well and truly stuck in the happiness trap.

How Can We Escape the Happiness Trap?

Increasing self-awareness is the first step. So notice all the little things you do each day to avoid or get rid of unpleasant thoughts and feelings—and carefully track the consequences. Ideally, keep a journal or spend a few minutes each day reflecting on this (or use the form in *The Happiness Trap: Extra Bits*). This is important, because the faster we can recognize we're stuck in the trap, the faster we can lift ourselves out of it.

Does this mean we just have to put up with difficult feelings and resign ourselves to a life of suffering and misery? Not at all! That would be an example of OBEY mode, where we allow our thoughts and feelings to command all our attention and dictate what we do. In part 2 of this book, you will learn new, more effective ways to handle unwelcome thoughts and feelings that are radically different from both STRUGGLE and OBEY. But before we get into that, there's one more piece of the puzzle we need to explore.

[4]

Dropping the Struggle

Have you ever seen one of those ancient cowboy movies where the bad guy falls into a pool of quicksand and the more he struggles, the faster it sucks him under? If you haven't, don't worry; they're terrible movies. The point is, if you ever fall into quicksand, struggling is the worst thing you can do. What you're supposed to do is lie back, stretch out, keep still, and let yourself float on the surface. (Then you whistle for your super-intelligent horse to come and rescue you!) Physically, this takes little effort. But psychologically, it's very challenging to do because every instinct in your body tells you to . . . STRUGGLE!

The same holds true when difficult thoughts and feelings arise within us: our immediate instinct is to struggle; we pull out all those struggle strategies we explored last chapter and use them to fight with or flee from our inner experience. But unfortunately, just as with quicksand, struggling only makes things worse.

So What's the Alternative?

Well, there's a radically different way of responding to painful thoughts and feelings that's far more effective than struggling—but it's so counterintuitive it can be hard to get your head around it. To help you understand it, I encourage you to do a simple three-part experiment. (And I guarantee you'll get much more out of it if you do it for real, instead of just reading about it. But if you're unable or unwilling to do that, then at least vividly imagine it.)

Part A

Wherever you are right now, imagine that in front of you is everything that matters to you. This includes both the enjoyable, pleasing aspects of life (favorite movies, books, music, sports, games, food, drinks, people, places, pets, and all the activities you love doing) and the difficult, unpleasant aspects of life (all the challenges and problems you are facing).

At the same time, pretend the book you're holding is comprised of all those difficult thoughts, images, memories, feelings, emotions, sensations, and urges that you usually tend to struggle with.

Part B

(Caution: If you have neck, shoulder, or arm problems, please do not do this part of the exercise; just vividly imagine it.)

When you reach the end of this paragraph, grip the book tightly with both hands, then hold it as far away from you as possible. (If you're reading this on a device, you can use that instead; alternatively, any book or even a sheet of paper will suffice.)

Once you're holding it firmly with both hands, straighten your arms fully (no bending at the elbows) and extend them as far as possible, so you are holding the book "at arm's length." (This should be effortful; if it's not, you need to extend more, push harder.) Then maintain that position for at least one minute—pushing hard, keeping the book as far away from you as you can. And as you do so, notice with curiosity how you find this experience; especially note what kinds of thoughts and feelings show up.

So, how was it? Uncomfortable, tiring, taxing? (Most people find that even just one minute of doing this exercise is annoying, wearying, and a source of significant discomfort.*)

Now imagine doing this exercise all day long, for hours on end; how utterly exhausting would it be? Imagine trying to type on a computer, play

---

* Occasionally I have a super-strong athletic client who says, "That was easy. I could do it all day." So I invite them to keep pushing, as hard as they can for another two minutes. After that I ask, "So would you honestly like to keep doing this for the remaining forty minutes of our session?" Even super-strong athletic types say no because they recognize it would be both draining and distracting.

video games, read a book, drive a car, cook dinner, eat a delicious meal, make love, play tennis, lie on the beach and sunbathe . . . at the same time as doing this exercise. How much would it distract you from what you're doing? Reduce your enjoyment or satisfaction? How hard would it be to do those activities competently? How much would you miss out on?

This is what it's like to struggle with our thoughts and feelings: we invest massive amounts of time and energy in trying hard to push them away. This is tiring, draining, and distracting. And because so much of our attention is invested in this internal struggle, it's very hard to be present, to focus on or engage in what we're doing, and almost impossible to respond effectively to life's many challenges.

Now let's try doing something radically different.

Part C

Again, pretend this book is all your difficult, unwanted thoughts and feelings. And again, when you reach the end of the paragraph, push this book away from you, as hard as you possibly can, for one minute. Then stop pushing and immediately rest the book on your lap. And really pay attention: what difference does it make when you stop struggling with this stuff? Allow the book to gently rest in your lap . . . and stretch out your arms . . . and take a slow and gentle breath . . . and with an attitude of curiosity, open your eyes and ears and notice what you can see and hear around you.

So what did you discover? What was it like to stop pushing; to put down the book and rest it on your lap? Was it less distracting? Less tiring? Less painful? A sense of relief? A sense of freedom? Was it easier to notice the world around you? Easier to move your arms and hands and take action?

This way of responding to unwanted thoughts and feelings is the very opposite of struggling. We open up and make room for our thoughts and feelings; we allow them to come and stay and go in their own good time. We don't let them push us around, nor do we invest our precious energy and attention in fighting with or trying to get away from them. This frees us up to invest our time and energy in toward moves. It also makes it easier for us to focus our full attention on what we're doing, which gives us two huge benefits. When we're focused, we:

- do things much better, and
- get more enjoyment and satisfaction from potentially pleasurable activities.

Much like floating in quicksand, this doesn't come naturally. But the research is crystal clear: when we respond to our thoughts and feelings in this way, symptoms are reduced. Anxiety levels fall; stress levels lower; depression symptoms drop; even physical pain decreases in conditions like chronic pain syndrome.

There's also a third benefit, which many people find surprising. Our difficult thoughts and feelings often contain useful information: among other uses, they can alert us to problems that need addressing, give us important feedback about life, and help us recognize when the things we're doing aren't working for us. We can't effectively use this valuable information while we are busy struggling with these inner experiences; but we can once we drop the struggle. (If that seems like psychobabble gobbledygook right now, no need for alarm; we'll explore this concept in depth in later chapters.)

Despite those three thousand published studies on the effectiveness of ACT, sometimes people are very skeptical about dropping the struggle. For example, Karl was a thirty-two-year-old businessman with high levels of anxiety. He was continually worrying about getting sick, losing his job, or his wife leaving him, and he had many self-judgmental thoughts about being unworthy, unlovable, and inadequate. In addition, he was prone to "unhealthy perfectionism" (constantly striving to do things perfectly, to such an extent it creates huge stress and anxiety). For example, at work, a simple task like writing an informal email could take Karl an age to complete, because he'd have to rewrite it four, five, six, or seven times, until it was "perfect." Often, he'd procrastinate on important tasks for fear he wouldn't be able to do them perfectly; and when he did eventually do them, his constant obsessing about the need for a perfect end result sucked all the joy out of every project.

When I first took Karl through the exercise above, using an old paperback, he said, "Can't I just do this?" and threw the book across the room.

"Yes," I said, "For sure. You've got so many struggle strategies that enable you to do exactly that: drugs, alcohol, distraction, procrastination, and so on. But for how long does it go away before it returns? And how much is it costing you to keep using those strategies?" Karl looked teary. I got up and picked up the paperback. "So throwing this book away is functionally the same as holding it at arm's length: you're struggling with it, trying to get it away from you. We're talking about doing something radically different. We're talking about doing this," I said, resting the book gently on my lap.

Karl looked doubtful. "You don't understand," he said. "My anxiety is debilitating. It's unbearable."

"Yes," I said. "Right now, your anxiety *is* debilitating. Of course, you can't bear feeling that way." I picked up the book, gripped it hard with both hands, and held it at arm's length. "As long as this is the main way you respond to anxiety, it will always be debilitating and unbearable. So would you like to change that? Would you like to learn a new way of responding; a way to drain its power, so that it's *not* unbearable and debilitating?" I dropped the book back into my lap.

Karl nodded. "Great," I said. "Of course, doing that with a book is easy. Let's try it with some real thoughts and feelings."

PART TWO

HOW TO HANDLE DIFFICULT THOUGHTS AND FEELINGS

[5]

How to Drop Anchor

Have you ever experienced an "emotional storm"? Distressing thoughts whirling through your mind like leaves tossed in a gale? Painful emotions surging through your body like a river that's burst its banks? "Emotional storms" vary enormously as to how intense they are, how often they happen, and what triggers them. And they can include any combination of thoughts and feelings you can imagine: anger, anxiety, sadness, loneliness, guilt, shame, worries, judgments, traumatic memories, terrifying images, painful sensations, intense urges—you name it. But whatever the nature of an emotional storm, one thing is for sure: it readily sweeps us away.

There are two main ways we respond to emotional storms: OBEY or STRUGGLE. In OBEY mode, the storm totally controls us. And in STRUGGLE mode we do whatever we can to make it go away. And often we both OBEY and STRUGGLE simultaneously. In other words, we get "completely hooked." Which makes it almost impossible to effectively deal with whatever problem or difficulty set off the storm.

Now let's discuss real storms for a moment. Imagine you have a boat, and just as you're sailing into harbor you hear on the radio there's a strong storm blowing in. You'd want to drop anchor in that harbor both quickly and securely because if you don't, the storm will sweep your boat out to sea. Of course, dropping anchor won't get rid of the storm, but it will hold the boat steady until the storm passes. And shortly, you're going to do something similar: learn how to "drop anchor" when emotional storms flare up inside you. But first let's discuss the importance of . . .

Noticing and Naming

Many of the unhooking skills in this book involve a process called "noticing and naming": noticing your thoughts and feelings with curiosity and naming them in a nonjudgmental manner (e.g., "Here's anxiety" or "Feeling anxious"). And because, for most of us, this doesn't come naturally and may initially seem like an odd thing to do, it's important to understand the point of it.

When we notice and name our difficult thoughts and feelings, it reduces their effect on our behavior. How so? Well, the simple act of noticing what we are thinking and feeling and putting it into words activates part of the "prefrontal cortex" (that portion of your brain directly behind your forehead) and this in turn moderates other parts of the brain that are stirring up those emotional storms inside you.

Basically, the less aware we are of our thoughts and feelings, the less control we have over our actions—over what we say and do. Remember when you were a kid and your teacher left the classroom? What happened? All hell broke loose, right? Well, the same principle applies to our inner world. Our awareness is like the teacher, and our thoughts and feelings are like the kids. If we're not consciously aware of them, they act up, create havoc, run wild. The less aware we are, the more they control our actions and the easier it is for them to pull us into away moves.

However, when the teacher returns to the classroom, the kids immediately settle down. And a similar thing happens when we bring awareness to our thoughts and feelings; when we notice and name them, they lose much of their ability to jerk us around. They're still there, but we no longer OBEY them or STRUGGLE.

It's often helpful to name our thoughts and feelings with terms like "I'm noticing" or "Here is." For example, you might say to yourself, "I'm noticing anxiety," "I'm noticing numbness," "Here is tightness in my chest," "I'm noticing my mind worrying," "Here's a painful memory," "Here's an urge to smoke."

When we first start doing this, it often seems odd or uncomfortable. But it usually helps us to unhook, at least a little. In everyday language, if I say, "I'm angry," it seems as if *I am* that feeling; but when I say, "I'm noticing anger," or "Here's a feeling of anger," it helps me to "step back" a little, see it as an emotion passing through me.

Similarly, if I say, "I'm a loser," it seems as if *I am* that thought; but when I say, "I'm noticing the thought that I'm a loser," it gives me a little distance, so I can recognize it as a thought passing through rather than the essence of who I am.

So I hope you're willing to experiment with noticing and naming (even if your reason-giving machine tries hard to dissuade you)—and feel free to invent your own methods for doing it.

A Simple Formula

So, ready to try dropping anchor? Please remember, it's not a way to avoid or get rid of those stormy thoughts and feelings (just as a real anchor does not control the weather). It's a way to hold yourself steady so the storm doesn't carry you off.

There are hundreds of ways to drop anchor when emotional storms blow up, but they all follow a simple three-step formula. I hope you'll play around with this formula and create your own exercises, which you can do any time, any place, for as long as you wish. You can remember it with the acronym "ACE":

A: Acknowledge your thoughts and feelings.
C: Connect with your body.
E: Engage in what you're doing.

Let's run through this exercise now, and I'll explain the steps as you do them. Before starting, take a few moments to reflect on something that's difficult in your life today, and see if you can tap into some anxiety, sadness, guilt, anger, loneliness, or other difficult thoughts and feelings, so you've got some material to work with. (If you're unable to do that, it's not a huge problem; you can practice this exercise no matter how you're feeling—calm, relaxed, cheerful, bored, depressed, or numb. But the results will be more obvious if you're somewhat distressed when you do it.)

A: Acknowledge Your Thoughts and Feelings

Young children are naturally curious about the world; they can stare with utter fascination at a bird, flower, or caterpillar that the adults around them barely register. Tap into that childlike sense of curiosity to notice what's going on in your inner world. Acknowledge whatever is "showing up" inside you: thoughts, feelings (including numbness), memories, sensations, urges.

(Note: Some people find it easier to notice thoughts than feelings; others find the opposite. Start by noticing whatever is easiest for you, then tackle the harder part. And if you can only notice one or the other, that's fine for now; as you work through the book that will change.)

Take about ten to twenty seconds to notice what thoughts are popping up in your head, and about ten to thirty seconds to scan your body from head to toe, and notice what sensations are present. As you're doing that, use a term like "I'm noticing" or "Here is" to name whatever you notice. For example: "Here is a feeling of anger," "I'm noticing thoughts about being worthless."

The aim here is to acknowledge your thoughts and feelings without OBEYING them and without STRUGGLING against them. Remember how you stopped pushing that book away and instead placed it on your lap in the previous chapter? Well, this is the first small step of that process. (It's just the first step, mind you—and only a small one; there are many more to follow, so please be patient.)

What you're aiming to do is simply acknowledge that here and now, in this moment, these thoughts and feelings are present (neither OBEYING them nor STRUGGLING against them). Notice and name them, and that's all. Please do this now for at least twenty to thirty seconds (that's the bare minimum; take much longer if you prefer) before reading on.

C: Connect with Your Body

Now keep acknowledging your thoughts and feelings and simultaneously connect with your physical body. Find your own way of doing this, as everyone differs in terms of what's most useful. Below are some suggestions to play around with, but please freely modify them or come up with alternatives that suit you better:

- Slowly and gently push your feet into the floor.
- Slowly and gently straighten up your back and your spine.
- Slowly and gently press your hands together, touching only at the fingertips.
- Slowly and gently stretch out your arms, stretch your neck, or roll your shoulders.

If there are limits to what you can do with your body because of illness, injury, or chronic pain—or if there are parts of your body you don't want to focus on—then modify this exercise to suit your needs. You may prefer to do the following:

- Slowly and gently, breathe in and out.
- In ultra-slow motion, ever so gently, adjust your position in your chair or bed to one that's more comfortable, really noticing which muscles you use.
- Slowly and gently, raise your eyebrows as high as you can, then lower them.

Use your creativity; anything you can do that helps you tune in to some part of your body, from tapping your fingers to wiggling your toes, is good. You could also try these movements:

- Push your palms hard against each other and feel the muscles contract in your neck, arms, and shoulders.
- Press your hands down on the arms of your chair or firmly massage the back of your neck and scalp.
- Slowly look around the room and notice how you're using your neck, head, and eyes.
- Slowly stretch (or do a yoga move).
- Twiddle your thumbs, cup your hands, give yourself a hug, slide your hands over your knees . . . or try any of the hundreds of other possibilities.
- If you're around other people but don't want them to know you're doing this, simply straighten up your spine and push your feet into the floor.

Remember, you're not trying to get rid of these difficult thoughts and feelings. (Anchors don't make storms go away.) Nor are you trying to distract yourself.

The aim is to keep acknowledging your thoughts and feelings and at the same time tune into and actively move your body. The reason for this is to give you more control over your physical actions—over what you do with your arms, hands, legs, feet, face, and mouth—so you can act more effectively while the emotional storm continues to rage.

Please do this now, before reading on: acknowledge your thoughts and feelings and connect with your body, for at least ten to twenty seconds (again, that's bare minimum; take as long as you like).

E: Engage in What You're Doing

Continue to acknowledge your thoughts and feelings and connect with your body ... and as you're doing so, get a sense of where you are and what's going on ... and then focus your attention on the activity you are doing.

Again, the idea is to be creative and find your own methods of doing this, but here are some suggestions to play around with:

- Look around the room and notice five things you can see.
- Notice three or four things you can hear.
- Notice what you can smell, taste, or sense inside your nose or mouth.
- Notice what you are doing.

Please do this now, taking ten to twenty seconds (bare minimum) to notice the world around you, and then bring your full attention back to your current activity of reading this book.

Well done. Now please run through the ACE steps again: Acknowledge your thoughts and feelings, Connect with your body, Engage in what you're doing. Take at least ten to fifteen seconds for each step, but more if preferred.

You're doing really well. Now run through ACE a third time. Again, take ten to fifteen seconds (or more) for each step.

And now, a fourth and final time, taking ten to fifteen seconds (or more) for each step. Finish the exercise by giving your full attention to the activity you're doing (which, in this case, is reading a book).

So what happened for you? Hopefully you experienced at least some of the following:

- Although your thoughts and feelings probably didn't change much, you were able to separate a little from them; to "step back" and notice them instead of getting swept away by them. You were less pushed around, bothered, or impacted by them.
- You were able to feel and move your body more readily and have a greater sense of control over your physical actions.
- You were more present, awake, or alert.
- You had a greater awareness of where you are, what you're doing, and what you're thinking and feeling.
- You had a sense of disentangling yourself from your thoughts.

If none of that happened, or if you had problems, please see the troubleshooting section at the end of this chapter. (And if your difficult thoughts and feelings decreased or disappeared—well, that's a lucky bonus, not the aim, as we'll discuss shortly.)

It's Not Working!

"This isn't working!" said Karl, when I took him through the exercise above.

"What do you mean by 'not working'?" I asked.

"I don't feel any better," he said. "It's not making these feelings go away."

"Yes, that's not the aim of it," I replied.

Comments like Karl's are incredibly common when people are new to this approach. Even after listing all their struggle strategies and realizing the costs they have on health and well-being. Even after learning about "dropping the struggle" and how this reduces the impact of difficult thoughts and feelings, without trying to avoid or get rid of them. And even despite knowing that anchors don't control storms.

Yes, even after all that, for many people this new way of responding to thoughts and feelings still takes a while to sink in. So if you're one of them . . . that's completely normal. When I was new to this approach, it took a while for me to get it, too. This is only to be expected; it's such a radically different way of responding.

Like Karl, most people initially misunderstand the point of dropping anchor and try to use it as yet another struggle strategy. But that's a recipe for failure and disappointment; this isn't some clever way to control your feelings. The aims of it are

- to gain more control over our physical actions so we can act more effectively when difficult thoughts and feelings are present;
- to reduce the influence of our thoughts and feelings: when we're on autopilot, they jerk us around like a puppet on a string (OBEY mode); but when we're consciously aware of them—acknowledging them with curiosity—they lose much of their control over us;
- to interrupt worrying, rumination, obsessing, or any other way we get lost inside our heads;
- to interrupt our away moves (i.e., to short-circuit problematic behaviors that take us away from the life we want to build); and
- to help focus (and refocus) our attention on the task or activity we are doing—especially if we're disengaged, on automatic pilot, or getting pulled out of it by our thoughts and feelings (this is why the exercise ends with the instruction to give your full attention to what you're doing).

There are other benefits, too, which we'll cover later in the book, but first I need to highlight something very . . .

Distraction Is Not the Aim

The word *distraction* comes from the Latin *distrahere*, which means "draw away from." Distraction techniques are struggle strategies, where the main aim is to *take your attention away from* unwanted thoughts and feelings. When dropping anchor, we do the very opposite: we actively *notice* the thoughts, feelings, emotions, sensations, urges, and memories that are present. If we attempt to distract ourselves—try to get away from these unwanted inner experiences, ignore them, pretend they aren't there—this is simply another form of struggling with them. (When you stopped pushing that book away and let it rest on your lap, you didn't try to ignore it or pretend it wasn't there.)

Distraction isn't "wrong" or "bad"—but hey, you already know how to do it. We've all got zillions of ways of distracting ourselves, and we know they often don't work, or they give short-term relief at best. So our aim here is to do something totally different: to step out of that struggle with thoughts and feelings and allow them to be as they are; to let them "rest in our lap" and allow them to come, stay, and go in their own good time.

If you're hurting badly—with crushing sadness, extreme anxiety, intense loneliness—your pain is unlikely to go as you drop anchor. However, it will often rapidly lose some of its impact; its power will drain away so it can't so easily push you around. And if you keep the practice going for several minutes—usually three or four is enough, but sometimes longer is needed—you'll often experience a sense of calmness, even as the storm continues to rage inside you.

On the other hand, if your pain isn't extreme—for example, if you're experiencing mild to moderate sadness, stress, or anxiety—then as you drop anchor the pain will quite often lessen and sometimes even completely disappear. When that happens, naturally appreciate and enjoy it, but always remember: it's a bonus, not the main aim. If you take any technique we cover in this book and try to use it to avoid, escape, get rid of, or distract yourself from painful thoughts and feelings . . . you'll soon be disappointed or frustrated. And then your mind will protest: "It's not working!"

Mixing It Up

I encourage you to create your own ways to drop anchor. There are hundreds of ways to use the ACE formula. And keep in mind, you don't have to stick to the sequence above: Acknowledge → Connect → Engage. Some people find it works better to first Connect with their body, and then to Acknowledge what's going on inside, and then to Engage in what they're doing. Yet others prefer to Connect → Engage → Acknowledge. The sequence doesn't matter as long as you include *all three* phases (don't skip the Acknowledging, or this will become distraction) and you run through several cycles. You can also experiment with different methods of naming; some people like to use just one or two words: "Anxiety," "Worrying," "Sadness," "Judging myself"; others prefer longer phrases like "I'm noticing a feeling of . . ." or "I'm having thoughts about . . ."

Now, please drop anchor again, and do at least three cycles of ACE. (You can use audio recordings in *The Happiness Trap: Extra Bits*, downloadable from "Free Resources" on www.thehappinesstrap.com.)

What Next?

You may be wondering, "After I drop anchor, what do I do next?" (Even if you aren't, I'm going to tell you.) Remember the concept of the choice point in chapter 2? Toward moves are things you do that are in line with the sort of person you want to be, taking you toward the life you want to build; and away moves are the opposite. So if you are doing a task or activity that's a toward move, then you keep doing it. And as you do it, you give it your full attention. Why? For two good reasons.

First, if we want to do anything well, what's the one thing we need most? It's not skills, knowledge, experience, or talent, although all those things help. What we need most is the ability to keep our attention on the task. It doesn't matter how skilled, knowledgeable, experienced, or talented you are; if you can't stay focused on what you're doing, you won't do it well.* This is what elite athletes mean when after an unexpectedly poor performance, they say, "My head wasn't in the game." But this doesn't just apply to people involved in sports. It applies to all of us, whatever we are doing—whether driving a car, cooking dinner, making love, playing football, studying, working out at the gym, supervising the kids, reading a book, or working at our job. If we're disengaged, unfocused, distracted, on autopilot, or simply going through the motions, we will not do these things well.

The second good reason to give our full attention to the activity we're doing is so that we can get the most out of it. Basically, the less attention

---

* Of course, there are exceptions to this rule. For example, if you want to get drunk or slump on the couch and zone out in front of the TV, you don't really need to give your full attention to those activities in order to do them well. But for most complex tasks and activities, the rule generally applies.

we give to what we're doing, the less satisfaction or pleasure we'll get from doing it (for reasons we'll explore later).

So if, after dropping anchor, you're currently doing a toward move, give your full attention to the activity. But if you're doing an away move, then stop that activity and switch to a new one that's a toward move. (Of course, that's a whole lot easier to say than do—especially if at this point you can't even think of any toward moves. But rest assured, by the time you reach the end of this book, you'll have plenty of toward moves up your sleeve, and if you've practiced your new skills, you'll readily be able to make these kinds of switches.)

When and Where?

The more we can practice dropping anchor, the better. Ideally, we want to get in as much practice as possible during milder emotional weather to ensure we're well prepared to handle the storms. So run through the steps of ACE repeatedly throughout the day whenever you're mildly to moderately stressed, anxious, angry, irritable, worried, or sad. Then as your skills improve, test them out in harsher weather conditions. It may take a while, but with continued practice you'll find you can drop anchor in even the roughest of storms. (But you do have to practice; just reading about it won't help.)

Also practice this any time you're unfocused, distracted, or on automatic pilot, to help you refocus and engage. Similarly, use it when you're feeling sluggish, drained, lethargic, or like you can't be bothered to do anything to help you wake up, energize, and regain control of your actions.*

The great thing about these exercises is that they are so incredibly easy to fit into your daily routine, you can do them anytime, anywhere, as often as you wish: a thirty-second version while you're stopped at a red light; a one-minute version first thing when you get out of bed; a two-minute version while waiting in a slow-moving line; or a three-minute version during your lunch break. You can even do it lying in bed.

---

* Every suggestion in this book needs to be adapted to your unique life situation. So, for example, if your lethargy is due to sleep deprivation or a medical condition, it may, at times, be better to go and have a lie down.

The more you do this, the better. If you can notch up to ten minutes a day, that's great. Twenty is even better. But even just one minute is better than nothing.

It's particularly useful to drop anchor

- when any type of emotional storm blows up;
- when you want to disrupt worrying, obsessing, or ruminating;
- when you want to interrupt any type of self-defeating behavior;
- when it's hard to focus on or engage in what you're doing;
- when you're sluggish, lethargic, or feel yourself "shutting down";
- when you keep "drifting off" into your thoughts and feelings;
- any time your body is starting to "lock up" or "freeze up" (a common occurrence with trauma-related issues);
- when distressing or traumatic memories arise;
- when strong addictive cravings or urges arise; or
- whenever you want to get out of OBEY or STRUGGLE mode.

This is just one of many unhooking skills we're going to cover in this book. You may not notice much benefit at first, or you may notice a dramatic difference rapidly, or you may be somewhere in between those extremes. But if you practice this regularly and often, even for just a few minutes a day, it will, over time, pay big dividends.

[TROUBLESHOOTING]

If you had no trouble dropping anchor, please skip this section and head to the next chapter.

It Didn't Work

When people say this, almost always they are trying to use this skill as a struggle strategy: to distract themselves from or get rid of unwanted thoughts and feelings. We've already addressed both issues in this chapter.

I Didn't Notice Any Difference

Usually this only happens when you aren't hooked by your thoughts and feelings to begin with; if you're not hooked, you won't get to experience unhooking. If this was the case, try the exercise again but first tap into some difficult thoughts and feelings by reflecting on some big problem or challenge in your life. The other possibility is that sometimes there's so much going on the first time around (reading all the instructions, etc.) you don't really get into the exercise; so again, please have another go.

Also keep in mind, sometimes the difference is only subtle: you are only slightly more alert or aware, or more connected with your body and in control of your actions.

My Feelings Intensified

Fortunately, this problem is rare. It usually happens when you've been avoiding your feelings for a long time—cutting off from them, pushing them away, ignoring them. So now you've stopped doing that, there's a rebound effect. It's as if this emotion (which is usually anxiety) is now jumping up and down excitedly saying, "Hey! About time you gave me some attention! Why have you been ignoring me for so long? Look at me! Look at me! Here I am! Look what I can do!"

With regular practice, as you keep acknowledging your feelings instead of pushing them away, this will stop. If it ever happens again, the trick is to continue dropping anchor for several minutes longer. Do another three or four rounds of ACE—taking at least one minute per round—and you should start to experience the outcomes described earlier in the chapter.

Do I Have to Name the Thoughts and Feelings When I Acknowledge Them?

No, you don't have to. (You don't have to do anything I suggest, ever. It's always a personal choice.) When we notice our thoughts and feelings with curiosity, without actually naming them, that is useful in itself. But when we *do* name them, this adds extra "oomph" to any unhooking skill.

I Can't Name What I'm Feeling

Some people have great difficulty naming their emotions. This is a skill you can learn, but for now, you can simply use general terms like "stress," "discomfort," "hurt," or "pain."

It's Hard to Notice What I'm Feeling

If you find it hard to tune in to your feelings, or you're only feeling a sense of numbness, just acknowledge, "I'm noticing numbness" or "I'm noticing a lack of feeling in my body." In later chapters, you'll learn new skills that will remedy this.

It's Hard to Notice My Thoughts

If you can't notice your thoughts or don't seem to have any, just notice your feelings.

I Can't Notice So Many Things at Once

If you get overwhelmed trying to notice so many things, then go more slowly and narrow your focus. In step A, just notice one feeling in your body or just notice your thoughts rather than your feelings. In step C, just move and notice one part of your body. In step E, just notice one or two things you can see or hear. Over time, gradually broaden your focus to notice more things simultaneously.

I Became More Aware of Physical Pain

Sometimes people become aware of neck aches, backaches, muscle tension, or other physical pain in their body as they do this. One option is to incorporate this into step C, stretching or massaging those areas as a way of connecting with your body. The other option is to incorporate it into step A, acknowledging this discomfort without struggling: "Here's back ache," "I'm noticing neck pain." Better still, do both of the above.

[6]

The Never-Ending Stories

Suppose you have a mind-reading machine that enables you to tune directly into my brain. If you used that machine to listen in to my mind whenever it's really beating me up, giving me a hard time, you would hear all of the self-judgments in the paragraph below. (Not all on the same day, mind you; you'd have to tune in over several months.) Now as you read them consider: does your mind ever say similar things to you?

Okay, here goes. My mind likes to tell me *I'm fat; I'm old; I'm stupid; I'm a fake; I'm incompetent; I haven't achieved enough; I'm not as smart as others; I'm a hypocrite; I'm weird; I don't fit in; if you knew what I was really like you, you wouldn't like me; I'm boring; I'm unattractive; I'm a lousy parent; I'm a lousy partner; I'm too selfish; I'm too disorganized; I'm clumsy.*

So there you have it. Now take a moment to notice what your mind is saying. Is it something like, "Wow! Russ's mind sounds like mine!"? Or is it more like, "What is wrong with this guy? Isn't he supposed to be a self-help guru?" At the time of writing this second edition, I'm fifty-four years old and looking at that list of my self-judgments I can see I've had most of them my whole adult life and quite a few since childhood. What's different now, though, is, most of the time, when these thoughts show up, they're like water off a duck's back. Most of the time, they have little or no impact, and even if they do, I can usually unhook pretty rapidly. (Did you notice the phrase "most of the time" in those last two sentences? You never perfect this stuff; there's always room for improvement.)

The fact is, negative thoughts are normal. I give presentations and trainings all around the world (to both health professionals and laypeople), with audiences varying in size from less than fifty to more than two thousand. And I share with them all those thoughts I just shared with you.

Then I say, "Please raise your hands if at times your mind says things like that to you—doesn't have to be *exactly* the same, but similar." And each time I do this, almost every single arm shoots high in the air. Then I say to them, "Keep your arms up and look around the room. Notice how it's not just you. Our minds all do the same things. It's part of being human."

For reasons discussed in chapter 1, we all have lots of negative thoughts. In fact, research shows that about 80 percent of our thoughts have some degree of negative content. So if your mind does a lot of negative thinking, welcome to the club.

The Great Storyteller

Now before we go any further, we'd best get clear about what thoughts actually are. Thoughts are basically words. When words are written down, we call them "text." When words are spoken aloud, we call them "speech." And when words are inside our head, we call them "thoughts."

In addition to those words inside our head, we also have pictures inside our head in the form of images or memories. And our thoughts, images, and memories are collectively known as "cognitions." We'll look at images and memories in later chapters; in this one, we're going to explore thoughts.

We humans rely a lot on these words inside our head. Our thoughts tell us about our life and how to live it. They tell us how we are and how we should be, what to do and what to avoid. And yet, they are nothing more or less than words—which is why, in ACT, we often refer to thoughts as "stories." Sometimes they are true stories (called "facts") and sometimes they are false. But most of our thoughts are neither true nor false. Most of them are either stories about how we see life (called "opinions," "attitudes," "judgments," "ideals," "beliefs," "theories," "morals," "viewpoints," "assumptions," etc.) or about what we want to do with it (called "plans," "strategies," "goals," "wishes," "desires," "values," etc.).

And how much does our mind love telling stories? It never stops, does it? (Not even when we're asleep). Our mind is constantly comparing, judging, evaluating, criticizing, planning, analyzing, remembering, predicting, and imagining. It's like the world's greatest storyteller: never at a loss for words and brilliant at grabbing our attention.

But the way ACT helps us to deal with these thoughts is different from many other psychological models. Our main interest in any given thought is not whether it's true or false, positive or negative. What interests us first and foremost is: Does this thought have something useful to offer us? If we let this thought guide us, will it help us to build the life we want to live?

"But hang on a minute!" I hear you say. "Aren't negative thoughts harmful or bad for us?" The answer is no! (That's not a misprint; the answer is definitely no.) Negative thoughts are never, in and of themselves, harmful or bad for you. "But how can that be?" I hear you ask. "Don't they cause things like stress, depression, anxiety?" The answer is no, they don't.

Now at this point, pause for a moment, and notice what your mind has to say about that. Chances are, it's going to disagree. Why? Because you've probably read, heard, or been told many times that negative thoughts are both abnormal and harmful. And if you've bought into these extremely popular myths, you're in for a surprise.

Popular Methods for Dealing with "Negative Thoughts"

Many psychological approaches regard negative thoughts as a major problem and point to them as the cause of depression, anxiety, low self-esteem, and so on. They then get you working hard, trying to eliminate them. Such approaches usually advise you to STRUGGLE against your thoughts, as follows:

- Get rid of negative thoughts by repeatedly telling yourself better, more positive ones.
- Distract yourself from such thoughts.
- Push the thoughts away.
- Argue with the thoughts; try to prove they're not true.
- Rewrite your thoughts, making them more positive.

But haven't you already tried methods like these? Almost everyone has! And the reality is, even if they give you short-term relief, they do not permanently get rid of negative stories; like zombies in a horror flick, those negative thoughts keep coming back. This is because . . .

There's No Delete Button in the Brain

Here's a quick experiment. The three sentences below are incomplete. As you read them, please don't try to guess or figure out which words are missing; just read each sentence slowly and as you get to the end, notice the word your mind automatically generates to complete it.

- Mary had a little . . .
- Twinkle, twinkle, little . . .
- The grass is always greener on the other . . .

If you grew up with English as your first language, in countries such as the United Kingdom, the United States, Australia, and New Zealand, your mind automatically completed these sentences with "lamb," "star" and "side." (So if you don't get these references, please bring to mind three well-known sayings from your own culture and read on.)

Now suppose I say to you, "Delete those sentences from your memory. Completely eliminate them from your brain, so those sentences never again pop into your head, under any circumstances." Could you do it? (If you think you can, have a go.) Those words are "in there" to stay.

And it's the same for all those difficult thoughts that have been showing up in your head for years and years. You can't simply get rid of them. There is no "delete button" in the brain.

You may have heard of neuroplasticity or brain plasticity: the ability of the brain to "rewire" itself, to change itself by adjusting its neural pathways (connections between the neurons inside the brain). But the brain doesn't change by subtraction, by pulling out neural pathways. It changes by addition—by laying down new neural pathways *on top of* the old ones. So we can't simply delete these unwanted thoughts. But we *can* lay down new neural pathways that enable us to respond differently— so that when these thoughts inevitably reappear, we can acknowledge them and allow them to freely come and stay and go without getting hooked.

A Different Approach

In this approach, our view of negative thoughts is different from most other psychological models. Negative thoughts are not a problem, in and of themselves. They only become problematic when we react to them in OBEY mode.

In OBEY mode, we give our thoughts our undivided attention or treat them as commands *we must obey* or regard them as *the absolute truth*. The technical term for responding to our thoughts in this way is *fusion*.

To say we are "hooked" by (or "fused with") our thoughts basically means they dominate us. They either dominate our awareness (e.g., we are worrying, obsessing, or otherwise lost in thought) to such an extent that it's hard for us to focus on anything else—or they dominate our physical actions, pulling us into self-defeating patterns of behavior, or away moves. To get a better sense of this, try the three-part experiment below. (It's similar to the one where you pushed the book away, but there are some significant differences.)

The Hands as Thoughts Experiment

Part A

Imagine that in front of you is everything that matters: the enjoyable, pleasing aspects of life (your favorite movies, music, games, foods, people, places, and events) and the difficult, unpleasant aspects of life (all the challenges, problems, and hassles you need to deal with). Now put your hands together, palms up, as if they are the pages of an open book and imagine they are comprised of all your thoughts, images, and memories.

Part B

When you reach the end of this paragraph, raise your hands to your face, until they are totally covering your eyes. Look around you and notice what your view of the world is like as you peer out through those gaps between your fingers. Do this for fifteen seconds before reading on.

So that's what it's like to be totally hooked by your thoughts. When those hands were covering your eyes . . .

- How much were you missing out on?
- How cut off and disconnected were you from all the important stuff out there?
- How difficult would it have been to focus on things?
- Imagine if the task you need to do, or the person you love, were in front of you; how hard would it have been to give them your full attention?
- How difficult would it have been to take action, to do the things that make your life work? How hard to drive a car or cook dinner or type on a computer?

Imagine going around like that *all day*; how much harder would your life be? When we're hooked by our thoughts, it's difficult for us to focus on or engage in what we're doing, hard to appreciate the enjoyable parts of life, and almost impossible to respond effectively to the problems and challenges we face.

Part C

Again, imagine your hands are your thoughts and around you is everything that's truly important to you. When you reach the end of this paragraph, again raise your hands to your face, covering your eyes, and look at the world around you. Do this for five seconds, then ever so slowly lower your hands to your lap, noticing how your view of the world changes. Let your hands rest there, and with genuine curiosity, look around you and notice what you can see and hear.

With your hands in your lap, how much easier is it to focus on and engage in the world around you? To give your full attention to the task you need to do or the person you're with? This is what it's like to unhook from our thoughts. (Technically, in ACT this is known as "defusion.")

And notice, your hands are still there; you haven't chopped them off and thrown them away. So if there's something useful you can do with them, like driving a car or cooking dinner or hugging the person you love, you're free to do so. But if there's nothing useful you can do with them, you just let them sit there. And the same goes for our thoughts. If we can make good use of them, let's do so. Even our most painful, distressing, negative thoughts often have at least some useful information for us, as we'll explore shortly. But if there's nothing useful we can do with them, we just let them sit there.

"But I don't want to let them sit there," said Michelle, after doing this exercise. "I want to get rid of them." (You may recall Michelle from chapter 3. She kept having thoughts such as "I'm hopeless," "I'm a lousy mother," and "Nobody likes me.")

"Of course, you do," I replied. "Who wouldn't want to get rid of all those harsh negative thoughts? And haven't you've been trying hard for years to do that? Look at all the struggle strategies you've used: positive affirmations, positive thinking, prayer, meditation, distraction, therapy, reading self-help books, disputing your thoughts, eating chocolate, drinking, avoiding the people and places and activities that trigger these thoughts . . . and that's just scratching the surface. You have struggled long and hard against these thoughts! And most of these things give you short-term relief—but in the long term what happens?"

Michelle sighed. "They come back."

"So are you ready to try something radically different?" I held my hands over my eyes. "Instead of doing this," I said, "Would you like to learn how to do this?"—and I lowered my hands to my lap.

"Yes," she replied. "But first, can you explain something? Why do our minds say these things?"

Your Mind Is Like an Overly Helpful Friend

Have you ever had one of those overly helpful friends, who was trying so hard to help you they actually became a nuisance? Although they had good intentions, they kept getting in the way or making things harder? Well, you may be surprised (and perhaps pleased) to know that when your mind is saying all those unhelpful things to you . . . it's actually trying to help.

To understand this better, let's take a look at some common categories of thought that repeatedly tend to hook us, and in each case you'll see, your mind is either trying to help you get things you want or avoid things you don't want.

Past and Future

Our mind continually pulls us into the future: worrying, catastrophizing, predicting the worst. Why? Well, this is your mind preparing you, getting you ready for action. It's saying, "Look out. You might get hurt. Protect yourself."

Our mind also frequently pulls us into the past: ruminating, dwelling on painful past events, blaming ourselves (or others) for things we (or they) did (or didn't do). This is your mind trying to help you learn from past events. It's saying, "Bad stuff happened. You need to learn from this so you're ready and prepared and know what to do if something similar should ever happen again."

Judgments

Our minds are judgment factories that never stop manufacturing their product: "This is good," "That's bad," "He's ugly," "She's beautiful," "You can't trust those people," "Life sucks," "I'm right, you're wrong!" "These feelings are awful," and so on. These judgments are your mind's attempts to map out your world for you: to point out what's "safe" and "good" and highlight what's "unsafe" and "bad."

And of course, we all do plenty of judging of ourselves. Harsh self-judgment and self-criticism is our mind trying to "whip us into shape," help us to change our behavior. The mind figures if it leans on us hard enough, beats us up enough, then we'll "sort ourselves out" or "do the right thing."

Reasons

Earlier, we discussed how our mind is like a reason-giving machine. As soon as we even think about doing something uncomfortable, challenging, or anxiety provoking, it cranks out all the reasons why we can't do it, shouldn't do it, or shouldn't even have to do it: "I don't have the time/energy/confidence," "I'm too anxious/stressed/depressed," and so on. This may take the form of worry ("Something bad might happen"), hopelessness ("It won't work"), meaninglessness ("There's no point"), perfectionism ("No point in doing it if I can't do it perfectly"), or self-judgment ("I'm too stupid/weak/lazy to do it").

All these reasons serve the same dual purpose: your mind is trying to spare you from uncomfortable thoughts and feelings or from trying out new things in case you get hurt.

Rules

Our minds love to lay down strict rules about what we can, can't, should, or shouldn't do. "Can't do this!" "Have to do that!," "Mustn't do it that way!"

This is your mind giving you guidelines for life: do this, and you'll be okay; do that, and you're in trouble. The aim, yet again: to help you get what you want and avoid what you don't want.

I could go on all day with similar examples, but I'd probably bore you to death. The take-home message: underlying almost any unhelpful thought or thinking process, our mind's main aims are to protect us, help us get our needs met, help us avoid pain, or alert us to important things that require our attention.

How Can We Tell If We Are Hooked?

When we are hooked, it seems as if

- our thoughts are commands we must obey or rules we must follow,
- our thoughts are very important—we have to give them our full attention,
- our thoughts are wise—we need to follow their advice, or
- our thoughts are the truth—we completely believe them.

I hope you're starting to see that negative thoughts—in and of themselves—are not problematic; they don't directly cause stress, depression, anxiety, and so on. It's only when we respond to them in OBEY mode that problems occur. As I mentioned, the technical term for such responses is *fusion*; however, in everyday language we have many different words and phrases that refer to this psychological process. We talk of being *lost, trapped, entangled, caught up in, dwelling on, carried away, jerked around, pushed around,* or *consumed by our thoughts.* Or we refer to their impact with expressions like *held back, pulled down, drowning, swamped, sinking, flooded, blinded* by, *stuck*, *crushed*, *preoccupied*, or *obsessed*. These metaphorical terms illustrate many of the common side effects of getting hooked, especially the drain on our energy and attention. But when we unhook from our thoughts, they lose their power.

Sometimes people ask me: "So, are you saying we should *never* be absorbed in our thoughts?" To which I reply . . . "NOOOOO!" (Well, I don't say it exactly like that.) To answer such questions, I always come back to the basic ACT principle of workability: is this working to help you build the sort of life you want?

There are plenty of times when it's useful and life enhancing to be absorbed in our thoughts: when we're making plans or solving problems or being creative, or mentally rehearsing a presentation, memorizing something important, or pleasantly daydreaming in a hammock on our summer vacation. No unhooking required. But when we're caught up in our thoughts in a way that's taking us away from the life we want . . . then it's time to unhook. So let's look at my all-time favorite method for unhooking from thoughts.

"I'm Having the Thought That . . ."

When Michelle was hooked by her thoughts, they completely dominated her awareness; she felt terrible, and it was hard for her to focus on anything else. But she found she could often unhook with the simple technique that follows. Please read the instructions, then have a go.

First bring to mind an upsetting self-judgmental thought that takes the form "I am X"; for example, "I'm not good enough" or "I'm incompetent." Pick a thought that often recurs and hooks you in some way—it brings you down, holds you back, pulls you into away moves, dominates your awareness, and so on. (If you can't think of a self-judgment, use a recurrent worry instead; for instance, "It's all going to go horribly wrong.")

Now focus on that thought and buy into it as much as you can for ten seconds.

Next, take that thought and, in front of it, insert this phrase: "I'm having the thought that . . ." Play that thought again, but this time with the phrase attached. Silently say to yourself, "I'm having the thought that I am X." Notice what happens.

Now do that again, but this time with a slightly longer phrase: "I notice I'm having the thought that . . ." Silently say to yourself, "I notice I'm having the thought that I am X." Notice what happens.

Did you do it? Remember, you can't learn to ride a bike just by reading about it—you actually have to get on the bike and pedal. Likewise, you won't get much out of this book if you only read the exercises; you need to actually do them. So if you skipped the exercise, please go back and do it now.

So what happened? You probably found that inserting those phrases instantly gave you some distance from the actual thought, as if you "stepped back" from it. (If you didn't notice any difference, please try again with another thought.)

You can use this technique with any difficult thought that tends to hook you. For instance, if your mind says, "Life sucks!" then acknowledge, "I'm having the thought that life sucks!" If you prefer, use the term "I'm noticing." So when your mind says, "I'll fail!" you acknowledge, "I'm noticing the thought that I'll fail!" Another option is "My mind's telling me." For example, "Here's my mind telling me I'm a bad person." Using these phrases means you're less likely to get beaten up or pushed around by your thoughts. Instead, you can step back and see those thoughts for what they are: words passing through your head.

We can get hooked by positive thoughts, too, which readily gives rise to problems like narcissism, arrogance, overconfidence, unrealistic optimism, or prejudice and discrimination. For example, have you ever known a relative or work colleague who believes, "I can do this better than anyone else; you need to do it my way to get the best results" or "I already know everything about this; there's nothing new you can tell me," or "I'm superior to you." Those thoughts are "positive" in the sense that they tell people positive things about themselves, but when people get hooked by those thoughts—boy, does that create problems!

When we unhook, or defuse, we recognize the following:

- Our thoughts are sounds, words, stories, or "bits of language."
- Our thoughts are not orders we need to obey; we don't have to do what they tell us to do.
- Our thoughts may or may not be important; we give them our full attention only if it's helpful to do so.

- Our thoughts may or may not be wise; we don't automatically follow their advice.
- Our thoughts may or may not be true; we don't automatically believe them.

Well, I think that's enough theory for one chapter. How about we do something more practical?

Unhooking Techniques Galore!

There are zillions of different unhooking techniques, and some may seem a bit gimmicky at first. So think of them like training wheels on a bicycle: once you are able to ride, you no longer need them. And as you try them out in this chapter and the next, remember to treat each one as an experiment, with an attitude of openness and curiosity.

I expect these experiments will be useful (or I wouldn't suggest them), but as I said earlier, nothing works for everyone. Any given technique may have a powerful effect, a moderate effect, or a mild one. (And sometimes even no effect at all.) And on rare occasions, a technique may have the opposite effect to that intended, so you end up more hooked than before. This is very unlikely, but if it does happen, clearly that technique is not right for you, so drop it and move on to another.

Let's Get Started

Remember as you use these unhooking techniques, the aim is not to *get rid of* a thought but simply to see it for what it is—a string of words—and to let it come, stay, and go in its own good time; neither struggling with it nor getting dominated by it.

The next technique calls on your musical abilities. But don't worry; no one will be listening except you.

Unhooking Technique 1: Musical Thoughts

Bring to mind a negative self-judgment that easily hooks you; for example, "I'm such an idiot." Now hold that thought in your mind and really buy into it as much as you can for about ten seconds. Notice how it affects you.

Now take that thought and silently sing it to yourself to the tune of "Happy Birthday to You." Notice what happens.

Now go back to the thought in its original form. Again, buy into it for ten seconds. Notice how it affects you.

Now silently sing the thought to the tune of "Jingle Bells" (or any other tune of your choice). Notice what happens.

As an alternative to the above, there are quite a few free phone apps that can add music to your voice. (My current favorite is Auto-Rap.) Basically, you record something, and the app adds a musical backing track. So the idea is you speak your thought aloud into the app, then play it back as a funky song.

So what happened? You probably found that after putting it to music, your thought isn't hooking you as much. And notice you haven't challenged the thought; you haven't tried to get rid of it, debated whether it's true or false, or tried to push it away and replace it with a positive thought. So what happened? By taking the thought and putting it to music, you saw its "true nature"; you realized that, like the lyrics of a song, it is nothing more or less than a string of words.

Unhooking Technique 2: Name the Story

Another simple way to unhook is to identify your mind's favorite stories and give them names: the "loser!" story or the "my life sucks!" story or the "I can't do it!" story. Often there will be several variations on a theme. For example, the "nobody likes me" story may show up as "I'm boring," the "I'm undesirable" story as "I'm fat," and the "I'm inadequate" story as "I'm stupid." When your stories show up, acknowledge them by name. For example, you could say to yourself, "Ah yes. I recognize this. That old favorite, the 'I'm a failure' story." Or "Aha! Here comes the 'I can't cope' story."

Once you've acknowledged a story, that's it—just let it be. You don't have to challenge it or push it away, nor do you have to give it much attention. Simply let it come and go as it pleases while you channel your energy into doing something meaningful.

Unhooking Technique 3: Name the Process

A variant on the previous method, name the process is especially useful when you have many different thoughts rapidly showing up. Rather than noticing and naming specific thoughts, you notice and name the thinking process itself. You silently say to yourself, "I'm noticing obsessing" or "There's my mind ruminating." Or you might prefer to drop phrases like "I'm noticing" and instead simply name it with one word: "Worrying" or "Daydreaming," or even just "Thinking." Or you can, if preferred, use several words: "Dwelling on the past," "Worrying about rejection," "Blaming myself," and so on.

This technique is often helpful to disrupt cognitive processes like worrying, ruminating, obsessing. Step 1 is to name the process (e.g., "Here's worrying"). Sometimes that is enough to unhook you. But if it doesn't, step 2 is to drop anchor, which pulls you out of your head and helps you refocus on what you're doing.

Practice Is Essential

So, back to Michelle. She was able to identify two major themes that repeatedly hooked her: the "I'm worthless" story and the "I'm unlovable" story. Acknowledging her thoughts by these names rapidly helped her unhook. But Michelle's hands-down favorite technique was musical thoughts. Whenever she caught herself buying into "I'm pathetic" or "I'm a bad mother," she would put the words to music and instantly they'd lose all their power.

But she didn't just stick to "Happy Birthday to You." She experimented with a wide variety of tunes, from Beethoven to the Beatles. After a week of repeatedly practicing this technique throughout the day, she found she was taking those thoughts a lot less seriously (even without the music). She hadn't eliminated them, but they bothered her much less.

Now you're no doubt brimming with all sorts of questions, so please be patient. In the next three chapters we're going to cover unhooking from thoughts (and memories and images) in much more detail and troubleshoot any difficulties you may have. In the meantime, please practice at least one or two of the methods we've covered so far: "I'm having the thought that . . .," "My mind's telling me . . .", musical thoughts, name the story, and name the process.

In addition, remind yourself frequently of the following:

- These difficult thoughts are normal; everyone has them.
- This is not your mind out to get you but the opposite; this is your mind trying way too hard to help.

Use these techniques regularly with difficult thoughts, as often as you possibly can (at least ten times a day, but more is better). Any time you're feeling stressed, anxious, depressed, agitated, or upset—or you're disengaged, distracted, or unfocused—ask yourself, "What story is my mind telling me now?" Then once you've identified it, unhook.

And your fallback option, when other methods fail: drop anchor.

It's important not to build up great expectations at this point. Sometimes it's easy to unhook; at other times, it seems almost impossible. So play around with these methods and notice what happens—but don't expect instant transformation.

And if all this seems too difficult, acknowledge, "I'm having the thought that it's too difficult!" It's okay to have thoughts such as "It's too hard," "This is stupid," or "It won't work." See those thoughts for what they are—chains of words—and let them be.

"That's all fine," you may say, "but what if the thoughts are true?"

Good question . . .

[7]

Off the Hook

"But it's true!" snapped Marco, "I really am fat!" He pulled up his shirt. "Look at that," he said, slapping his belly. Marco was, indeed, seriously overweight. Like many of us, he used eating as a struggle strategy. He often felt sad, lonely, anxious, ashamed, unworthy, and inadequate, and when he ate his favorite foods (chocolate, chips, pizza, nuts, burgers, and ice cream) that would, for a little while, help him escape from those unwanted thoughts and feelings. But of course, long term, this strategy was making him feel even worse.

So I said to Marco, "The important question here is not whether your thoughts are true or not, but whether they are helpful." He looked a bit surprised. "Let me explain," I said. "Suppose I have a magic wand here, a real one. And I wave it, and magic happens—so all your difficult thoughts and feelings suddenly lose their impact. They're like water off a duck's back; they no longer hold you back in any way from doing the things you really want to do. If that happened, how would you treat your body differently?"

"Well," he said, "for a start I wouldn't eat so much shit."

"What would you eat?"

"More healthy stuff, I guess. And less of it."

"Okay. Anything else you'd do differently? If you could treat your body the way you really want to treat it, deep in your heart?"

"Well, I'd definitely exercise more."

"Okay. So it's seems like you've hit on a really important value there. I'm going to call it 'self-caring.' And if you were really living by this value of self-caring, you'd be doing different things: eating more healthily, exercising more. That right?"

"Yeah."

"Okay. So at the moment, when your mind starts beating you up, calling you all those names—fat, lazy, disgusting, and so on—you get hooked by them straight away, right?"

"Yeah."

"And then what happens?"

"I get depressed."

"And then what?"

"I eat shit."

"Right. In other words, getting hooked by those thoughts doesn't help you to live your value of self-caring."

"No. It doesn't."

"So whether your thoughts are true or not isn't the issue here. The point is, if you let them push you around, that's not helpful. So would you like to learn how to unhook from them, so it's easier to start doing those toward moves of eating well and exercising?"

"Yes," he said.

Helpfulness versus Truth

Truthful or not, our thoughts are nothing more or less than words. If those words are telling us something useful, something that can help us, then it's worth paying attention to them. But if not, why bother?

Suppose I am making some serious mistakes in my work and my mind tells me, "You are incompetent!" This is my mind trying hard to help: it's pointing out an issue that needs addressing. But aside from that, it's of no help at all. It doesn't tell me what I can do to improve the situation; it's merely demoralizing. Putting myself down is pointless. Instead, what I need to do is take action: correct the mistakes I'm making, brush up on my skills, or ask for help.

You can waste a lot of time trying to decide whether your thoughts are actually true; again and again your mind will try to suck you into that debate. But although at times this is important, most of the time it is irrelevant—and wastes a lot of energy.

The more useful approach is to ask, "Does this thought offer anything useful? If I let it guide me, will it take me toward or away from the life

I want?" If this thought is offering something helpful, then make good use of it; allow it to guide what you do. But if it's not offering anything of value, unhook.

"But," I hear you ask, "what if that negative thought actually is helpful? What if telling myself, 'I'm fat' actually motivates me to exercise?" Good point. Harsh, judgmental, self-critical thoughts *can* sometimes motivate us—but the costs of relying on this form of motivation are huge. Although at times self-critical thoughts kick us into action, often they have the opposite effect: we feel guilty, stressed, depressed, frustrated, or anxious, and we end up demoralized or demotivated.

This is what happens with "unhealthy perfectionism." You get hooked by the rule "I have to do it well and achieve great results." As long as you're successfully following the rule, working hard, getting those good results, your mind is (somewhat) satisfied. But if you "slack off," it judges you mercilessly, calls you all sorts of names. This kicks your arse back into action, and you start working hard again—but at what cost? Usually the long-term result is stress, burnout, or exhaustion.

In later chapters we'll look at much healthier ways to motivate yourself; methods that will enhance your life rather than drain it. For now, suffice to say, thoughts that criticize you, insult you, judge you, put you down, or blame you are, in the long term, likely to lower your motivation rather than increase it. So when troublesome thoughts pop into your head, it may be useful to ask yourself one or more of the following questions:

- "Is this an old thought? Have I heard this one before? Do I gain anything useful from listening to it again?"
- "If I let this thought guide my actions, will that help me to improve my life?"
- "What would I get for buying into this thought?"

And if you're wondering how to tell whether a thought is helpful or not, ask yourself, "If I use this thought for guidance, will it help me to

- be the sort of person I want to be;
- do the things I really want to do; and
- in the long term, build a better life?"

If the answer to any or all of these is yes, then the thought is probably helpful. (And if not, it's probably *un*helpful.)

Thoughts and Beliefs

How do we know which thoughts to believe? There are three parts to this answer. First, be wary of holding on to any belief too tightly. We all have beliefs, but the more tightly we hold on to them, the more inflexible we become in our attitudes and behaviors. If you've ever tried having an argument with someone who absolutely believes they are right, then you know how pointless it is—they will never see any point of view other than their own. We describe them as being inflexible, rigid, narrow-minded, blinkered, or "stuck in their ways."

Also, if you reflect on your own experience, you'll recognize that your beliefs change over time; that is, the beliefs that you once held tightly, you might now find laughable. For instance, at some point in your life you probably used to believe in at least some of the following: dragons, goblins, fairies, vampires, witches, wizards, magic, Santa Claus, the Easter Bunny, the tooth fairy. And almost everyone changes some of their beliefs about religion, politics, money, family, or health at some point, as they grow older. So by all means, have your beliefs—but hold them lightly. Keep in mind that all beliefs are thoughts (i.e., words inside your head) whether or not they're "true."

Second, if this thought helps you to create a rich, full, and meaningful life, then it makes sense to use it for guidance and motivation. And at the same time remember that it is still, in its essence, a story: a string of words, a segment of human language. So for sure, let it guide you, but don't clutch it too tightly.

Third, pay careful attention to what is *actually happening* rather than just automatically believing what your mind says. For example, you may have heard of "impostor syndrome." This is where someone who does their job competently and effectively believes they're just an impostor; they don't really know what they're doing. Impostors think of themselves as frauds, bluffing their way through everything, always on the verge of being "found out."

People with impostor syndrome are not paying enough attention to their direct experience; to the clearly observable facts that they are doing their job effectively. Instead, they are paying attention to a hypercritical mind that says, "You don't know what you're doing. Sooner or later, everyone will see you're a fake." A high-profile example is the phenomenally successful rock star Robbie Williams, who is often tortured by thoughts that he can't sing.

In my early years as a doctor, I had a bad case of impostor syndrome myself. If one of my patients said, "Thank you. You're a wonderful doctor," I used to think, "Yeah, right. You wouldn't say that if you knew what I'm really like." I could never accept such compliments because although in reality I did my job well, my mind kept telling me I was useless, and I believed it.

Whenever I made a mistake, no matter how trivial, two words would automatically blaze into my head: "I'm incompetent." Back then, I used to get really upset, believing that thought was the absolute truth. Then I'd start doubting myself and stressing out about all the decisions I'd made. Had I misdiagnosed that stomachache? Had I prescribed the wrong antibiotic? Had I overlooked something serious?

Sometimes I would argue with the thought. I'd point out that everyone makes mistakes, including doctors, that none of the mistakes I made was ever serious, and that, overall, I did my job very well. At other times I would run through lists of all the things I did well and remind myself of all the positive feedback I'd had from my patients and work colleagues. Or I'd repeat positive affirmations about my abilities. But none of that got rid of the negative thought or stopped it from bothering me.

These days the "I'm incompetent" story still often pops up when I make a mistake, but the difference is, now it rarely bothers me. I know that those words are just an automatic response, like the way your eyes shut whenever you sneeze. So instead of ruminating about how incompetent I am, I simply correct the mistake and get on with my life.

The fact is, we don't choose most of the thoughts in our head. For sure, we choose *some* of them, *sometimes*—but most of the thoughts in our head just show up of their own accord. We have many thousands of useless or unhelpful thoughts every day. And no matter how harsh, cruel, silly, vindictive, critical, frightening, or downright weird these thoughts may be, we can't prevent them from popping up.

But just because they appear doesn't mean we have to OBEY them. We can treat such thoughts like those ads that appear when you're scrolling through social media or surfing the net. You can't stop the ads from appearing—but you don't have to click on them or buy what they're selling. Alternatively, treat your thoughts as if they're spam emails in your inbox: once you realize they're junk, you don't have to open them and read them. (Unfortunately, unlike spam emails, we can't simply delete our spam thoughts; but I trust you get the point.)

In my case, the "I'm incompetent" story was there long before I became a doctor. In many different aspects of my life, from learning to dance to using a computer, any mistake I've made has triggered the same thought: "I'm incompetent." Of course, it's not always those exact words. Often it's "Idiot!" "You're useless!," or "Can't you do anything right?" But these thoughts are not a problem as long as I see them for what they really are: a bit of "old programming" that popped into my head.

Basically, the more we can tune in to our direct experience of life (rather than to the mind's running commentary), the easier it is to do things that take us toward the life we want. (This is why at the end of any anchor-dropping exercise, we give our full attention to whatever we're doing; and in later chapters, we'll work on developing this ability.)

So without further ado, let's play around with three more methods for unhooking from thoughts.

Unhooking Technique 4: Thank Your Mind

This is one of the simplest ways to unhook. When your mind starts coming up with those same old unhelpful stories, then, with a sense of humor and playfulness . . . you thank it. You silently say to yourself, "Thank you, Mind! How very informative!" or "Thanks for sharing!" or "Is that right? How fascinating!" or simply, "Thanks, Mind!" When I use this method, this is what it sounds like inside my head:

MY MIND: You're so pathetic!

RUSS: Thanks, Mind.

MY MIND: You can use that unhooking technique, but you're still pathetic!

RUSS: Thanks, Mind. Thanks for sharing.

MY MIND: You think you're so clever with that technique, but really you're just a loser.

RUSS: Thanks, Mind. I appreciate the feedback. I know you want to chat, but sorry, I have other things to do.

It's important we don't do this sarcastically or aggressively, because that can easily pull us into conflict with our thoughts (in much the same way as sarcasm and aggression pull us into conflict with other people). We want to do this playfully, with warmth and lightness and humor. (To see a humorous video demonstrating this method, go to YouTube and type in Russ Harris Thanking Your Mind.)

There are many ways to modify this technique. For example, you can combine it with naming the story: "Ah yes, here's the 'I'm a failure' story. Thanks, Mind!" Or you can acknowledge your mind's good intentions: "Thanks, Mind. I know you're trying to help—but it's okay, I've got this covered." (And if you don't like the "thanking" part, you can simply acknowledge, "Ah, there you are, Mind, trying to help.")

Unhooking Technique 5: Play with Text

If you're good at visualizing, you can do this exercise in your imagination. But if you find visualization hard (as I do), then do it on your computer or smartphone: type your thought out in a PowerPoint or Keynote presentation, or into one of the many smartphone apps for sketching, drawing, or painting.

Find a thought that often hooks you. Put it into a short sentence (less than ten words) and for about ten seconds see if you can really let it hook you. Buy into it. Get caught up in it. Get as hooked as possible.

Now imagine that thought as black text on a computer screen (or type it out, for real, on your device).

Now without changing any of the words, play around with the formatting. First, space the words out, with large gaps between them: I   am useless.

Then run the words together, with no spaces between them: Iamuseless.

Now put the words back the way they were (normal formatting, black text) and this time play around with different colors and notice what happens. (For example, you might find bright red tends to hook you, but pale pink helps you unhook.) Try at least three different colors.

Now play around with the font. See it written in *italics*, then in *stylish graphics*, then in one of those big PLAYFUL FONTS you see on the covers of children's books.

Now put it back as plain black text and this time animate the words: get them jumping up and down, bouncing, or spinning around.

Now put it back as plain black text, and this time imagine a karaoke ball bouncing from word to word. (And if you like, at the same time, hear it sung to "Happy Birthday to You.")

So what happened? Did you get a sense of distance or detachment from the thought? Did it lose some of its impact?

Unhooking Technique 6: Silly Voices

This technique is particularly good with recurrent harsh self-judgments. Find a self-critical thought that often hooks you and buy into it as much as you can for about ten seconds. Get as hooked as possible.

Next, pick an animated cartoon character with a humorous voice, such as Mickey Mouse, Bugs Bunny, Shrek, SpongeBob SquarePants, or Homer Simpson. Now silently replay that self-judgment, but this time "hear" it in the voice of the cartoon character. Notice what happens as you do this.

Now get the thought back in its original form and again let it hook you for ten seconds. (You might find that's a bit harder to do now).

Next pick a character from a movie or television show. Consider fantasy characters such as Darth Vader, Yoda, or Gollum, someone from your favorite sitcom, or actors with distinctive voices, like Arnold Schwarzenegger, Chris Rock, Ellen DeGeneres, and Jada Pinkett Smith. Once again, replay the thought, and "hear" it in this new voice. Notice what happens.

Now try that one more time, using any kind of voice you think might help you unhook: a politician, sports commentator, newsreader, world leader, someone with an outrageous accent. Notice what happens.

As an alternative to the above, you can download a "voice changer" app onto your smartphone. There are many free ones, and they all work the same way. You record your voice, and the app then modifies it; for example, it can make you sound like a robot, a ghost, or a chipmunk. So the idea is, you speak your thought aloud into the app, then play it back in several different voices.

So how did you do? By now, I'm guessing you're a lot less hooked by that thought. (Actually, although this isn't the aim, many people find themselves grinning or chuckling as they do this exercise.) And notice that you haven't STRUGGLED against the thought at all: you haven't tried to change it, get rid of it, argue with it, push it away, debate whether it's true or false, replace it with a more positive thought, or distract yourself from it. Rather, you have seen it for what it is: a bit of language. By taking that segment of language and hearing it in a different voice, you become aware that it is a string of words—nothing more, nothing less—and thus it loses its impact.

Some people dislike the silly voices technique; they feel like it's trivializing something serious. If this technique (or any other) feels that way to you, please don't use it. Unhooking is not about trivializing genuine problems in your life. It's aimed at freeing us from oppression by our mind; freeing up our time, energy, and attention so we can invest it in meaningful activities (rather than dwelling uselessly on our thoughts).

Jana, who suffered from chronic depression, found this particular method extremely helpful. She had grown up with a verbally abusive mother who constantly criticized and insulted her. The insults that had once come from her mother had now turned into recurrent negative thoughts: "You're fat," "You're ugly," "You're stupid," "You'll never amount to anything . . . nobody likes you." When these thoughts came to mind during our sessions, Jana would often start crying. She had spent many years (and thousands of dollars) in therapy, trying to get rid of these thoughts, to no avail.

Jana was an avid fan of the British comedy troupe Monty Python, and the character she picked was from their best-known film, *The Life of Brian*. In the film, Brian's mother, played by male actor Terry Jones, is always criticizing Brian in a ridiculously high-pitched, screeching voice. When Jana "heard" her thoughts in the voice of this screeching old woman, she couldn't take them seriously. The thoughts did not immediately disappear, but they quickly lost much of their power over her, which helped in lifting her depression.

When Thoughts Are Both True and Serious

What do we do if a thought is both true and serious? One of my clients, Amina, had severe cardiomyopathy (heart disease) and was desperately hoping for a heart transplant, without which she would soon be dead. She told me she couldn't focus on anything; she spent all day lost in a thick smog of anxious thoughts. These were all *true and serious* thoughts, about her heart condition, the chances of finding a donor, the risks of surgery, the chances of dying, the importance of writing a will, and so on. The problem was, while all caught up in those thoughts, she was missing out on life; she couldn't be present with her loved ones; she couldn't focus on the movies, books, and music that she loved. So I listened compassionately, validated all of her perfectly natural fears, and taught her how to drop anchor. Then we talked about naming the story, and she chose to call it the "time's running out" story.

She agreed to practice noticing and naming the "time's running out" story whenever it showed up during the day and to alternate this with thanking her mind: "Thanks, Mind. I know you're trying to help me deal with my illness and make the most of my remaining time. And it's okay, I've got this handled." And if that didn't help, she was to drop anchor and refocus.

At her next session, only a week later, she was so much better at unhooking from all those thoughts. She still *believed* them, 100 percent. Of course, she did; they were true! However, she was now able to notice and name them and let them freely come, stay, and go without getting hooked. (Not everyone responds this dramatically, of course. So if you find, despite lots of practice, you're still getting hooked, you'll need additional methods, such as those in chapter 18.)

Interestingly, when we unhook from our thoughts, they often do reduce in believability. But that's not the aim. We're not primarily interested in whether or not the thought is true or false. Our main interests are: Does this thought offer you anything useful? Can it help you make the most out of life? If you let this thought guide you, will it take you toward the life you want?

Create Your Own Unhooking Techniques

The techniques we've covered so far are like those inflatable armbands young children use in swimming pools: once you can swim, you don't need them anymore. Down the line, you'll be able to unhook without the need for such contrived methods. (However, going forward, there will still be times when it's useful to pull them out of your psychological tool kit.) In the meantime, while you're still using "armbands," why not have some fun inventing your own techniques?

All you need do is put your thought in a new context where you can "see" it or "hear" it, or both. You might visualize your thought spray-painted as graffiti on a wall, printed on a poster, emblazoned on the chest of a comic book superhero, carved on the side of a tree, trailed on a banner behind an airplane, tattooed on the arm of a movie star. Or imagine it as a text message, spam email, or "pop-up" ad. Or you could paint it, draw it, or sculpt it. Or you could imagine it dancing, bouncing, or spinning or moving down a TV screen, like the credits of a movie. Alternatively, you might "hear" your thought being broadcast from a radio, emanating from a robot, or being sung by a rock star. Let your creative juices flow freely.

Four Things to Remember

When practicing unhooking, it's important to keep these four things in mind:

1. The aim is not to get rid of unpleasant thoughts but rather to see them for what they are—simply words—and drop the struggle with them. At times they will quickly disappear, but at other times, they won't.
2. Often when you unhook from a troublesome thought, you will feel better. But this is a beneficial by-product, not the main goal. The primary aim of unhooking is to free you from the tyranny of your mind, so you can invest your time, energy, and attention in more important things. When unhooking *does* make you feel better, obviously enjoy it. But please don't *expect* it.

3. Remember that you're human, so there will be plenty of times you forget to use these new skills. And that's okay. The moment you realize you're hooked—even if it's been happening for hours—you can instantly use one of these techniques.

4. No technique is foolproof. There may be times when you try these methods but find they are of little or no help. If so, go back to dropping anchor. Apply the ACE formula: Acknowledge your thoughts and feelings, Connect with your body, and Engage in what you're doing.

Putting It into Practice

In this chapter and the last, we've covered "I'm having the thought that . . .," "My mind's telling me . . .," naming the story, naming the process, musical thoughts, thanking your mind, playing with text, and silly voices, as well as how to create your own techniques. So pick your preferred methods (if it's hard to decide which, toss a coin) and use them as often as you can, every day. And if one method doesn't work, try another. I usually recommend the following sequence (but please change this as required; experiment and find what works for you):

1. The first step is simply to notice and name what's hooking you (e.g., name the story, name the process, thank your mind, or use a phrase like "I'm noticing . . .").

2. If you're still hooked, use a playful technique (musical thoughts, silly voices, playing with text).

3. If you're still hooked after that, drop anchor.

And now, some words of caution. From here on out, in almost every chapter you're going to learn new skills, and if you try to do them all, to the maximal extent, every single day—you're sure to get overwhelmed. So please be flexible; adapt everything to suit your way of living. For example, you might practice one particular technique on one day of the week and a different technique on another. Ideally, you'll put aside at least five to ten minutes a day to focus on building new skills; but if that's not realistic, try every second or third (or fourth or fifth) day.

And rotate the skills you work on from day to day or week to week or month to month.

Also keep in mind, many of these skills can be incorporated into your daily routine without the need to free up extra time. You don't have to "stop your life" to do them; instead, let them become a part of your life.

One final caution: This is not some "quick fix" approach. Over time, as you apply your new skills more and more, you'll experience profound changes; but it does require patience and persistence. So go slowly, take your time, and simply notice what happens as you incorporate these practices into everyday life.

[TROUBLESHOOTING]

The Thought(s) Didn't Go Away!

Unhooking isn't about getting rid of thoughts. It's about seeing them for what they really are and making peace with them; allowing them to exist in your world without fighting them. Sometimes they will rapidly move on. Other times, they'll hang around for a while. Sometimes they'll go away—and then come back when you're least expecting them.

I Didn't Feel Any Better!

If you use these techniques to try to control your emotions, you will soon be disappointed. That's not their purpose. (If this doesn't make sense to you, please go back to p. 73 and redo the hands as thoughts experiment.) True, unhooking will often reduce unpleasant feelings, but that's a bonus, not the aim.

I Got Even More Hooked!

This usually means the technique you chose is not a good fit for you. In this case, please try a different one. Sometimes you need to try quite a few to find what works best for you. And if all else fails, drop anchor.

But I Don't Like These Thoughts! I Want Them Gone!

You don't have to like your thoughts in order to drop the struggle. It's okay to want to get rid of them. In fact, that's expected. But wanting to get rid of something is quite different from actively struggling with it. For example, suppose you have an old car that you no longer want, but you won't have an opportunity to sell it for at least another month. You can *want* to get rid of the car; and you can simultaneously acknowledge that you still have it and allow it to stay in your garage without a struggle. You don't have to try to smash the car up or make yourself miserable or get drunk every night on account of the fact you still have that old car.

So if you do find yourself struggling with a thought (as we all do at times), just notice it. Pretend you're a curious scientist observing yourself and notice all the different ways in which you STRUGGLE.

[8]

Frightening Images, Painful Memories

Roxy trembled. Her face was pale and drawn, her eyes teary.

"What's the diagnosis?" I asked.

"Multiple sclerosis," she whispered.

Roxy was a thirty-two-year-old lawyer, dedicated to her profession. One day at work she noticed weakness and numbness in her left leg, and within a few days she was diagnosed with multiple sclerosis, or MS. MS is a disease in which the nerves in the body degenerate, creating all sorts of physical problems. In the best-case scenario, you may have one fleeting episode of neurological disturbance from which you fully recover, never to be bothered again. In the worst case, the MS steadily worsens, and your nervous system progressively deteriorates until you are severely physically disabled. Doctors have no way of predicting how it will affect a patient.

Not surprisingly, Roxy was very frightened by this diagnosis. She kept imagining herself in a wheelchair, her body horribly deformed, her mouth twisted and drooling. Every time this image popped into her head, it terrified her. She tried telling herself all the usual common-sense things: "Don't worry . . . it will probably never happen to you," "Your chances are excellent . . . cross that bridge if and when you come to it," "What's the point of worrying about something that may never happen?" Friends, family, and doctors also tried to reassure her with similar advice. But did that get rid of this scary image? Not in the least.

Roxy found she could sometimes distract herself or push the image out of her head, but it wouldn't stay away for long, and when it returned it seemed to bother her even more than before. This commonly used but ineffective struggle strategy is known as "thought suppression," which means actively pushing distressing words or pictures out of your head. For example, each time an unwanted cognition appears, you might say to yourself, "No, don't think about it!" or "Stop!" or you might snap an elastic band against your wrist or just mentally shove it away.

Unfortunately, while thought suppression comes naturally to us all, the research on this is crystal clear: in the short term, it makes distressing thoughts, memories, or images go away, but in the long term, there's a rebound effect and they return with greater frequency and intensity than before.

We see dramatic examples of this in trauma-related disorders. Horrific memories of traumatic events (e.g., rape, violence, sexual abuse) repeatedly appear, accompanied by painful emotions. Many people find they can, in the short term, push those memories away through various methods: distraction, drugs, alcohol, and all the other usual suspects. But in the long term, they return with a vengeance.

Trauma aside, most of us have a tendency to get hooked by frightening images of the future or painful memories of the past. (We can actually store memories with all five senses—sight, sound, smell, taste, and touch—but in this chapter, we're focusing on the visual elements.) How often have you "seen yourself" failing, being rejected, getting sick, dying, doing something bad, or getting into trouble of some kind? And how much time have you spent dwelling on or reliving painful events from the past? If you're anything like me, the answer is "a lot."

(Note: around 10 percent of the population find it difficult, or even impossible, to visualize or "think in pictures." If you're one of them [as I am], you may not relate to much of this chapter, but please still read it, so you can understand and support your loved ones when they get hooked by mental pictures. And also keep in mind, throughout the book, whenever I use the word *imagine,* you don't need to "see" mental pictures; you can imagine with words, concepts, and ideas.)

Your mind creates these cognitions because it's trying hard to keep you safe: "You need to be prepared for this," "Don't let this happen," "Protect yourself," "Stay safe," "Look what happened in the past; don't let that happen again." Your mind operates on the rule "Safety first!" and it will never relinquish its number one job of looking out for you. This means that unpleasant or unnerving images and memories will pop up repeatedly—especially when we face significant challenges; and we can waste a lot of precious time and energy if we respond to them in OBEY or STRUGGLE mode. Moreover, sometimes when we get hooked by these cognitions, they become so frightening that they can scare us away from doing the things we'd like to do.

For example, many people avoid air travel, public speaking, or socializing because they get hooked by images of things going badly. Similarly, painful memories of being hurt or abused in previous relationships may scare you away from entering new, healthier relationships.

When we are hooked by images or memories, we

- give them our undivided attention (so it's hard to focus on anything else),
- react to them as if the events they depict are happening here and now, and
- treat them as threats we need to avoid or get rid of.

In contrast, when we *unhook* from images and memories, we

- recognize their true nature—we see they are pictures occurring in our mind,
- give them our full attention only when they are offering something of use, and
- realize that no matter how unpleasant they may be, these images and memories are not threats; they can trigger unpleasant emotions, but they can't actually harm us.

Of course, these troublesome cognitions are accompanied by unpleasant emotions, urges, and sensations, and in later chapters we'll look at how to deal with those feelings. For now, let's explore how to unhook from images and memories.

First Steps In Unhooking from Images and Memories

You already know quite a few ways to unhook from "words inside your head." Unhooking from images and memories is similar. Often, noticing and naming is enough: "I'm having the image of . . .," "I'm noticing a memory of . . .," "Imagining the future," "Reliving the past."

However, for terrifying images or truly horrible memories, your best bet is to drop anchor. After several rounds of ACE (Acknowledging the image or memory and the feelings that go with it, Connecting with your body, Engaging in what you're doing), you'll likely unhook.

Going Further

Let's now look at some techniques that can help us see these cognitions for what they truly are: mental pictures that can't harm us. Once we recognize this, we can let them freely come and stay and go in their own good time, without STRUGGLE: no fighting or judging them, no trying to avoid them.

A word of caution: The playful techniques in this section are usually helpful for painful memories, such as times you have failed or screwed up, been rejected or humiliated, or done something you regret. But they are not appropriate for truly horrific memories. So if you are distressed by traumatic memories, please *don't* use the methods below; stick to noticing, naming, and dropping anchor.

And again, a reminder: Do these exercises as experiments, genuinely curious as to what will happen. If you can't do a given technique, or it doesn't work, acknowledge your disappointment and move on to a different one. For each experiment, first read the instructions, then bring to mind a troublesome image or memory. And if it's a moving image, condense it into a ten-second "video clip." Then put the book down and try the method (while skipping any technique that seems inappropriate).

Television Screen

Bring up a difficult image or memory and notice how it's affecting you.

Now imagine there's a small TV screen across the room from you. Place your image on the screen and play around with it: flip it upside down, turn it on its side, spin it around and around, stre-e-e-etch it sideways.

If it's a moving video clip, play it in slow motion. Then play it backward in slow motion. Then play it forward at double speed; then reverse it at double speed.

Turn the color down, so it's all in black-and-white.

Turn the color and brightness up until it's ridiculously fluorescent and lurid.

The idea is not to get rid of this image/memory but see it for what it is: a harmless picture. You may need to do this for anything from ten seconds to a minute. If you're still hooked after that, try the next method.

Subtitles

Keep that cognition on the television screen and add a subtitle. For example, an image of you failing might be subtitled: "The 'failure' story." If preferred, you could make it a humorous subtitle, like "Doh! Done it again!" (as long as that doesn't seem trivializing). If you're still hooked after thirty seconds, try the next technique.

Adding a Soundtrack

Keeping that cognition on the screen, add a musical soundtrack of your choice. Experiment with a few different soundtracks: jazz, hip-hop, classical, rock, or your favorite movie theme. And if the image still hooks you after that, move on to the next method.

Shifting Locations

Imagine this cognition in a variety of different locations. Stay with each scenario for twenty seconds before shifting to a new one.

Imagine it on the T-shirt of a jogger or a rock star.

Visualize it painted on a canvas, or on a banner flying behind an airplane.

See it as a bumper sticker, as a magazine photo, or as a tattoo on someone's back.

Imagine it as a "pop-up" on a computer screen or as a poster in a teenager's bedroom.

Visualize it as the image on a postage stamp or as a drawing in a comic book.

Use your imagination with this; the sky's the limit. And if you're still hooked after all this, then I suggest you practice running through some or all of the above exercises every single day, for at least five minutes. Initially, we need to focus on these images in order to practice unhooking. But the ultimate aim is to be able to let these images come and go without giving them much attention—like having the television on in the background, without really watching it.

I asked Roxy to do this practice daily, and within a week that image of herself in a wheelchair was no longer bothering her. It still appeared from time to time but no longer frightened her, and she was able to let it freely come and stay and go while she focused on more important things. Paradoxically, the less she tried to push this image away, the less often it appeared. This was not the intention, but it's something that usually happens as a pleasing side effect.

Exposure

In psychology jargon, the technical term for what you've just been doing is *exposure*. (In everyday language, we use terms like *facing your fears* or *leaving your comfort zone*.) Exposure means deliberately getting in contact with difficult stuff so that you can learn more effective ways of responding to it. This difficult stuff may be in the external world (people, places, situations, activities, events) or your internal world (thoughts, emotions, memories, etc.).

Exposure is the single most powerful intervention in the entire field of psychology; nothing has larger effects on human behavior. And almost everything in this book, at least to some extent, involves exposure. For example, all the unhooking techniques we've so far covered, from dropping anchor to naming the story to thanking your mind, involve deliberate contact with difficult stuff inside you (i.e., your unwanted thoughts and feelings), so you can learn more effective responses.

Going back to the concept of neuroplasticity: exposure enables you to lay new neural pathways on top of the old ones. Thus, when your old neural pathways fire up and those difficult thoughts and feelings reappear, your new neural pathways activate in response: your new learning kicks in and you unhook.

Now time for the "broken record." When you practice these techniques, your unpleasant images/memories will often disappear or lessen in frequency, and you will often feel much better. But those outcomes are "bonuses," not the main aim. Enjoy them when they happen, but don't make them your main intention or you'll soon be disappointed. (I'm sorry if this is repetitive, but many people find it's very hard for these ideas to sink in.) The aim of unhooking is to free you up, to do those toward moves and focus on what matters. (And if this doesn't make sense, please go back and repeat the hands as thoughts experiment on p. 73.)

If you use the techniques as intended, they'll help keep you free of the happiness trap. And they'll also help you to appreciate . . .

[9]

The Stage Show of Life

Life is like a stage show. And on that stage are all your thoughts and feelings and everything you can see, hear, touch, taste, and smell. And this show is continually changing from moment to moment. At times, what appears on that stage is absolutely wonderful; at other times, it's absolutely dreadful. And there's a part of you that can step back and watch that show; zoom in to any part of it, take in the details, or zoom out and take in the big picture. And that part of you is always there, always observing.

In everyday language, we don't have a good word for this part of you. I like to call it the "noticing self." And there's another part of you I like to call the "thinking self": this is the part of you that thinks, plans, judges, compares, creates, imagines, visualizes, analyzes, remembers, daydreams, and fantasizes. Whenever I use the term *mind* in this book, I'm always referring to the thinking self, not the noticing self. It's important to remember this, because in everyday language, the word *mind* usually refers to both the thinking self *and* the noticing self, without distinguishing between them.

The noticing self is fundamentally different from the thinking self. For a start, the noticing self doesn't think; it only notices. (Some people call it the "silent self" or "silent witness" because it never speaks; or the "observer self" because it silently observes.) This part of you is responsible for focus, attention, and awareness. It notices your thoughts but can't create them. The thinking self thinks about your experience—describes it, comments on it, analyzes it, compares it, or judges it—whereas the noticing self notices your experience directly.

For example, if you are playing baseball, cricket, or tennis and you are truly focused, all your attention is riveted on that ball coming toward you. That's your noticing self at work. You are not thinking about the ball; you are noticing it.

Now, suppose thoughts start popping into your head like, "I hope my grip is correct," "I'd better make this a good hit," "Wow, that ball is moving fast!" That's your thinking self at work. And of course, such thoughts can often be distracting. If you pay too much attention to those thoughts, you're no longer focused on the ball and your performance will be impaired. (How often have you been focused on a task, only to be distracted by a thought such as, "I hope I don't screw this up!"?)

The Thinking Self and the Noticing Self

Close your eyes for about a minute and simply notice what your mind does. Stay on the lookout for any thoughts or images, as if you are a wildlife photographer waiting for an exotic animal to emerge from the undergrowth. If no thoughts or images appear, keep watching; sooner or later they will show themselves—I guarantee it. (Your mind will say, "I'm not having any thoughts," "I can't do it," or "It's not working"—and of course, those *are* thoughts.)

With your eyes closed, you'll "see" black, empty space. So as thoughts or images pop up, notice where they are located within that space: in front of you, above you, behind you, to one side of you, or within you.

Are they moving or still?

If they are moving, what speed and what direction?

Alternatively, if you tend to "hear" your thoughts, a bit like a voice inside your head, notice: Where is that voice located?

Is it at the top or bottom, front or back of your head?

Is it loud or soft, speaking quickly or slowly?

Once you've done this experiment for about a minute, open your eyes again. That's all there is to it. So please read these instructions once more, then put down the book and give it a go.

Hopefully you experienced two distinct, but overlapping, processes. The thinking self was generating thoughts or images (and usually also giving a commentary on the experiment: "Am I doing it right?" "What am I supposed to notice?"). The noticing self was noticing whatever thoughts and images appeared (including any commentary).

In all those notice and name exercises, your noticing self notices the cognition, and your thinking self names it. This distinction between thinking and noticing is important, so please do the above experiment once more. Close your eyes for about a minute and notice what thoughts or images appear (including any commentary) and where they seem to be located.

Hopefully, this experiment helped you to "separate" a little from your cognitions: thoughts and images appeared, then disappeared again, and you were able to notice them come and go. In other words, your thinking self produced some cognitions, and your noticing self noticed them coming and going.

Our thinking self is a bit like a radio, constantly playing in the background. Most of the time it's the Radio Doom and Gloom Show, broadcasting negative stories twenty-four hours a day. It reminds us of pain from the past, warns us of dangers in the future, and gives us regular updates on everything that's wrong with us, others, life, the universe, and everything. At times, it broadcasts something useful or cheerful, but nowhere near as often as the negative stuff. So if we're constantly tuned in to this radio, listening to it intently and believing whatever we hear, it's a sure-fire recipe for stress and misery.

Unfortunately, there's no way to switch off this radio. Not even Zen masters can achieve this feat. Sometimes the radio will stop of its own accord for a short span of time. But we can't deliberately *make it* stop (unless we short-circuit it with drugs, alcohol, or brain surgery). In fact, generally speaking, the more we try to make this radio stop, the louder it plays.

But there is an alternative approach. Have you ever had some music playing in the background . . . and you were so intent on what you were doing that you hardly even noticed it was there? You could hear the music, but you were hardly paying it any attention. Well, that's what we're aiming to do with our cognitions. Knowing they are basically "words and pictures inside our head," we can treat them like background noise—let them come and stay and go in their own good time, without giving them much attention. When an unhelpful thought pops up, instead of focusing on it, we acknowledge its presence, allow it to be there, and return our attention to what we're doing.

In other words,

- if the thinking self is broadcasting something unhelpful, we treat it like music playing in the background and focus our attention on whatever we are doing here and now; but
- if the thinking self is broadcasting something useful or helpful, then we tune in, pay attention, and use it.

Radio Doom and Gloom versus Radio Happy and Joyful

What I'm suggesting here is very different from positive thinking, which is like bringing a second radio into the room, tuning it to a different channel (like Radio Happy and Joyful, or Radio Logical and Rational), and playing it alongside the first radio, in the hope of drowning it out. It's pretty hard to focus on what you're doing when you have two different radios playing two different channels in the background.

Notice, too, that when we let music play on in the background without giving it much attention, that's very different from actively trying to *ignore* it. Have you ever heard music playing and tried to ignore it? Or a loud voice in a restaurant? Or an alarm going off in your street? What happened? The more you tried to *ignore* it or *not* hear it, the more it bothered you, right?

The ability to let thoughts come and go in the background while you keep your attention on what you are doing is useful. Suppose you're in a social situation and your mind is saying, "I'm so boring! I have nothing to say. I wish I could go home!" It's hard to have a good conversation if you're focusing on those thoughts. Similarly, suppose you're learning to drive, and your thinking self is saying, "I can't do it. It's too hard. I'm going to crash!" It's hard to drive well if you're focused on those thoughts rather than on the road. So the following technique will teach you how to let your thoughts pass on by while you keep your attention on what you're doing. First read the instructions, then give it a go.

Ten Slow Breaths

In this experiment, it's essential to keep your breathing as sl-o-o-o-w and gentle as possible. If you breathe too fast, too deeply, or too forcefully, you may experience dizziness, pins and needles, or anxiety. (Such reactions are very rare, but if something like this happens for you, make sure to sl-o-o-o-ow your breathing even further, breathing in as *shallowly* and gently as possible; do not take deep breaths or this will worsen your dizziness. And if that doesn't fix the problem, forget this technique and follow the advice in the section on alternative methods, near the end of this chapter.)

- Find a comfortable position and either close your eyes or fix them on a spot in front of you.
- Take ten slow, gentle breaths.
- For each breath, first exhale fully, emptying your lungs. Do this for a count of three seconds—or longer if possible.
- Then, once your lungs are empty, inhale gently.
- When your lungs feel comfortably full, hold your breath for another count of three seconds.
- And then, once more slowly exhale (for at least a count of three seconds).
- Focus on the rise and fall of your rib cage and the air moving in and out of your lungs.
- Notice the sensations as the air flows in: your chest rising, your shoulders lifting, your lungs expanding.
- Notice what you feel as the air flows out: your chest falling, your shoulders dropping, the breath leaving your nostrils.
- Focus on completely emptying your lungs. Gently push out every last bit of air, feeling your lungs deflate.
- Then pause for three seconds before breathing in again.
- As you breathe in, slowly and gently, notice how your tummy moves and your chest expands.
- As you do this, let your thoughts and images come and go in the background, as if they are cars passing by outside your house. (You don't rush out and try to stop the traffic; you let it come and stay and go in its own good time.)

- When a new cognition appears, briefly acknowledge its presence, as if nodding at a passing motorist. You might find it helpful to silently say to yourself, "Thinking."
- As you do this, keep your attention on the breath, following the air as it flows in and out of your lungs.
- From time to time a thought will hook you and pull you out of the exercise, so you lose track of what you're doing. The moment you realize this, acknowledge it. Silently say to yourself, "Hooked," and acknowledge the thought that hooked you. Then gently refocus on your breath.

Please read through the instructions once more, then put the book down and give this a go.

How did you do? Most people get hooked quite a few times. This is completely normal; it happens to all of us, over and over and over, throughout every day. One moment we're focused, the next moment our mind hooks us and whisks our attention elsewhere. So if you practice this exercise regularly, you'll learn three important skills:

1. How to let your thoughts freely come and go, without OBEYING them or STRUGGLING against them. (Needless to say, you aren't trying to clear your thoughts away or empty your mind. You're aiming to let them come and stay and go, in their own good time, as they choose.)
2. How to focus on a task or activity and recognize when your attention has wandered.
3. How to gently unhook from the thoughts that pull you off task and refocus your attention on what you're doing.

Like dropping anchor, we can practice this technique anytime, anywhere, and the more the better. I encourage you to practice it often throughout the day: while you're stuck at traffic lights, waiting in line, on hold on the telephone, waiting for an appointment, during commercial breaks on the TV, and even in bed. Basically, try it any time you have a moment to spare. (And if you don't have time for the full ten breaths, even three or four can be useful.)

And remember when you're doing this, it doesn't matter how many times you get hooked. Each time you notice and unhook, you're building a valuable skill.

Also, as usual, let go of any expectations. Do it as a genuine experiment and notice what effect it has. Many people find it relaxing or calming, but—yes, you guessed it—that's not the primary goal; it's merely an enjoyable bonus. At other times it's likely to be boring, frustrating, or even anxiety provoking. So naturally, appreciate that relaxation or calmness when it occurs, but please don't make that the aim.

Up for a Challenge?

Are you up for a challenge? Something that will help you enormously in developing the skills above? Here's what it involves.

In addition to all those ultra-brief exercises above, put aside five minutes twice a day to practice focusing on your breath. For example, you might do five minutes first thing in the morning and five minutes during your lunch break. Or if you really want to go for broke, do a fifteen-minute session, guided by my free audio recording, "Focusing on Your Breath." You'll find this in chapter 9 of *The Happiness Trap: Extra Bits*, downloadable from the "Free Resources" page on www.thehappinesstrap.com.

Alternatives to Focusing on Your Breath

Some people dislike any sort of exercise that involves focusing attention on the breath, either because it makes them light-headed, dizzy, or anxious, or because they find it really boring. If this is you, no sweat; there are many other options.

Remember, the aims of this practice are to

1. train up our ability to focus our attention—and to catch ourselves quickly when it wanders, and
2. treat our thoughts like music playing in the background, allowing them to freely come and stay and go.

And we're doing this for two main reasons:

1. we get much more satisfaction from the things we do when we give them our full attention, and
2. we handle any challenge or perform any complex task much better when we are focused (as opposed to distracted, disengaged, zoned out, lost in our thoughts).

The good news is, we can develop these skills with almost any task or activity whatsoever. Here are three suggestions for now (we'll cover more later):

Activity 1. Focusing on Walking

Go for a five-minute walk, and with as much curiosity as you can muster, really notice the things around you. Notice what you can see and hear and touch and taste and smell.

Pay attention as if you're a curious child who has never encountered these kinds of things before.

As you do this, let your mind chatter away like a radio playing in the background but don't try to ignore it or silence it.

Keep noticing the world around you as you walk.

From time to time, your mind will succeed in hooking you, and you'll lose track of the exercise. The moment you realize this has happened, acknowledge the thought that hooked you, then refocus on the walk.

Activity 2. Focusing on Your Body

In chapter 17 you'll find a practice called a "body scan," which involves slowly scanning your body, from your toes upward to your head, and focusing on the sensations you encounter. Feel free to skip ahead to chapter 17 now, try it out, and use that method if you prefer it.

Activity 3. Focusing on Stretching

Focused stretching is another good option. You probably know at least a few basic stretches for your body. (If not, Google "basic stretches." And if you're bedbound, Google "bedridden stretches.") Choose two or three stretches and do them very sl-o-o-o-wly and gently, noticing what it feels like as your muscles stre-e-e-e-etch. Notice the sensations in your body as your muscles lengthen and the feeling of warmth as blood flows into the area. Notice that sense of loosening, lengthening, and flexibility. Notice how the sensations in your body continually change—at times painful, at other times pleasant.

Do this for five minutes, focusing entirely on the movements you're doing and the feelings in the areas you're stretching. Focus and refocus repeatedly, as described above, while letting your mind chatter away in the background.

And if doing this seems odd, unnatural, or uncomfortable . . . that's good! It means you're trying something new, something different. It's a sure sign that you're . . .

[10]

Leaving the Comfort Zone

Here's my guarantee to each and every reader of this book. As soon as you start to stretch yourself, to take your life in a new, meaningful direction, difficult thoughts and feelings will arise (100 percent guaranteed, or your money back!). This is because of your mind's overriding imperative: "Safety first!" As soon as we start to do something new, our mind will send us warnings in the form of negative thoughts, disturbing images, bad memories, and uncomfortable emotions, urges, and sensations.

And all too often, we let these "warnings" stop us from doing what matters; instead, we keep doing the same old things. Some people call this "staying in your comfort zone." But personally, I don't think that's a good name for it, because life inside the comfort zone is definitely not comfortable. It should be called the "misery zone," "stagnant zone," or "missing-out-on-life zone."

Whatever you wish to call it, there are two interweaving strategies for leaving this desolate place: (1) continually expand the range of your unhooking skills, and (2) connect with something that makes it worthwhile leaving. We'll focus on the first strategy over the next few chapters; in this one, we're going to look at the second strategy, beginning with a discussion of . . .

Values and Goals

Values are your heart's deepest desires for how you want to treat yourself and others and the world around you; personal qualities you want to bring into play in the things you say and do. For example, if deep in your heart you desire personal qualities such as being open, honest, loving, and caring, then we'd call those things your values. (But if you don't wish to behave in that manner, then they are not your values.) Once we know what our values are, we can use them for inspiration, motivation, and guidance, to help us do things that make our lives more meaningful and rewarding.

Values are very different from goals. Goals are things you're aiming for in the future: things you want to get, have, achieve, or do. Most of our goals fall into three categories: emotional goals, behavioral goals, and outcome goals.

Emotional Goals

Emotional goals describe how we want to feel (e.g., "I want to feel happy," "I want to stop feeling anxious," "I want more confidence," "I want inner peace").

Behavioral Goals

These goals describe how we want to behave and actions we want to take (e.g., "I want to exercise more," "I want to spend more quality time with my friends or family," "I want to travel").

Outcome Goals

These goals describe the outcomes we desire: what we want to *get* or *have* (e.g., "I want more friends," "I want other people to love me, treat me well, respect me," "I want a good body, great job, lovely house," "I want financial security, good health, equal opportunity," "I want power, status, fame").

It's very important to understand the difference between outcome goals and values, for reasons I'll explain shortly. So, for example, if you want to be loving and kind, those are values. But if you want to get married, that's an outcome goal. Notice you can live your values of being loving and kind even if you never achieve the outcome goal of marriage. (For example, you can be loving and kind to yourself, your dog, your cat, your friends, or your family.)

On the other hand, you can achieve the outcome goal of getting married yet neglect your values of being loving and kind (in which case, your marriage will suffer).

Here's another example: Suppose when you're at work you want to be open, honest, and cooperative; if so, those are (some of) your workplace values. In contrast, if you want to have a great job, that's an outcome goal. And notice, you can live your values of being open, honest, and cooperative whether your job is awesome or totally sucks. You can also live those values if you're retired, unemployed, or unable to work due to sickness or disability.

This difference between values and goals is of huge importance when it comes to . . .

Personal Empowerment

Have you ever seen pictures of those vast refugee camps in African and Middle Eastern countries: thousands of tents clumped together in the middle of a dry, barren wasteland? Some of these camps contain up to four hundred thousand refugees, struggling to survive amid the most awful hardships and deprivation. Could ACT help people in these terrible circumstances, many of whom have suffered terrible trauma?

The WHO thought it might. So back in 2015, they asked me to write a program, based on ACT, that they could roll out in refugee camps to help people cope with the enormous ongoing stress of camp life. The ten-hour program (two hours a week for five weeks) was delivered via audio recordings to groups of about twenty people at a time. At the time of this writing (2021), the WHO has been using that program for over five years, in camps in Syria, Turkey, and Uganda. And did it help? Remarkably, yes. The WHO carefully researched the program, and in 2020 they published their results in one of the world's top medical journals, the *Lancet*. Astonishingly, the refugees experienced significant improvements in their psychological health, including major reductions in depression and PTSD.

A big part of that program was the sense of personal empowerment among the participants, through connecting with their values. You see, in a refugee camp, there are many outcome goals that are impossible: get a paid job, get a car, have plentiful delicious food, live in a house instead of a tent, reunite with loved ones left behind, and so on and so on. Chances are, if you're reading this book, you take many things for granted that someone in a refugee camp would dearly love to have, from unlimited electricity and running water to plentiful food and clothes.

So what happens to any of us—whether our lives are very privileged or extremely deprived—if we become preoccupied or obsessed with achieving outcome goals that are (at least for now) unachievable? That's right: we will experience frustration, dissatisfaction, disappointment, sadness, or even hopelessness, because we're not getting what we want.

But values are a different story. We can live our values right here and now, in a thousand different ways, even when our goals are impossible. To clarify this in the refugee program, we used the following example. Suppose your goal is to get a paid job so you can support the people you care about. And suppose your values—the way you want to treat your family, friends, or people around you—are to be kind, caring, loving, and supportive. It might be impossible to achieve your goal . . . but you can still live your values. You can find little ways to be kind, caring, loving, and supportive to the people around you.

"What's so empowering about that?" you may be wondering. Well, the more preoccupied we are with what is *out of* our control (such as things we can't have), the more miserable and disempowered we become. But our values connect us with what is *in* our control: the ability to act like the sort of person we want to be.

This is important, because the only way you can influence the world around you is through your "actions": what you do with your arms, hands, legs, feet, and speech. And the more you take control of your own actions, the more you can influence the world around you: the people and situations you encounter every day.

For example, if you live in a refugee camp, you share a tent with other people. And you can act on your values of being kind, warm, and caring toward those others, or you can move away from your values and act in ways that are unkind, cold, or hostile. So your actions will influence what it's like to live inside that tent. Your actions won't end the war you fled or bring back loved ones from the dead or transform your flimsy tent into a brick house. But your actions can either improve or worsen the atmosphere within your tent; that is very much within your control.

The better we know our values, the easier it is to act on them, and the more we act on our values, the more we can shape our life in meaningful ways. So am I suggesting you give up on all your goals? NOOOOO! Not at all. In fact, later in the book, we'll look at practical strategies to help you get better at actually achieving your goals. What I'm saying is, values are instantly empowering in a way that goals never can be. Why? Because we can always live our values in little ways, no matter what life is like.

For example, if someone is living in poverty, living with severe chronic illness, or continually subjected to prejudice and discrimination on the grounds of sex, religion, or skin color, they're at a huge disadvantage to many others, and because of this disadvantage, they may have many goals that are not currently—and perhaps never will be—achievable. However, they can still live by and act on their values; they can still choose how to treat themselves and others and the world around them as they continue living in difficult circumstances.

For a more extreme example, suppose you have an incurable, progressive, terminal illness. If so, you will never achieve the goal of "good health," but you *can* live your values of being kind and caring to yourself.

I often use the term *reality gap* to describe difficult circumstances such as those above. A reality gap is any painful gap between the reality you want and the reality you've got. And the bigger that gap, the greater the pain that goes with it. (So if you are currently facing a huge reality gap, many difficult thoughts and feelings will arise, and you'll need all the unhooking skills in this book to handle them well.)

Some reality gaps can never be closed. For example, when someone you love has just died, there's no way to close that gap. Other reality gaps *can* be closed (for example, if you get cancer, but it's curable); however, it can take a long, long time and a huge amount of effort to get there. Values empower us to handle large reality gaps more effectively, whether we can close them or not.

Are you finding any of this a tad confusing? If so, you're not alone. The concept of values is so different from the much more familiar concept of goals, it often takes a while to wrap your head around it. Which is why we'll be exploring this concept repeatedly, starting right now with a quick look at . . .

A Values Checklist

As I mentioned earlier, values are your heart's deepest desires for how you want to behave as a human being. They describe how you want to treat yourself, others, and the world around you. Below is a list of common values. They are not the "right" values; there are no "right" or "wrong" ones. Values are like your taste in ice cream. If you prefer chocolate but someone else prefers vanilla, that doesn't mean their taste is right and yours is wrong, or vice versa. It just means you have different tastes. So these aren't the "right" or "best" values; they're just to give you some ideas. (And if your values aren't listed, there's room at the bottom to add them.)

Pick an area of life you want to improve (e.g., work, health, leisure, relationships). Then consider which values in the list below best complete this sentence: *In this area of my life, I want to be . . .*

As you read through the list, if a value seems very important, put a V by it; if somewhat important, put an S; and if not that important, put an N. (Alternatively, use the values checklist inside *The Happiness Trap: Extra Bits*, downloadable from www.thehappinesstrap.com.)

Common Values: A Checklist

In this area of my life, I want to be . . .

1. Accepting: open to, allowing of, or at peace with myself, others, life, my feelings, etc. V
2. Adventurous: willing to create or pursue novel, risky, or exciting experiences S
3. Assertive: calmly, fairly, and respectfully standing up for my rights, asking for what I want, and declining unreasonable requests V
4. Authentic: being genuine, real, and true to myself V
5. Caring/self-caring: actively taking care of myself, others, the environment, etc. V
6. Compassionate/self-compassionate: responding kindly to myself or others in pain V
7. Cooperative: willing to assist and work with others S
8. Courageous: being brave or bold; persisting in the face of fear, threat, or risk S
9. Creative: being imaginative, inventive, or innovative S
10. Curious: being open-minded and interested; willing to explore and discover S

11. Encouraging: supporting, inspiring, and rewarding behavior I approve of ⊆

12. Expressive: conveying my thoughts and feelings through what I say and do ⊆

13. Focused: focused on and engaged in what I am doing S

14. Fair/just: acting with fairness and justice toward myself and others S

15. Flexible: willing and able to adjust and adapt to changing circumstances S

16. Friendly: warm, open, caring, and agreeable toward others ∨

17. Forgiving: letting go of resentments and grudges toward myself or others ∨

18. Grateful: being appreciative for what I have received ⊆

19. Helpful: giving, helping, contributing, assisting, or sharing ∨

20. Honest: being honest, truthful, and sincere with myself and others ∨

21. Independent: choosing for myself how I live and what I do ∨

22. Industrious: being diligent, hardworking, dedicated S

23. Kind: being considerate, helpful, or caring to myself or others ∨

24. Loving: showing love, affection, or great care to myself or others ∨

25. Mindful/present: fully present and engaging in whatever I'm doing S

26. Open: revealing myself, letting people know my thoughts and feelings S

27. Orderly: being neat and organized ∧

28. Persistent/committed: willing to continue, despite problems or difficulties ∨

29. Playful: being humorous, fun-loving, lighthearted S

30. Protective: looking after the safety and security of myself or others S

31. Respectful/self-respectful: treating myself or others with care and consideration S

32. Responsible: being trustworthy, reliable, and accountable for my actions S

33. Skillful: doing things well; utilizing my knowledge, experience, and training ∨

34. Supportive: being helpful, encouraging, and available to myself or others √

35. Trustworthy: being loyal, honest, faithful, sincere, responsible, and reliable √

36. Trusting: willing to believe in the honesty, sincerity, reliability, or competence of another ら

37. Other: _Monogamy not really a_
38. Other: _good value, seems_
39. Other: _more like an_
40. Other: _outcome goal._
Would doing be better?

© Russ Harris, 2020, www.ImLearningACT.com

Please write down or mentally note any values that seem especially important to you, so you have them for future reference.

The Journey and the Destination

You've probably heard the saying, "It's not the destination that counts; it's the journey." Personally, I would say it's both. The destination clearly matters; a visit to Sweden is not the same as a visit to Afghanistan. But the journey to get there is also very important, especially as there's never any guarantee that you'll make it all the way.

The destination you head for is a goal. In contrast, your values describe the sort of traveler you want to be: How do you want to treat yourself, other people, and the things you encounter on your voyage? As you're traveling toward your destination, do you want to be kind and helpful to other travelers you meet, or mean, aggressive, or distant? Do you want to be open to, curious about, and appreciative of your experiences? Or closed off, uninterested, or disapproving? Do you want to treat your body caringly or neglectfully?

Notice you can live your values as a traveler, every step of the way toward that goal—even if you ultimately end up at a different destination. So, keeping this distinction in mind, let's do a different exercise to tease out some goals.

Suppose Magic Happens . . .

Please take a few moments to reflect on the questions below. There are quite a few, so feel free to skip some, but please reflect on at least two or three.

Suppose magic happens, so that all your difficult thoughts and feelings become like water off a duck's back; they lose their power over you; they no longer bring you down or hold you back . . .

- What projects, activities, or tasks would you start, resume, or continue?
- What or who would you stop avoiding?
- What would you start doing or do more of?
- How would you treat yourself differently?
- How would you treat others differently, in your most important relationships?

Please take a few minutes to think deeply about at least two or three of these questions. Better yet, write down your answers for future reference.

When you contemplate the questions above, what shows up? Images of things going badly? Memories of failure? Feelings of anxiety? A tight chest, knots in the stomach, or other uncomfortable sensations? Reasons not to do it?

If any of those things appeared, that's completely normal. And here's my guarantee: these troublesome thoughts and feelings will repeatedly appear. We can't eliminate them, but we can get very good at unhooking from them. Soon you'll learn how to unhook from emotions, sensations, and urges; but for now, stick with cognitions.

And I do strongly encourage you to practice, practice, practice those unhooking skills; because the more you can see your cognitions for what they are—words and pictures inside your head—the less negative influence they'll have over your life. (And if your reason-giving machine cranks out some excuse for not practicing, please notice and name it. And maybe even thank your mind: "Thanks, Mind. I know you're trying to save me from the discomfort of doing something challenging; and it's okay, I can handle this.")

In addition to all that unhooking practice, I encourage you to start playing around with your values. But please don't make a big deal out of it. All you need do is pick one or two values every day and look for opportunities to "sprinkle" them into your activities. For example, suppose you pick "kindness"; then as you go through your day, look for little ways to act kindly—kind things you can say, kind actions you can do. Do this as an experiment and notice what happens.

Be warned: your mind can tie you up in knots with questions like "Which values do I pick?" or "How do I know if they're the right ones?" There are only two purposes to this exercise: (1) play around with some values, and (2) notice what happens. So it doesn't really matter which values you pick. If it's hard to decide, do it in numerical order, as in the list. Play with one or two values for a few days and notice what happens. Then pick one or two more and play with those. And so on and so on.

Meanwhile, in the next chapter, we're going to look at a quality that's incredibly important for coping with pain and suffering. And if this quality is not yet one of your values, I hope it will soon become so. What I'm talking about is . . .

[11]

The Value of Kindness

Imagine you're on a grueling and dangerous journey, and all sorts of terrible things keep happening. You've encountered obstacle after obstacle, been knocked around over and over, you're exhausted and sore and you're struggling to keep going. But you're not totally alone on this journey; you have a companion by your side.

Now, let's suppose you have a choice between two different companions. Option 1: a companion who says, "This isn't so bad. You're pathetic. Just suck it up and get on with it!" Option 2: a companion who says, "This is really shit. But hey, we're in this together. I've got your back, and I'm with you every step of the way."

I've asked literally thousands of people, "Which companion would you prefer?" So far, everybody has chosen the second (often while looking at me as if I've just asked a stupid question). I then ask, "So what kind of companion are you being to yourself? Do you treat yourself more like the first one, or the second?" Almost everyone replies, "The first."

The absurd thing is, when our close friends or loved ones are deeply suffering, most of us are instinctively kind, understanding, and supportive; yet we find it extremely hard to treat ourselves the same way. Indeed, when I first introduce the idea of self-kindness, it's amazing how often people react negatively—especially if I call it by its other name: "self-compassion." Often when people hear the word *self-compassion*, their reason-giving machines go into overdrive, cranking out a long list of reasons to steer clear of it. They perceive it as weak, stupid, useless, passive, selfish, or demotivating. Sometimes they'll even insist that they're such bad people, they don't deserve it. We'll address these objections very shortly; but first let's clarify . . .

What Does *Self-Compassion* Mean?

There are many different definitions of *self-compassion*, and no universal agreement on any one of them. My own definition is only six words long: "acknowledge your pain; respond with kindness." In other words, self-compassion is consciously acknowledging your pain, hurt, and suffering—and in response, treating yourself with kindness and caring.

For most of us, self-compassion doesn't come naturally; we usually only learn it when we go down the path of therapy, personal growth, or spiritual development. When pain shows up, our default response modes are to OBEY it (allow it to push us around, dictate what to do) or STRUGGLE.

Self-compassion is radically different from both. We simply acknowledge our pain and treat ourselves kindly. And although for thousands of years people mainly learned about this concept through religion, these days it's well and truly in the realm of science. Hundreds of scientific studies published in top psychology journals have demonstrated the many benefits of self-compassion for health, well-being, and happiness. And the good news is, you've already started doing this.

How so? Well, self-compassion begins by simply being honest with ourselves about how much pain we're in—but without dwelling on it or wallowing in it. And that's completely different from self-pity, which sounds something like this: "I can't bear it any longer. I've never felt so bad. Why me? It's not fair. No one else has to go through this. I can't handle it." Self-pity never helps; it only makes things worse.

Self-compassion means we acknowledge our pain in a simple, kind, and honest way—just as we'd acknowledge the pain of a friend who was suffering. You've been practicing this for the past four chapters, in the Acknowledge phase of ACE, and whenever you notice and name difficult thoughts and feelings.

If you can't pinpoint the exact thoughts and feelings, you can use terms like *suffering*, *hurt*, *pain*, *heartbreak*, and *loss* (e.g., "Here is suffering" or "I'm noticing pain"). You may also like to add extra phrases, such as "here and now" or "this is a moment of." Why? Because when we say, "Here and now, I'm noticing anxiety" or "This is a moment of loneliness," it helps us remember that, much like the weather, our thoughts and feelings are changing all the time. Even amid great suffering, our cognitions and emotions change from moment to moment; sometimes we feel better, other times, worse. "Here and now" we may be noticing sadness, but later we'll be noticing different feelings. Please play around with these words and create a phrase that suits you. Psychologist Kristin Neff, the world's top researcher on self-compassion, suggests, "This is a moment of suffering"—a poetic phrase that appeals to many. However, some folks (like me) prefer more everyday language, such as "This really hurts."

Acknowledging our pain is just the first step in self-compassion; we then need to respond with genuine kindness. But before we get into that, let's revisit those . . .

Objections to Self-Compassion

Earlier I mentioned some common objections to self-compassion. Let's take a look at them and see if they have any substance. Let's start with "weak" or "stupid." If a good friend or a loved one were suffering, and you acknowledged their pain and said or did kind things to support them, would that be weak or stupid? Of course not. So neither is it weak or stupid to treat yourself that way (even if your mind says it is).

How about "useless" or "passive"? Well, the hundreds of studies I mentioned above show it's clearly not useless, if you value your health and well-being. Self-compassion helps you cope with adversity and handle stress much better, protects you from depression, and facilitates recovery after setbacks. And it's definitely not a "passive" response to life's challenges. It's a form of actively supporting yourself. It doesn't mean you give up or stop trying; self-compassion gives you more energy, so you can rise to your challenges, tackle your problems, do those toward moves.

So what about the notion that it's "selfish"? Well, if you've ever flown on a plane, you'll know what flight crew say about oxygen masks: put your own on first before you try to help anyone else. You can think of self-compassion the same way: if you take better care of yourself, you'll be able to take better care of others.

How about "demotivating"? Let's go back to Michelle (from chapter 3). This was her main objection to self-compassion. "I need to be hard on myself," she said. "That's how I get things done. It motivates me. If I was kind to myself, I'd never do anything." This idea is incredibly common, especially among perfectionists and high achievers. And yes, in the short term, being hard on yourself can often be motivating; but the long-term costs of this motivational method are enormous: stress, anxiety, depression, exhaustion, low self-esteem, or burnout.

To understand this better, think of your favorite team sport. Imagine two teams of equally talented players, and they each have a coach. The first coach motivates the players through being harsh, judgmental, and critical; focusing on everything the players do wrong: "That was pathetic!" "You're useless!" "You're not even trying!" "I can't believe you did that!" "How many times do I have to tell you?" "You screwed up this, you messed up that, and you completely stuffed up the other."

The second coach motivates the players through kind, supportive feedback and encouragement, acknowledging what they do right as well as what they do wrong: "You did A, B, and C really well today. And I can see you're improving at D and E. And I was stoked you remembered to do H and I when J happened. I notice you seem to be struggling a bit with P, Q, and Z; let's have a look at what's going on there and see how you can improve on that. Yeah, I know you messed up with X and Y, but hey— we're all human; we all make mistakes. Don't beat yourself up about it; let's go over it and see what you can do differently next time something like that happens."

There's been a huge amount of scientific research on this topic, and the results are crystal clear: harsh, critical, judgmental coaching may get positive results in the short term, but in the long term it leads to demotivated players and poor performance. Kind, supportive coaching is far more effective in the long term; players are more motivated and perform better.

Have you ever had a coach/teacher/manager/parent who used the harsh, critical method with you? If so, how did you find it? (No need to answer.) Later in the book, we'll explore much more effective methods of motivation that, in conjunction with self-compassion, will not only get you started and keep you going but also keep you healthy and thriving.

Finally, let's consider the objection "I'm so bad I don't deserve kindness!" This story is common if you've had an awful childhood—neglect, abuse, trauma, abandonment, and so on. Your parents or caregivers may have directly called you bad (in any of a thousand different ways) or indicated it through the way they mistreated you. But it is also common in people who had pretty good childhoods. And again, this is your mind trying to be helpful in its own misguided way; like the first coach in the scenario above, your mind thinks being hard on you is the best way to get results: to get you to shape up, sort yourself out, be a better person. So look at that story in terms of workability: if you let it dictate your actions, boss you around, tell you what you can and can't do . . . does that take you toward or away from the life you want?

Obviously, if it's helping you to do toward moves—to behave like the sort of person you want to be, build the sort of life you want—and it's contributing to your health, well-being, and happiness . . . there's no problem. But if it's taking you in the other direction, there's a choice to make: Are you going to go along with it? Or are you going to unhook and experiment with a different approach?

Kindness in Words and Actions

If someone you deeply care about were suffering—struggling with painful thoughts and feelings, or grappling with major problems—how would you treat them? If you wanted to send them the message, "I see you're hurting, I care about you and I'm here for you," what sort of things would you say and do?

Please reflect on this for at least two minutes, before reading on . . .

Self-compassion means treating ourselves the way we would a loved one; so whatever you came up with while reflecting on the question above, now it's time to apply that to yourself. Let's kick off with a look at . . .

Kind Self-Talk

Kind self-talk means speaking to ourselves in ways that are kind, encouraging, and supportive, much like the second coach and the second traveling companion. But remember: the brain changes through addition, not subtraction. So we're not trying to delete those old neural pathways that give rise to harsh self-talk; we're laying down new ones on top of them to bring in self-kindness. (So if harsh, judgmental self-talk shows up—as it often does, for most of us—then we don't try to dispute, avoid, or get rid of it; we simply notice and name it.)

What kind of things should we say to ourselves? There are soooo many options. Suppose we're struggling to complete a difficult but important task, and our mind's saying, "This is too hard" or "I can't do it." First, we might thank our mind, "Thanks, Mind, I know you're trying to make me give up, to spare me from discomfort, but it's okay, I've got this covered." Then we can try some kind self-encouragement: "I can handle this," "I can do this," "I'll get through this."

Or suppose after making a mistake we get hooked by "I'm a loser." Our kind self-talk might go like this: "Aha. Here's the 'loser' story again. Okay, I know I screwed up. But hey, I'm human. Everyone makes mistakes."

If you're hooked by a perfectionistic rule, you could say, "I'm having the thought I need to do this perfectly. But hey, I really don't have to. 'Good enough' is okay."

If you're struggling to make changes in your behavior and you fall back into an old pattern, your mind might say, "This is hopeless, I can't change." Your self-compassionate response might be, "Here's the 'give up' story—but I'm not buying it. What I'm trying to do here is really difficult—and today was a bad day. I'll have another crack at it tomorrow. Over time, I'll get better."

At this point, an important practical tip: It's not just the words you say that count but also the way you say them. So be aware of the tone of your "inner voice." If it's harsh, sarcastic, or uncaring, it will not have the desired effect. It needs to sound kind and caring.

So throughout the day, whenever difficult thoughts and feelings arise, the idea is to acknowledge they're present, acknowledge it's painful or difficult to have them, and then remind yourself to respond with kindness and caring. To help with this, it's useful to have a simple catchphrase you can say to yourself. Kristin Neff, the self-compassion expert I mentioned earlier, recommends this one: "This is a moment of suffering. May I be kind to myself." However, personally I prefer something a bit shorter and simpler. My self-compassion catchphrase is "This really hurts. Be kind." If either of those appeal to you, feel free to use them; but if you prefer to come up with your own phrase, all the better.

Play around with kind self-talk (using a kind tone of voice). And find your own way of doing it, using your own style of speaking (which might sound nothing like the examples above). And if you're ever stuck for ideas, consider this: "What would I say to a friend who was going through something similar?"

Now, moving on from kind self-talk, let's explore the equally important role of kind actions . . .

Kind Actions

Self-compassion is not just about what we say to ourselves; it's also about what we *do* for ourselves: actions of kindness, caring, and support. And really, the sky's the limit. Self-compassionate actions could include reading this book; practicing your unhooking skills; spending quality time with others; doing basic self-care such as healthy eating and regular exercise; making time for rest and relaxation; doing hobbies or sports or other pleasurable, restorative activities; and so on.

The great thing is you don't have to do anything dramatic. Even the tiniest little act of self-kindness counts. To give you an idea, here are some little acts of self-kindness I did today. I did some stretching of my back and neck; had a long, hot shower; played around with the dog; had a laugh with my son watching some silly YouTube videos; ate some healthy stuff for breakfast; and at one point I sat outside for a few minutes and closed my eyes—just to hear the birds and feel the sun on my face.

Now take two minutes to consider this: what are some kind actions you can do for yourself in (a) the next few hours and (b) the next few days?

Please write your answers down. (If you wish, you can use the "Kind Words and Actions Worksheet," which you'll find in *The Happiness Trap: Extra Bits.*) Over the next few hours and days, actually do these things and notice what it's like to do so; truly savor those actions of kindness and caring. (And if you don't do them, notice how your mind talked you out of it: What reasons did it give you not to? What rules did it impose on you?)

Where to from Here?

We've so far covered three important elements of self-compassion: unhooking from harsh, judgmental self-talk; acknowledging our pain and suffering; and treating ourselves kindly. Over the next few chapters, we're going to cover another important element: unhooking from painful emotions.

[TROUBLESHOOTING]

It Feels Weird; This Isn't Me; I Don't Do This

At first, self-compassion may seem odd or unnatural—like it's not really you. If so, that's a completely normal reaction. This is a new psychological skill. Maybe after you've practiced it ten thousand times it *will* seem natural; but it definitely won't to begin with. Are you willing to do something that feels weird, odd, or "not like you" in the service of building a better life?

It Makes Me Feel Anxious

If you've got a long history of deeply entrenched self-judgment, self-hatred, or self-loathing, self-compassion might initially trigger anxiety. It's such a radically different way of treating yourself. Your mind is suspicious: "What is this? I don't know what this is. It's different. It's weird. I don't know what might happen." You may not be aware of those thoughts—you might just feel anxious—but that's what's going on inside your head.

Another way to make sense of this anxiety is that it's like you're "breaking the rules." For a long time, your mind has ruled you like a tyrant, laying down the laws and commandments and forbidding you to break them. This includes the rule "YOU ARE NOT ALLOWED TO BE KIND TO YOURSELF!" Breaking this rule feels risky (something bad might happen if you get caught). So naturally, anxiety appears.

Over time, if you practice self-compassion regularly, until it becomes a familiar experience, that anxiety will lessen; but in the early stages, it will be there. So the question is this: are you willing to have some anxious thoughts and feelings in the short term in order to build a better life in the long term?

It Stirs Up My Negative Self-Talk

Sometimes kind self-talk can trigger a barrage of harsh self-judgment. Over time, you can expect these barrages to lessen, and then stop.

Whenever they occur, notice and name them—and if that doesn't help, drop anchor.

It Didn't Make My Feelings Go Away

It's not supposed to. It's not a struggle strategy. The aim is to acknowledge and allow your feelings to be present, without a struggle (like resting the book on your lap in chapter 4), while also being kind and supportive to yourself. When difficult thoughts and feelings lessen or disappear—as often happens—that's a bonus, not the main aim.

[12]

Hooked on a Feeling

You're trekking through the snowy wilderness of Alaska, and you suddenly come face-to-face with a huge grizzly bear. What do you do? Scream? Call for help? Run away? We'll return to this tricky situation shortly, but first let's tackle another challenging question: What *are* emotions?

Scientists have a hard time reaching any kind of consensus on what emotions are, but most experts agree on two things:

1. Underlying any emotion is a complex series of changes throughout the body, involving your brain and nervous system, heart and blood flow, lungs and airflow, abdominal organs, muscles, and hormones.
2. These physical changes prepare us for action.

As these changes happen in our body, they give rise to sensations such as "butterflies" in the stomach, a "lump" in the throat, or a "pounding" heart. At the same time, urges arise to act in particular ways: for example, to cry, laugh, scream, shout, or hide. The likelihood that we will act in a particular way when experiencing a particular emotion is called an "action tendency." But notice the key word here: *tendency*. A tendency means we have the *inclination* to do something; it doesn't mean we *have to* do it, that we have no choice.

So, for example, when you're anxious about running late, you might have the *tendency* to drive above the speed limit, but you can *choose* to drive legally and safely if you wish. However, as discussed in chapter 2, the less our ability to *unhook* from our emotions, the less choice we have.

In other words, the better our unhooking skills, the more control we have over our physical actions—our body posture, our facial expression, the words we say, the volume and tone of our voice, and the movements we make with our arms, legs, hands, and feet. This ability is incredibly useful. If we can control our physical actions when feeling strong emotions, this enables us to act in ways that get better results: we can feel anxious but act courageously; feel angry but act calmly.

For example, suppose I'm feeling truly furious with my teenage son (yes, it happens). When I'm being the sort of father I want to be, I silently acknowledge the raging anger storm inside me, and I drop anchor and take control of my actions; I speak to him in a soft, patient voice, with my arms by my side and my hands open, and I explain to him assertively and patiently what the problem is and what I would like him to do. And when I do that, it's so much healthier for our relationship than at other times when I get completely hooked by my anger and behave like a silverback gorilla: jutting out my chest and jaw, waving my arms around, and yelling.* As any parent knows, yelling at the kids often works in the short term to get your needs met. However, in the long term it doesn't work well for building a healthy relationship. (Plus, it's really bad role-modeling; sorry, son!)

The first skill we learned in this book was how to drop anchor, which offers a way to unhook from emotions while taking control of our physical actions. But that is just the very tip of the iceberg. Over the next few chapters, we'll explore what emotions are, the purpose they serve, how to unhook from them, and how to actually use them to enhance your life. We'll kick off with a look at the . . .

The Fight-or-Flight Response

The fight-or-flight response is a primitive survival reflex that originates in the midbrain. We find it in all mammals, birds, reptiles, amphibians, and most fish. it. It operates on the basis that if something is threatening you, your best chance of survival is either to run away (flight) or to stand your ground and defend yourself (fight). So whenever the brain perceives

---

* I can't stand those self-help books where the author seems to be perfect, flawless, and infallible. We're all human, and we all screw up.

something to be a significant threat, the fight-or-flight response immediately activates. Our body floods with adrenaline; the large muscles in our arms, legs, neck, and shoulders tense up, ready for action; and our heart and lungs speed up to pump well-oxygenated blood to our muscles. All of this primes us to effectively flee or fight.

In truly dangerous situations—running through a war zone or fighting off a wild animal—this response is lifesaving. But in modern life, most of us rarely find ourselves in genuinely life-threatening predicaments—and, unfortunately, our fight-or-flight response often fires up in situations where it's more of a hindrance than a help.

Once again, this is due to our overly helpful mind working with our body to keep us safe. Operating in "Safety first!" mode, our mind sees potential danger almost everywhere: in a moody partner, a controlling boss, a parking ticket, a new job, a traffic jam, a long line at the bank, a big mortgage, an unflattering reflection in the mirror—you name it. In addition, our mind may interpret our own thoughts, memories, images, emotions, and sensations as threats. Obviously, these inner experiences are not life-threatening, but our brain and body react as if they are. This gives rise to emotions such as fear, anxiety, or panic (related to "flight"), and irritation, anger, or rage (related to "fight").

The Freeze Response

Earlier I mentioned how when we're in great pain, the vagus nerve can cut off painful feelings in the body, resulting in emotional numbness. This same large nerve can also temporarily "freeze" or "lock up" the body. This happens when a threat is so extreme that our brain perceives fight or flight as futile (e.g., when someone is pinned under a rockslide, or a young child is abused by an adult).

When the threat is extreme and attempts to fight or flee appear futile, the vagus nerve takes the helm and switches us into "emergency shutdown" mode. This immobilizes the body, slows down the heart and lungs, drops blood pressure, and pauses nonessential activities such as digestion. In the early stages of shutdown, someone may be "frozen stiff," "rooted to the spot," or "completely paralyzed." The vagus also cuts off your feelings in these awful situations, trying to spare you from terror and physical pain.

So the freeze response is a powerful survival mechanism. It can keep you alive in situations when fight or flight is impossible or only likely to make things worse. However, freeze responses can continue to activate long after the traumatic situation(s) is over—even many decades later—often triggered by strong emotions or painful memories. If you are experiencing this kind of trauma-related freezing on a regular basis, dropping anchor is an extremely useful practice; it helps you to "unlock" your body, regain control of your actions, and reengage in life. The idea is to practice it often, immediately start doing it at the first sign of locking up, and keep going with it until you're back in control of your body and present in your life.

Numbness is the most common side effect of the freeze response, but it can also foster states such as apathy, despair, or hopelessness.

Elements of an Emotion

Any emotion we experience—anger, sadness, guilt, fear, shame, disgust, love, joy, curiosity, and so on—is always comprised of three interweaving elements: sensations, cognitions, and urges. Let's explore these elements with regard to anxiety.

Sensations

For most (but not all) of us, physical sensations in the body are a strong aspect of an emotion. For example, when feeling anxiety, we might notice muscle tension in various parts of the body, shaking, sweating, numbness, knots in the stomach, a lump in the throat, tightness in the chest, a racing heart, and so on. (Keep in mind, no two people experience any given emotion in exactly the same way; what you feel in your body could be very similar to the above, or completely different.)

Cognitions

Cognitions are an intrinsic element of all emotions. For example, when experiencing anxiety, we might have thoughts like, "It's not going to work," "Something bad will happen," "I can't stand this," and so on. Cognitions might also include the name we give to the experience (e.g., do we describe it as "anxiety" or do we talk of feeling "nervous," "jittery," "shaken," "on edge"?);

- the meaning we make of it (e.g., "I feel scared so that means I'm in danger"); and
- the images or memories that go with it (e.g., memories of other times you've felt afraid, or images of what you fear).

Urges

All emotions come with urges. For example, with anxiety there might be urges to worry, seek reassurance, take drugs, drink alcohol, smoke a cigarette, distract oneself, avoid or leave a difficult situation, and so on. However, an urge is itself comprised of cognitions and sensations. For example, if you have an urge to drink alcohol, you will have words and images inside your head to do with drinking that alcohol. And if you tune in to your body, you will notice the (often subtle) sensations of that urge: perhaps warmth and wetness inside your mouth or a tingling in your tongue and throat or increased tension and restlessness in your limbs or jaws. So basically, any emotion or urge is a loose bundle of sensations and cognitions, continually interacting with each other in a myriad of complex ways.

Do We Have to OBEY Our Emotions?

The answer to this is, quite simply, no! If we lack unhooking skills, then naturally our emotions will dominate us. But the greater our ability to unhook, the more freedom we have to choose how we behave in their presence. I'm sure that at some point in your life you have felt afraid, yet you did what you needed to do, even though you felt like running away. We all have experienced this when taking an important test, asking someone for a date, going for a job interview, speaking before a group, or partaking in a dangerous sport.

Whenever I give a speech in public, I experience anxiety. And yet, when I reveal this to my audience, they are always amazed. "But you look so calm and confident," people often say. That's because even though I'm *feeling* anxious (racing heart, churning stomach, and my hands literally dripping with sweat), I am not *acting* anxiously. I have the urge to fidget, breathe rapidly, and talk fast; yet I do the very opposite of these things. I consciously choose to talk slowly, breathe slowly, and move slowly. The same is true for virtually all public speakers: even after years of experience, they still commonly feel anxious, but you'd never know it because they *act* calmly.

Now let's get back to that trek through the Alaskan wilderness where you suddenly come face-to-face with a grizzly bear. Your fight-or-flight response will kick in, you will feel intense fear, and you'll feel the urge to turn and run. But if you've read your survival manual, you'll know that's a bad idea. If you turn and run, this will incite the bear's pursuit instinct. It will chase after you, easily outrun you—and hey presto, you're snack food. What you need to do is back away v-e-e-e-ry sl-o-o-o-wly, make no sudden moves or loud noises, and never turn your back on the bear. (So don't say you didn't learn anything in this book!)

Many people have survived by following this advice. Here's the point I'm trying to hammer home: although we have little control over our feelings, we have huge amounts of control over our actions. This will have important practical applications later, because when making important changes in your life, it's far more useful to focus on what you *can* control rather than on what you can't.

When strong emotions hook us, we might do all sorts of things we later regret. While we are in OBEY mode, we might smash things, shout, abuse people, drink excessively, or engage in any number of destructive or self-defeating behaviors. But if we consciously bring our awareness to how we are feeling and pay careful attention to how we're behaving, then no matter how intense our emotions are, we can switch out of OBEY mode and take effective control of our actions. Even if we're furious, sorrowful, or scared, we can still choose to stand up or sit down, close or open our mouth, drink a glass of water, answer the telephone, talk calmly, or scratch our head.

How Our Emotions Help Us

Emotions are like the weather—they're always present and constantly changing. They continually ebb and flow, from mild to intense, pleasant to unpleasant, predictable to utterly unexpected. A "mood" refers to the general "tone" of emotion across a period of time. Thus a "bad mood" is like an overcast day, whereas a specific emotion such as anger or anxiety is like a shower of rain. But what's the point of emotions? How do they help us?

Our emotions serve three main purposes: communication, motivation, and illumination. Let's take a quick look at each.

Communication

Emotions allow us to communicate to others in valuable ways. Here are a few examples:

- Fear communicates "Watch out; there's danger!" or "I find you threatening."
- Anger communicates "This isn't fair or right," "You're trespassing on my territory," or "I'm defending what's mine."
- Sadness communicates "I've lost something important."
- Guilt communicates "I've done something wrong, and I want to put it right."
- Love communicates "I appreciate you," "I want you to stay close."

When we're interacting with trustworthy, caring people, such communication is often valuable. For example, if a good friend sees you're scared or sad, they'll often respond with kindness and support. If they see you feel guilty for something you did that hurt them, they're more likely to forgive you. If they see you're angry about something they're doing, they might back off and reconsider it. Obviously, this form of communication isn't a perfect system. At times we send the wrong signals or others misinterpret them. But much of the time, the system works well.

Motivation

Our emotions also motivate us. The words *emotion, motivate, motion,* and *move* all originate from the Latin word *movere*, which means "to move." Emotions prepare us to move our body in particular ways and to act in ways that are likely to be helpful and life-enhancing. The following are some examples:

- Fear motivates us to take evasive action, to protect ourselves against danger.
- Anxiety motivates us to prepare ourselves for things that might hurt or harm us.
- Anger motivates us to stand our ground, to fight for what we care about.
- Sadness motivates us to slow down, ease up, take a break, rest up, and recuperate.
- Guilt motivates us to reflect on our behavior and how it's affecting others, and to make amends if we've hurt them.
- Love motivates us to be loving and nurturing, to share and to care.

Illumination

Finally, our emotions illuminate what's important to us. They alert us that something important is happening; something we need to attend to or deal with. They shine a light on our deepest needs and wants; they remind us what we care about, what truly matters to us. They are messengers bearing gifts: they point us toward issues we need to address and actions we can take to improve our life. Here are some examples:

- Fear illuminates the importance of safety and protection.
- Anger illuminates the importance of defending our territory, protecting a boundary, or standing up and fighting for what is ours.
- Sadness illuminates the importance of rest and recuperation after a loss.
- Guilt illuminates the importance of how we treat others and the need to repair social bonds.
- Love illuminates the importance of connection, intimacy, bonding, caring, and sharing.

When strong emotions arise, we can often extract their wisdom with two simple questions: "What does this emotion tell me really matters? What does it suggest I need to attend to?" However, we won't be able to access this wisdom when we're in OBEY or STRUGGLE mode: fighting or fleeing from the emotion, or letting it jerk us around like a puppet on a string. We first need to learn a radically new way of responding to our emotions, starting with how to turn off . . .

[13]

The Struggle Switch

Imagine that at the back of your mind is a "struggle switch." And when it's switched on, you will struggle vigorously against any emotional pain that comes your way.

Now let's suppose some anxiety shows up. With the struggle switch on, we perceive that feeling as a *huge problem*. "Oh no!" says our mind. "Here's anxiety. I hate this feeling. It can't be good for me. I wonder what it's doing to my body. I wish it would go away."

So now we've got anxiety about our anxiety. "Oh no," says our mind. "This anxiety is *GETTING BIGGER!* This is awful." At this point, we might then get sad about our anxiety: "Why does this keep happening? I wish I didn't have to live this way." And then, on top of that, we could get angry: "This isn't fair! I hate this!" So now we've got anger about our sadness about our anxiety about our anxiety; our emotional pain is skyrocketing. Spot the vicious cycle, anyone?

However, things go very differently when our struggle switch is off. Whatever emotion shows up, no matter how unpleasant, we don't struggle with it. We acknowledge it and allow it to be there. Anxiety shows up, and sure, it's unpleasant and we don't want it or like it—but we *allow* it.

With the struggle switch off, our anxiety levels are free to rise and fall as the situation dictates. Sometimes they'll be high, sometimes low, and sometimes there'll be none at all. But however high or low they may be, we don't waste precious time and energy in STRUGGLE.

Basically, the struggle switch is an emotion amplifier. Switch it on, and we can have anxiety about our anxiety, or anger about our anxiety, or sadness about our sadness, or guilt about our anger, or any other combination you can think of. But it doesn't stop there. With the switch firmly on, we pull out all our favorite struggle strategies (the ones we explored in chapter 3). And as you know, *in moderation* that's not a problem. However, with the switch on, we use these strategies *excessively* and *inappropriately*, which leads to health problems, missed opportunities, relationship issues, wasted time and energy, more emotional pain, greater psychological suffering, and so on.

So with the struggle switch off,

- our emotions can freely flow through us; come and stay and go in their own good time;
- we don't waste time and energy on STRUGGLE, which means we can invest it in more meaningful activities; and
- we don't create extra suffering by amplifying our emotions.

But with the struggle switch on,

- our emotions are stuck; they hang around for a looong time;
- we waste a huge amount of time and energy struggling with them; and
- we amplify our emotions and create a lot of unnecessary extra pain.

Take the case of Rachel, a forty-three-year-old legal secretary. Rachel lives with a panic disorder, a condition characterized by sudden episodes of overwhelming fear known as "panic attacks." During a panic attack, the person typically has an intense feeling of impending doom, associated with distressing sensations such as breathlessness, chest pain, a thumping heart, choking, dizziness, tingling in the hands and feet, hot and cold flushes, sweating, faintness, and trembling. This is a common disorder, affecting up to 3 percent of the adult population in any given year.

Rachel's major problem is not anxiety. The problem is her STRUGGLE against anxiety. She sees it as something terrible and will do anything possible to avoid or get rid of it. As soon as she feels any physical sensation that even remotely resembles anxiety—such as a racing heart or tightness in the chest—that sensation will itself trigger further anxiety.

And hey presto—vicious cycle. Her anxiety level rises; those unwanted sensations grow even stronger; this triggers even more anxiety; and soon she is in a state of full-blown panic.

Rachel's world is steadily shrinking. She now avoids drinking coffee, watching thrillers, or doing any physical exercise. Why? Because all these things make her heart beat faster, which sets off the whole vicious cycle. She also refuses to ride in elevators or airplanes, drive on busy roads, visit crowded shopping centers, or attend large social gatherings. Why? Because she knows she might feel anxious in those situations, which is something she wants to avoid at any cost!

Rachel's case is extreme, but to a lesser extent we all do the same. All of us, at times, avoid challenges to escape the stress or anxiety that goes with them. And in moderation, this isn't a problem. But the more extensive our avoidance, the more we suffer in the long run.

So how do we turn that struggle switch off? With another unhooking skill called . . .

14

Making Room

Every painful feeling tells you something important. It tells you that you care; that you have a heart; that there's something that really matters to you. And this is something you have in common with every living human on this planet. When there's a gap between the reality we want and the reality we've got, painful feelings arise. And the bigger that reality gap, the greater the pain that arises.

All those painful feelings you have are not signs of weakness, mental illness, or defectiveness. They're signs that you're a normal, living, caring human being. And going into battle against them achieves nothing helpful. So can you drop the struggle, and make peace with them?

Up for a Challenge?

Are you up for a meaningful challenge that could make a huge impact on your life? Earlier we talked about the technical term *exposure*: putting yourself in contact with difficult stuff so you can learn more effective ways of responding to it. That's what this challenge involves: contacting a difficult feeling and learning how to make room for it, instead of responding in OBEY or STRUGGLE mode.

You may recall that emotions are comprised of two interweaving elements: cognitions and sensations. We've already looked at cognitions, so let's focus on sensations—that is, on what we *feel in our body*—in our limbs, head, neck, back, chest, tummy, and pelvis.

Because this work is often quite challenging, good preparation is essential for success. The sections below describe five things to do before starting.

Task 1. Get Clear on Your Motivation

What matters enough that you'd be willing to deliberately contact an uncomfortable emotion and practice making room for it? If your answer is "Because I want to feel good/happy/calm/confident/relaxed" or "I want to stop feeling anxious/sad/lonely/angry/guilty," that won't do. We know, in the long term, you will feel a lot better with the ACT approach to life—again, over three thousand scientific studies confirm this—but if that is your *primary* motivation, then you're falling back into the happiness trap, trying to control your feelings.

So you want your motivation to be based on toward moves. Ask yourself the following: If you were better at unhooking from these emotions . . .

- What toward moves would you do?
- What projects, activities, or tasks would you start, resume, or continue?
- How would you treat yourself differently?
- What would you say or do differently in your most important relationships?

If you already have answers to these questions from chapter 10, great. But if not, please think about this now. Then complete this sentence (in your head or on paper): I am going to learn this new skill so I can do important toward moves such as . . . _____

_____

_____.

Task 2. Choose the Degree of Difficulty

Making room for your feelings is a transferable skill; you can apply it to any sort of emotion, urge, or sensation, no matter how great or small, intense or mild. It's best to start with a smaller feeling that's not too difficult; then next time try something more challenging.

No one expects a sailor apprentice to steer a boat through a massive storm without any training. The apprentice first learns the basics of sailing in safe weather conditions on calm waters. Once they've practiced in milder conditions, become familiar with the equipment, and learned all the drills and maneuvers—then they may safely venture out into rougher seas and weather. A similar approach is wise when you make room for difficult feelings. Don't begin with the ones that completely overwhelm you. Start with smaller, less challenging feelings. If necessary, start with just one small sensation somewhere in your body. Then gradually, over time, work up to bigger ones.

Task 3. Expect Your Mind to Interfere

Your mind is not likely to help you with this. It's far more likely to pass judgment on your feelings, tell you scary stories about them, or claim that you can't handle them. Alternatively, it might say: "Don't bother with these exercises; reading about them is enough." (It may even suggest that you "do them later," knowing full well that you probably won't.)

Here's an opportunity to apply the skills you've been learning. Treat your thoughts like cars driving past your house—you know they're there, but you don't have to peer out the window each time one goes by. Let them come and go as they wish, while you keep your attention focused on the task. And if a thought does hook you (in the same way that the sound of screeching tires might pull you to the window), then the moment you realize it, gently acknowledge it and refocus.

Task 4. Be Ready to Drop Anchor (If Needed)

When emotional storms blow up, your best first-line response is to drop anchor. I'm not expecting that to happen with this exercise—but if it does, drop anchor. Then once you're fully anchored, make a choice: either continue the experiment from where you left off or end it and try again later with something less challenging.

Task 5. Contact a Difficult Feeling

The technique that follows is suitable for all emotions, urges, and sensations, so once you know the drill, you can apply it to literally *any* feeling at all (even numbness or emptiness). If a difficult feeling is already present, work with it. But if not, tap into one using any of the methods below.

- One method is to vividly recall a painful memory. (Please heed my earlier caution: Don't pick some truly horrific memory. Pick something that's relatively distressing—a fight with a loved one, a painful rejection, or a mistake you regret—but not traumatic). Make that memory as vivid as you can; relive it as if it's happening right now and tap into the emotion.
- Another method is to bring to mind an unpleasant event that's looming in the near future—something you're very scared of or worried about—and vividly imagine that event as if it's actually happening here and now.
- A third method is to dwell, for a minute or so, on a major current problem you're finding stressful, such as an important task you're procrastinating on, a health issue, or a relationship issue.

How to TAME Your Emotions

Preparation done? Then let's get started. I call this exercise "TAME your emotions." TAME is an acronym for the four steps involved:

T: Take note (notice and name what's showing up in your body).
A: Allow (give your feeling permission to be there; "let it be").
M: Make room (open up to this feeling and let it freely flow through you).
E: Expand awareness (broaden your focus to include the world around you).

You'll note this exercise overlaps a lot with dropping anchor. The "Take note" and "Allow" components of TAME are like the "Acknowledge" phase of dropping anchor, with its emphasis on noticing, naming, and allowing. And the "Expand awareness" component of TAME combines both the "Connect" and "Engage" phases of dropping anchor. The main difference between these exercises is the "Make room" component of TAME; this is the part where we work hard on opening up to these feelings.

There are four basic steps to TAME, but "Take note" and "Make room" are each comprised of several smaller components. So after you've done the whole thing several times, I encourage you to create your own version by mixing and matching the smaller components in any sequence you want (and leaving out any you dislike).

Please read through all the instructions at least once, so you know what's involved; then go back to the start and put them into practice. A row of three dots indicates you are to pause for about three to five seconds, focusing intently on whatever has been suggested.

Please do take your time with this exercise; don't rush. (You may like to use my free audio recording, "Making Room for Emotions," downloadable from chapter 14 of *The Happiness Trap: Extra Bits*.) And if there's any part of it you can't do, or you don't understand, just skip it and move on to the next bit; there's no one element that's essential.

To start the exercise, sit upright in your chair with your back straight and your feet flat on the floor. Then either close your eyes or fix them on a spot in front of you. And once you have a difficult feeling to work with . . .

Take Note

PART A. NOTICE WHAT YOU'RE DOING: Tap into a sense of curiosity, as if you're a curious child discovering something you've never encountered before. And with that sense of genuine curiosity, notice how you are sitting . . . notice your feet on the floor . . . the position of your back . . . where your hands are, and what they are touching . . .

And whether your eyes are open or closed, notice what you can see . . . and notice what you can hear . . . and smell . . . and taste . . .

And notice what you are thinking . . . and feeling . . . and doing . . .

PART B. NOTICE YOUR BODY: Now quickly scan your body from head to toe. Start at your scalp and move downward . . .

(If there are particular parts of your body you wish to avoid, do so for now—but carefully note what you're avoiding, as you'll need to work on this later, as we'll discuss in chapter 17.)

Notice the sensations you can feel in your head . . . face . . . jaws . . . throat . . . neck . . . shoulders . . . chest . . . upper arms . . . forearms . . . hands . . . abdomen . . . pelvis and buttocks . . . thighs . . . lower legs . . . and feet.

PART C. NOTICE YOUR FEELING: Now zoom in on the part of your body where you're most intensely feeling this emotion (or numbness). And observe that feeling closely, as if you're a curious child who's found something new and fascinating . . .

(As you do this, let your mind chatter away like a radio playing in the background, and keep your attention focused on the feeling. And at any point, if your thoughts hook you and pull you out of the exercise, the moment you realize it's happened, acknowledge it, unhook, and refocus.)

Notice where this sensation starts and stops . . . Learn as much about it as you can . . .

If you drew an outline around it, what shape would it have? . . . Is it 2D or 3D? On the surface of the body or inside you, or both? . . . How far inside you does it go? . . . Where is it most intense? . . . Where is it weakest? . . .

(And if at any moment you realize you've been hooked, simply acknowledge it, unhook, and refocus on the sensation.)

Observe it with curiosity . . . How is it different in the center than around the edges? Is there any pulsation or vibration within it? . . . Is it light or heavy? . . . Moving or still? . . . What is its temperature? . . . Are there any hot spots or cold spots? . . .

Notice the different elements within it . . .

Notice that it's not just one sensation; there are sensations within sensations . . .

Notice all the different layers to it . . .

PART D. NAME THE FEELING: Take a moment to name this feeling . . .

Silently say to yourself, "I'm noticing a feeling of XYZ" . . .

(If you don't know what to name it, "pain," "hurt," or "discomfort" will do.)

Allow

See if you can just allow this feeling to be there.

You don't have to like it or want it; just allow it . . .

Just let it be . . .

Silently say to yourself something like, "I don't like or want this feeling, but I will allow it." Or simply state the word "Allowing."

You might feel a strong urge to fight with it or push the feeling away. If so, acknowledge the urge is there without acting on it. And continue observing the sensation . . .

Don't try to get rid of it or alter it. Your aim is simply to allow it . . .

Let it be . . .

Make Room

PART A. BREATHE INTO IT: And as you're noticing this feeling, breathe into it . . .

Imagine your breath flowing into and around this feeling . . .

Get a sense of breathing into and around it . . .

PART B. EXPAND AROUND IT: And it's as if, in some magical way, all this space opens up inside you . . .

You open up around this feeling . . .

Make space for it . . .

Expand around it . . .

(You're aiming to get a sense of opening up around the feeling instead of squeezing in on it. Another option is to tense as hard as possible all the muscles around this spot and then slowly ease off the tension.)

Breathing into it . . . opening up . . . expanding around it . . .

And as you continue to observe this feeling, see if there's anything underneath it. For example, if anger or numbness is at the surface, perhaps underneath it is fear, sadness, or shame.

Don't try to make a new feeling appear; if a new one emerges, that's okay; if it doesn't, that's okay too. Whatever feeling is present in this moment, let it have its space . . .

PART C. SENSE IT AS AN OBJECT: Get a sense of this feeling as if it is a physical object (you don't have to visualize it; just sense its physical properties) . . .

As an object, what shape and size does it have? . . .

Does it seem to be liquid, solid, or gaseous? . . .

Is it moving or still? . . .

If you could touch the surface, what would it feel like? . . . Wet or dry? Rough or smooth? Hot or cold? Soft or hard? . . .

Get a sense of this "object" inside you, and observe it from all sides . . .

If you like visualizing, imagine its color—and whether it's transparent or opaque . . .

Curiously observe this object. Breathe into it and open up around it . . .

You don't have to like it or want it. Just allow it . . .

Expand Awareness

Life is like a stage show . . . and on that stage are all your thoughts, all your feelings, and everything you can see, hear, touch, taste, and smell . . .

And what we've been doing here is dimming the lights on the stage and shining a spotlight on this feeling . . . and now it's time to bring up the rest of the lights . . .

So keep this feeling in the spotlight and also bring up the lights on your body . . .

Notice your arms and legs and head and neck . . .

And notice that you're in control of your arms and legs, regardless of what you're feeling; move them around to check this out for yourself . . .

Now take a stretch and notice yourself stretching . . .

And also bring up the lights on the room around you . . . Open your eyes, look around, and notice what you can see . . . and notice what you can hear . . .

And notice that there's much more here than this feeling; that feeling is inside a body, inside a room, where you are working on something very important . . .

So now that you've read through the whole exercise, the idea is to go back and actually do it, step by step. (Or better still, use the audio recording; it's not exactly the same as the script above, but it's close enough.)

And if you're not keen on a particular component (e.g., breathing around it, visualizing its color), then skip that bit. However, I do encourage you to try every component at least once.

Ready to try it for real? Off you go!

So how did you do? Hopefully, you had a sense of dropping the struggle with this feeling, a sense of "letting it be" (like resting the book in your lap back in chapter 4). And if you found that hard to do, you're not alone. Most people do. Raising kids, keeping fit, nurturing a relation-ship, developing a career, creating a work of art, caring for the envi-ronment . . . all these meaningful challenges involve some difficulty. So why should making room for painful feelings be any different? Like any new skill, it's difficult to begin with—but with practice, it gets easier.

Keep in mind, that was a long exercise; you can chunk it up into much shorter versions. You can take any component and turn that into a one-minute exercise. Or combine two or three components into a two- to three-minute exercise. Basically, take the bits you like, tweak them as desired, and create your own making room exercises, of whatever dura-tion you prefer.

In addition, when difficult emotions arise, some kind self-talk often helps. You might like to try kindly reminding yourself of some simple truths about the nature of emotions:

"This emotion is normal; it's a natural reaction to a difficult situation."
"Emotions are like waves: they rise and they peak and they fall."
"I'm willing to make room for this feeling, even though I don't like it."
"I don't have to let it control me; I can have this feeling and choose to
    do toward moves."
"Like all feelings, this will come and stay and go in its own good time."
"This is a moment of great pain. Everyone feels this way at times."

Also remember, one of the main purposes of emotions is illumina-tion. So after you've made room for an emotion, if you can spare an ex-tra minute, you may like to tap into its wisdom. Ask yourself two simple questions: "What does this emotion tell me really matters? What does it suggest I need to attend to?" Often (not always) you will quickly find use-ful answers: your emotion is pointing to a problem you need to address, a fear you need to face, a behavior you need to change, a loss you need to come to terms with, or a relationship that truly matters. (But if no an-swers come to mind, don't start ruminating about it! Instead, treat is a reminder to practice self-compassion.)

Throughout each day, practice making room with a range of different feelings—both strong and mild. Use every opportunity. Experiment with longer versions and shorter versions; you can even do twenty- or thirty-second versions. If you're stuck in traffic, caught in a slow-moving line, or waiting for a friend who's running late, practice making room; then at least you're using your time constructively to develop a life-changing skill. And notice how the more you develop this skill, the easier it becomes to choose toward moves. Each and every time you TAME an emotion, it's a step toward the life you want.

[TROUBLESHOOTING]

I Don't Feel Emotions in My Body; They're All in My Head

This suggests you're disconnected from your body. Chapter 17, "Reinhabiting Your Body," will remedy this.

I Don't Feel Anything; I'm Just Numb

For now, practice making room for your numbness. Find the area that feels most numb, dead, hollow, or empty, and practice the TAME exercise. Often as you do this, other feelings arise. However, the key to overcoming numbness is covered in chapter 17, "Reinhabiting Your Body."

I Can Feel My Emotions, but I Find It Hard to Know What They Are; I Can't Name Them

If you have difficulty recognizing and naming your emotions, it's a skill well worth developing. Why? Because a wealth of scientific research shows the less your ability to do this, the more your emotions will hook you and jerk you around. For advice on how to develop this skill, see *The Happiness Trap: Extra Bits*, chapter 14.

I'm Feeling Overwhelmed by All These New Skills; I Don't Have Time to Practice Them

Yes, if you try to do too much, it will be overwhelming! So please follow the advice near the end of chapter 7 (just before the troubleshooting section).

What Do I Do after Making Room?

After making room, do something meaningful and life-enhancing, in line with your values. Get those toward moves happening. (Interestingly, once we make room for unpleasant feelings and immerse ourselves in meaningful activities, pleasant feelings will often start to emerge. In which case, enjoy them. But as I've said countless times, that's not the main goal. Our aim is to engage in meaningful activities, no matter what feelings are present. It is this that, in the long run, makes life fulfilling.)

I Tried to Make Room for the Feeling, but It Was Too Overwhelming

Just pick *one* troublesome sensation and keep your focus on it. Aim to make room for just that one sensation. Once you've done that, if you're game for more, go ahead and pick another one. If not, call it a day, and next time see if you can extend to two sensations, and so on. If that's too hard, work on the strategies we cover in chapter 17, then come back to this chapter.

It's Hard to Stay Focused on One Sensation

It gets easier with practice. Meanwhile, give it your best shot, and if your attention wanders to another sensation, then as soon as you realize it, refocus.

The Feelings Gradually Moved On— but Then They Came Back

Many uncomfortable feelings will surface repeatedly. If someone you love has died, then waves of sadness may keep washing over you for many weeks or months. And if you've been diagnosed with cancer or some other serious illness, waves of fear will surge again and again. As the saying goes, "You can't stop the waves, but you can learn to surf them."

How Does This Apply to Panic Attacks?

A panic attack has three elements:

1. Getting hooked by scary thoughts: "I'm going mad," "I'm going to have a heart attack," "I'm going to die."

2. STRUGGLE against the anxiety, which instantly amplifies it.

3. Hyperventilating (breathing very rapidly), which creates unpleasant but harmless sensations like dizziness, flushing, headache, pins and needles. Hyperventilating also gives rise to a sense of being unable to breathe properly, as if you can't get enough air in. This happens because you're breathing so fast you're not emptying your lungs properly on the out-breath; therefore, on your next in-breath, you're trying to draw air into lungs that are already half full.

The solution is as follows:

1. A panic attack is a type of emotional storm, so your first step is to drop anchor. During the Acknowledge phase, make sure to notice and name your thoughts: "I'm noticing thoughts about dying," "Here's the 'heart attack' story."

2. Stop struggling against the anxiety; stop trying to avoid, control, or get rid of it. Instead, TAME it.

3. Instead of hyperventilating, practice the slow, gentle breathing method described in chapter 9. This will empty your lungs completely on the out-breath—which is precisely what you need to do if it feels like you can't get air in. Only when your lungs are empty will you be able to inhale normally. (Note: very rarely, this type of slow, gentle breathing doesn't help—in which case, drop it and seek expert advice from a doctor or therapist.)

Do You Recommend "Self-Soothing" Strategies When You're Feeling Bad?

Lots of self-help approaches suggest self-soothing strategies, like having a hot bath, listening to music, reading a good book, savoring a hot chocolate, getting a massage, walking the dog, playing a sport we love, or spending time with friends. If you do these activities *primarily* to distract yourself from unpleasant feelings, they are unlikely to be satisfying or fulfilling; it's hard to appreciate an activity when you're doing it mainly to avoid something threatening or disturbing. Plus, with any type of distraction, there's always that risk of a rebound effect. So I recommend you first TAME your feelings. Then, *after* you've opened up and made room for them, ask yourself, "What meaningful, life-enhancing activity would I like to do now?" This may be a "self-soothing" activity such as those above, or it might be something else entirely. Whatever it is, go ahead and do it, and give it your full attention so you can do it well and get the most out of it.

I Allowed My Feelings for a Little While, but Then I Started Struggling Again

This is common. We often need to run through this practice again and again and again. (And again and again and again.)

What Do I Do If Strong Feelings Come On When I'm at Work or in Some Other Situation Where I Can't Just Sit Down and Practice This Method?

With practice, it takes only a few seconds to drop anchor or take a slow, gentle breath and TAME your feelings. You can then focus your attention on effective action.

I Don't Really Like Making Room

You don't have to like it (I certainly don't). The question is: Even though you don't like it, are you *willing* to make room for painful feelings in order to build a meaningful life? If not, please revisit chapter 3 and remind yourself what it's costing you to STRUGGLE.

15

TAME It with Kindness

"What's this new age bullshit?" That was Karl's initial response when I suggested a kind hands exercise. Quite a few people are initially reluctant to try such an exercise, because they think it's weird, flowery, "hippy shit," or too "touchy-feely." This is understandable, because a kind hands exercise involves (a) placing one or both hands on various parts of your body (or letting them hover just above the surface) and (b) sending kindness inward. However, almost always, when people unhook from their doubts and judgments, and actually try it, they find it's a very effective method for simultaneously unhooking, making room, *and* practicing self-compassion. And although in chapter 11 we focused on kind self-talk, many people find kind self-touch is far more powerful. It can help us to truly be there for ourselves in a caring, supportive way, at a level much deeper than words.

Personally, kind hands exercises are my go-to, whenever I'm in intense emotional pain; and always the first thing I suggest to clients, friends, and family when they're coping with grief, loss, or deep hurt. So even if you're highly skeptical, I encourage you to experiment with this process and notice what happens. The script below is just one example of a kind hands exercise; after going through it, we'll explore other options. (And if you'd like my voice to guide you, download the free audio MP3 from *The Happiness Trap: Extra Bits*, chapter 15.)

An Exercise in Kind Self-Touch

Get yourself into a comfortable position. And if a difficult feeling is not already present, trigger one as described in the previous chapter.

Now notice where in your body you feel it most . . .

Where is it? What's it like?

Observe it with curiosity . . .

And name it . . .

Now take one of your hands and turn it palm upward. And see if you can fill this hand with a sense of kindness . . .

You've used this hand in a lot of kind ways. Maybe you've held someone's hand when they were upset, or cuddled a crying baby, or hugged a distressed friend, or helped someone out with a difficult task. So put that sense of kindness into your hand right now . . .

Now rest this hand gently on your body, either on top of the feeling or on top of your heart. (If you prefer not to touch your body, let your hand hover just above the surface.)

And see if you can send that kindness inward—you might feel it, imagine it, or sense it—a sense of warmth and kindness and support, flowing into you . . .

Let your hand rest (or hover) there, lightly and gently . . .

Sense its warmth flowing into your body . . .

Imagine your body softening around the pain, loosening up, making space . . .

Hold this pain or numbness gently. Hold it as if it is a crying baby, a whimpering puppy, or a fragile work of art . . .

Infuse this gentle action with caring and warmth, as if reaching out to support someone you care about . . .

Let the kindness flow from your fingers . . .

Now, use both of your hands. Place one of them over your heart and the other on your stomach, and let them gently rest there (or hover above) . . .

Hold yourself kindly and gently, connecting with yourself, caring for yourself, giving comfort and support . . .

And silently say a few kind words to yourself; the sort of thing you'd say to a loved one who was feeling something similar . . .

If you're not sure what to say, try, "This really hurts; be kind" or "This is difficult—but I can do this" . . .

And keep sending in that warmth and kindness . . .

Not trying to get rid of your pain but rather making room for it . . .

Allowing it to be as it is in this moment . . .

Giving it plenty of space . . .

And sending in warmth and kindness . . .

Taking a moment to acknowledge, this feeling is a sign you *care* . . .

It tells you there's something important that really matters to you . . .

A gap between what you want and what you've got . . .

This is something you have in common with every living, caring human on this planet . . .

The bigger that reality gap, the greater the pain we feel . . .

So can you make peace with it . . . even though it hurts?

And continuing to send in warmth and kindness to yourself . . .

While bringing this exercise to an end . . .

And having a stretch, and moving your body . . .

And engaging with the world around you . . .

So how'd you do? If you didn't get much out of it, maybe it's not for you; but I encourage you to try it once more, using the suggestions below. If you did find it helpful, I encourage you to use it often and add it in to your TAME routine: do the entire TAME exercise with your hands on (or hovering above) your body, sending in kindness. It's also a useful exercise to practice in bed when you're having a sleepless night due to anxiety or waking early with a sense of dread or despair.

As an alternative to the exercise above, you might like to experiment with some of these options:

- Placing both hands on your chest
- Placing both hands on your tummy
- Hugging yourself gently
- Hugging yourself while also gently stroking your arms
- Gently massaging an area of tension or tightness
- Gently holding your face in your hands—plus or minus massaging your temples

You can also use kind hands to help with a powerful exercise known as . . .

Urge Surfing

Have you ever sat on the beach and watched the waves? Just noticed them coming and going? A wave starts off small and builds gently. Then gradually it gathers speed and grows bigger. It continues to grow and move forward until it reaches a peak, known as a crest. Then, once the wave has crested, it gradually subsides. The same thing happens with urges. They start off small, steadily increase, reach a peak, then drop off.

When urges show up, we usually respond with OBEY mode (giving in to them) or STRUGGLE mode (resisting them). In urge surfing, we neither give in to nor resist our urges; instead, we open up and make room for them. If you give an ocean wave enough space, it will reach a crest and then harmlessly subside. But what happens if that wave encounters resistance? Ever seen a wave *crash* onto the beach or *smash* against the rocks? It's loud, messy, and potentially destructive!

So "urge surfing" means exactly what it says: we treat our urges like waves, and "surf" them until they dissipate. The term was coined back in the 1980s by psychologists Alan Marlatt and Judith Gordon, as part of their groundbreaking work with drug addiction. The same principles they used for unhooking from addictive urges can be readily applied to *any* urge, whether it's an urge to stay in bed all day, quit a course, eat chocolate, get revenge, drink alcohol, procrastinate on an important task, harm yourself, smash something, hide away from friends and family, or yell at someone you love.

Do keep in mind, this isn't a way to avoid or get rid of our urges; we are allowing them to rise and fall in their own good time, without acting on them. Which naturally begs the question . . .

How Long Do Urges Last?

Most urges—from the start to the end of one "wave"—last about three minutes (although sometimes they can go for longer). Sometimes when I say this, people protest that their waves go "on and on for ages." To which I compassionately reply, "Yes, that's right. At the moment, they do. And there's a good reason for it. It's because you're doing the same thing that we all naturally and instinctively do: you're resisting them."

There are so many ways we resist our urges: we may fight with them, ruminate about them, worry about them, try to distract ourselves, try to push them away, or dozens of other emotion control strategies. And when we respond that way (when we flick the struggle switch on), yes, that *does* make them go on for ages. But when we make room for them, the waves usually rise and fall pretty quickly.

Of course, in challenging situations there will be more than one wave. As long as the challenge persists, those waves will continue to rise and fall—and then rise and fall again. And although they typically rise and fall quite quickly, they often don't go all the way down to zero. But as long as we give them space, rather than STRUGGLE, we are free to invest our energy in doing something meaningful.

Urge Surfing in a Nutshell

To surf an urge rather than be "wiped out" by it, we slightly modify the TAME technique, you tried in the previous chapter.

T: TAKE NOTE: Notice and name the urge. Where do you feel it most in your body? Is it located in a specific area (e.g., is your mouth salivating?) or is it more like a sense of restlessness in your legs or tension in your neck? Name it: "Here's an urge to . . ."

A: ALLOW: Give your urge permission to be there. "Let it be."

M: MAKE ROOM: Open up to this urge. Allow it to freely rise and peak and fall in its own good time.

E: EXPAND AWARENESS: Broaden your focus. Acknowledge the urge and also connect with your body and notice the world around you.

The main modification to the TAME technique is that while we're doing this, we think of the urge as a wave and watch it with curiosity as it rises, crests, and subsides. And to help with this, we can score the urge on a scale of 0 to 10. This enables us to keep track of whether it's rising, peaking, or falling. For example, "I'm having the urge to smoke, and it's now a 7." "Oh, it's rising to an 8." "And now it's a 9." "Still at a 9." "Now dropping to an 8." "Now down to a 6." And so on.

For an added boost with this practice, we can bring in kind words and kind hands. We can silently say to ourselves, with genuine caring and kindness, "This is difficult, but I can surf this" or "I'm so tempted to OBEY this urge, but I'm going to let it rise and fall without acting on it." And we can lay a kind hand (or two) on the body, as described earlier.

[16]

Being Present

When Soula turned thirty-three, her best friend organized a surprise birthday party in a local café. At first Soula was delighted, thrilled that all her closest friends and family had come together in her honor. But as the evening wore on, she began to feel sad and lonely. When she looked around the room, her mind started telling her the "single and lonely" story. "Look at all your friends. They're all in long-term relationships, or married and having kids, and you haven't even got a boyfriend! You're thirty-three now, for heaven's sake! Time's running out . . . Soon you'll be too old to have kids . . . Just look at them all, having so much fun . . . They don't know what it's like to go back to an empty apartment night after night . . . What's the point of celebrating? All you have to look forward to is being old, lonely, and miserable . . ."

On and on it went, Radio Doom and Gloom, broadcasting at full volume. And the more Soula tuned in to it, the more she lost track of the party going on all around her. She hardly tasted the food, hardly heard the conversation; she became increasingly disconnected from the warmth, joy, and love that surrounded her.

Of course, it is true that Soula was single and getting older and that most of her friends were in long-term relationships. But remember the key question: Is this story helpful? In this case it clearly wasn't. It was yet another example of the mind being an overly helpful friend, trying to alert her to *a problem that must be solved*! And this was by no means an isolated episode. For most of a year now, the "single and lonely" story had been a major source of misery for Soula, hooking her repeatedly, feeding her depression.

Sadly, scenarios like this are all too common. The more entangled we are in our thoughts and feelings, the more we lose touch with whatever is happening in the world around us. This particularly tends to happen with depression and anxiety. With anxiety we tend to get hooked by stories about the future, about things that might go horribly wrong and how badly we're sure to handle them. With depression, we tend to get hooked by stories from the past about all the things that have gone wrong and how badly they've affected us. But even if you've never suffered from anxiety or depression, for sure you've often been hooked by worrying, ruminating, or obsessing. How do I know? Because you're human, and it happens to all of us.

The reality is, we all repeatedly get hooked by our thoughts and pulled out of our lives as a result. Typically, this happens many times a day. Ever been for a drive in a car and reached your destination with no real memory of the journey? Ever been asked, "What did you do today?" and not been able to remember? Ever find yourself snacking on something without even realizing it? Ever reached the end of a page and found you haven't taken in a single word? Ever walked into a room to get something, only to find you can't remember what you want? Ever been having a conversation and suddenly realized you have no idea what the other person just said (because you were a million miles away)? We've all experienced these kinds of things, many times. Caught up in our thoughts, our attention wanders away from what we're doing: we're physically present but not psychologically present.

Suppose you're trying to have a conversation with someone, and you're caught up in thoughts like, "He thinks I'm boring," "I've got to get my taxes done," or "I hope I remembered to lock the front door when I left home." The more those thoughts hook you, the less involved you are in the conversation. And the same goes for everything you ever do, whether you're driving a car, cooking dinner, or making love: the more absorbed in your thoughts, the less engaged in the activity.

Now obviously there are times when being absorbed in our thoughts is useful and life-enhancing; for example, if we're dreaming up ideas for a creative project, mentally rehearsing a speech, planning an important event, or simply solving a crossword puzzle. When we're absorbed in thoughts in useful, life-enhancing ways that help us move toward the life we want, the term *hooked* (or *fused*) wouldn't apply. We only use the term *hooked* when we're caught up in our thoughts in ways that take us *away* from the life we want.

What Goes Wrong When We're Not Present?

When we're not psychologically present, that is, not giving our full attention to what we're doing, we suffer in two main ways: we miss out or we do things poorly. Let's take a quick look at each.

Missing Out

This is the only life we've got, so we want to make the most of it. If we're only half present, we're missing out. It's like watching your favorite movie with sunglasses on or listening to your favorite music while wearing earplugs or having a massage while wearing a thick wetsuit. How often have you missed out on a deep connection with a good friend or loved one because you weren't fully present? How often have you missed out on much of the pleasure from your food because you wolfed it down on autopilot? To appreciate the richness and fullness of life, you have to "be there" while it's happening!

Doing Things Poorly

To quote the great novelist Leo Tolstoy, "There is only one time that is important: *now*! It is the most important time because it is the only time when we have any power." To build a meaningful life, we need to take action. And the power to act exists only in this moment. The past has already happened, and the future doesn't exist yet, so we can only ever take action here and now. And in order to act effectively, we need to be psychologically present: aware of what is happening, how we are reacting, and how we wish to respond. When we operate on autopilot, go through the motions, do things in an unfocused or disengaged manner, we do them poorly. We slip up, make mistakes, and often say or do things we later regret.

So How Can We Be More Present?

Good question. You've been learning many different ways to unhook from your thoughts and feelings: dropping anchor, noticing and naming, focusing and refocusing attention, making room for emotions, and urge surfing. All these different unhooking techniques are technically known as "mindfulness skills."

I haven't mentioned mindfulness until now because there are so many inaccurate and misleading notions around it. For example, people often think it's a religious practice, a type of meditation, a relaxation technique, a way to "empty your mind" or control your feelings, or a form of positive thinking. But you can clearly see from what you've been reading in this book that none of those ideas is correct.

There are many definitions of *mindfulness* floating around, with no universal agreement on any one of them. I define it like this: *Mindfulness is a set of psychological skills for effective living that involve paying attention with openness, curiosity, and flexibility.*

So when we drop anchor, unhook from unhelpful stories, make room for difficult feelings, surf urges, focus and refocus repeatedly on the task at hand, those are all different ways of practicing mindfulness. And central to these skills is a particular way of paying attention: with openness, curiosity, and flexibility. As we notice, name, allow, and make room, that's *openness*—the very opposite of struggle. And in addition, we aim for *curiosity*—thus my repeated instructions to observe "like a curious child." This is important, because even if something is very difficult and unpleasant, if we are genuinely curious, we can learn something useful—either about its true nature or about how to respond to it effectively.

And as well as being open and curious, we aim to pay attention *flexibly*. If I'm talking to you over dinner at a restaurant, I want to be focused on our conversation. But if I suddenly smell smoke coming from the kitchen, I want to shift my attention to find out what's going on.

Let's revisit the idea that life is like a continually changing stage show. And on that stage are all your thoughts, feelings, memories, urges, and sensations, and everything you can see, hear, touch, taste, and smell. And there's a part of you that can zoom in and out of that show, lighting up any aspect at any time. And this part of you that does all the noticing—

your "noticing self"—is centrally involved in every mindfulness skill. Sometimes you use it to illuminate your thoughts or put a particular emotion in the spotlight. At other times, you direct it toward the world around you, shining a light on sights, sounds, and smells. Sometimes you use it to zoom in and spotlight one area. At other times, you use it to zoom out, floodlighting the entire stage.

What we're talking about here is *flexible* attention: the ability to narrow, broaden, sustain, or shift your focus, depending on what's most useful in the moment. If you're walking mindfully through the countryside, taking in all the sights, sounds, and smells, that's a very broad focus of attention. But if you're mindfully doing your job as a bomb disposal expert, you want an extremely narrow focus (or ka-boom!).

The noticing self, flexible attention, unhooking, making room, surfing urges, noticing and naming, dropping anchor: all these terms describe various aspects of mindfulness. And we learn all these skills for the same overarching purpose: they help us to be present, so we can act more effectively and get more fulfillment out of life. And you'll note, there's nothing religious about any of these practices;* no meditation; no positive thinking; and no attempt to relax, "empty your mind," or control your feelings. (Of course, as we do these practices, uncomfortable emotions often lessen, difficult thoughts frequently disappear, and pleasant feelings of calm and relaxation often arise; but these outcomes are bonuses, not the main aim.) What follows are four simple mindfulness practices you can easily incorporate into your daily routine without needing to put aside time to do them.

Four Simple Practices

I'm now going to take you through four simple practices for being present. In each case, I'll ask you to focus your attention on some aspect of your experience in this moment—and if distracting thoughts and feelings should arise, the aim is to

---

* People often attribute mindfulness to Buddhism, but this is inaccurate. Buddhism is only 2,600 years old, whereas mindfulness practices can be found in Judaism, Yoga, and Taoism dating back over four thousand years. However, ACT is not based on ancient Eastern traditions; it is a modern, secular, science-based approach originating from a branch of behavioral psychology with the mind-boggling, tongue-twisting name of "functional contextualism."

- let them come and go like passing cars, and keep your attention on the task; and
- when you realize your attention has wandered (and it will, I promise), gently acknowledge it, then refocus on the exercise.

Each experiment lasts only thirty seconds (so there's no excuse for not doing them all).

Experiment 1: Noticing the Environment

Once you've finished reading this paragraph, put down the book and notice your surroundings. Notice as much as you can about what you can see, hear, touch, taste, and smell. What's the temperature? Is the air moving or still? What sort of light is there and where is it coming from?

Notice at least five sounds you can hear, at least five objects you can see, and at least five things you can feel against the surface of your body (such as the air on your face or the chair against your back or your feet on the floor). Put down the book now and do this for thirty seconds. Notice what happens.

Experiment 2: Noticing Your Body

As you're reading this paragraph, connect with your body. Notice where your legs and arms are and the position of your spine. Inwardly scan your body from head to toe; notice the sensations in your head, chest, arms, abdomen, legs. (And if there are parts of your body or sensations within it that you dislike, notice how you try to avoid them.) Put down the book, close your eyes, and do this for thirty seconds. Notice what happens.

Experiment 3: Noticing Your Breath

As you're reading this, notice your breathing. Notice the rise and fall of your rib cage and the air moving in and out of your nostrils. Follow the air in through your nose. Notice how your lungs expand. Feel your abdomen push outward. Follow the air back out as your lungs deflate. Put down the book, close your eyes, and do this for thirty seconds. Notice what happens.

Experiment 4: Noticing Sounds

In this experiment, just focus on the sounds you can hear. Notice sounds coming from you (e.g., from your breathing and your movements), sounds coming from the room around you, and sounds coming from outside. Put down the book now, close your eyes, and do this for thirty seconds. Notice what happens.

So what did you notice? Hopefully, three things:

1. We are always in the midst of a sensory feast; we just don't usually realize it.
2. It's sooooo easy to get distracted by thoughts and feelings.
3. The moment we realize we're distracted, we can unhook and refocus.

Now let's explore the connection between being present and . . .

Curing Boredom

Being present involves bringing our full attention to what is happening here and now, with openness and curiosity. When we're present in this way, we don't get into a struggle with reality.

Struggles with reality happen when we get hooked by judgments that things are bad or wrong. Our mind tells us that things shouldn't be as they are, that we shouldn't be as we are, that reality is in the wrong and we are in the right. It tells us that life would be better somewhere else, or we would be happier if only we were different. When these thoughts hook us, they pull us into a thick psychological smog that dims and obscures our view of the world.

But life is very different when we pay attention with openness and curiosity. For a start, it's a lot less boring. Boredom arises when we get hooked by the story "there's nothing of interest here." This is usually followed by another story about how life would be so much more interesting or enjoyable if we were doing something else. Our mind is easily bored because it thinks it already knows it all. It's been there, done that, seen the show, and bought the T-shirt. Whether we're walking down the street, driving to work, eating a meal, having a chat, or taking a shower, the mind takes it all for granted. After all, it's done all this stuff countless times before. So rather than help us engage with reality, it carries us off to a different time and place. As a result, we spend much of our time only half awake, scarcely aware of the richness of our experience. The stage show of life carries on—but the lights are so dim, hardly anything is visible.

However, the good news is, our noticing self is always on standby. And in any moment, we can use it to bring up the lights on that stage show. Through paying attention with openness and curiosity, we can connect with the vast length, breadth, and depth of human experience, regardless of whether it is new and exciting or familiar and comfortable. The fascinating thing is that when we pay attention in this way to an experience we consider familiar, boring, or mundane, we often see it in a new and interesting light. To experience this for yourself, notice what happens when you . . .

Focus Attention on This Book

In this experiment, the aim is to take a fresh look at the book in your hands, to see it with "new eyes." (If you're reading this on a device or listening to it as an audiobook, please go and get a book—any book will do—so you can participate.) Imagine you're a curious scientist, and you've never seen an object like this before. Pick up the book and feel the weight of it in your hands. Feel the cover against your palms. Run your finger slowly down a page and notice the texture. Bring the open book to your nose and smell the paper. Slowly turn a few pages and notice the sound it makes. Look at the front cover of the book. Notice how the light reflects off the surface. Notice the shapes, colors, textures, and lines. Then turn to any page at random and notice the shapes of the white space surrounding the text.

How did you find that? You've been reading this book for quite a while, and until now you've probably taken all these different aspects of it for granted. And the same is true for just about every aspect of our life. Which is why I'm about to introduce you to . . .

A Thoroughly Enjoyable Practice

The easiest way to develop our ability to be present is to bring our full attention to everyday activities that are potentially pleasant and enjoyable. We often do this spontaneously in novel, stimulating, or pleasurable situations. Perhaps while on a walk in the countryside you feasted your eyes on the fields, the wildlife, the trees and flowers; enjoyed the touch of a balmy summer breeze; and listened to the songbirds. Or during an intimate conversation with the one you love, you hung on their every word, gazed into their eyes, and felt the closeness between you. Or while playing with a child or a beloved pet, you were so involved in the fun of it all that you lost all track of time and didn't have a care in the world.

Unfortunately, these moments rarely last for long. Sooner or later, the mind grabs our attention with a gripping story and pulls us out of the experience. But with practice, we can realize when that happens, unhook, and refocus. And we can go a step further and actively savor the experience; to truly appreciate it. The greater our ability to do this, the more satisfaction and fulfillment we'll get from life's many pleasures (many of which we take for granted or miss out on because we're on autopilot). So to develop this ability, we can . . .

Focus Attention on Something Pleasurable

Do this practice with at least one or two pleasant activities every day. Make sure it's a values-driven activity, not an avoidance-driven activity—that is, it's something you're doing because it's important, meaningful, and life-enhancing and not just an attempt to avoid "bad feelings." The activity doesn't have to be anything mind-blowing. It can be something as simple as eating lunch, stroking the cat, walking the dog, listening to the birds, cuddling your kids, sitting in the sunshine, or listening to a favorite piece of music.

As you do this activity, pretend that this is the first time you've ever done it. Really pay attention to what you can see, hear, smell, touch, or taste, and savor every moment. Totally focus on what you are doing, using all your five senses. For example, you could do this the next time you have a warm shower. Notice the various sounds of the water as it sprays out of the nozzle, as it hits your body, as it gurgles down the drain. Notice the sensations of the water running down your back and legs. Notice the smell of the soap and the shampoo. Notice the clouds of steam billowing upward. Notice how your body responds. Notice the feelings of pleasure that arise.

When thoughts and feelings arise, acknowledge their presence, let them be, and refocus on the shower. As soon as you realize that your attention has wandered (as it definitely will), acknowledge it, unhook, and refocus on the shower—and savor every moment.

Two Not-as-Enjoyable-but-Very-Valuable Practices

We're going to end this chapter with two valuable practices for developing your ability to be present. And the great thing is, you don't have to carve out time to fit them into your day. You do your daily routines as usual, but you practice being present as you do them. They won't be as enjoyable as the previous exercise, though, because you're going to deliberately challenge yourself. The idea is to pick at least two activities each day that you find boring, tedious, or annoying. Pick tasks you normally do resentfully or on automatic pilot or rush through as fast as possible.

If the suggestions below don't suit you, come up with your own versions. And ideally do them both at least once a day. (If you can do more than that, great; the more the merrier. But even once a week is a lot better than nothing.)

Focus Attention on Your Morning Routine

Pick an activity that's part of your daily morning routine, such as brushing your teeth, combing your hair, making the bed, shaving, or putting on makeup. (Having a shower doesn't count because that's a naturally pleasurable activity; you want to pick something that's boring, tedious, or "a hassle.") Give this activity your full attention, noticing what you can see, hear, touch, taste, and smell, as if you're a curious child discovering this activity for the very first time. Allow your thoughts and feelings to freely flow, and if you get hooked, you know the drill: acknowledge, unhook, refocus.

For starters, practice this with just one part of your morning routine each day. Then, as your ability improves, extend it to other parts.

Focus Attention On a Useful Chore

Pick a chore that you don't like but you know is helpful in the long run. It could be ironing clothes, washing dishes, cleaning the car, cooking a healthy meal, bathing the kids, massaging your pet donkey*—any task you'd just as soon avoid. Then each time you do it, give it your full and curious attention.

For example, if you're ironing clothes . . .

- Notice the color and shape of the clothing.
- Notice the patterns made by the creases and shadows.
- Notice how the patterns change as the creases disappear.
- Notice the hiss of the steam, the creak of the ironing board, the faint whispery sound of the iron moving over the material.
- Notice the grip of your hand on the iron and the movement of your arm and your shoulder.
- If boredom or frustration arises, acknowledge it, make room for it, and refocus on what you're doing.
- Let your thoughts and feelings flow freely and acknowledge, unhook, and refocus as required.

Putting This into Practice

As Soula practiced and improved her ability to be present, she began to appreciate the things she had in her life instead of always focusing on what she lacked. She was able to connect more with the people she loved, focus much better on difficult tasks at work and at home, and get significantly more enjoyment and satisfaction from the small pleasures in life. All of which played a big role in lifting her depression. (However, I wouldn't want you to think this was some "quick fix" that transformed her life overnight. It was only part of Soula's journey. We'll revisit her later in the book to see what else she did.)

I'm expecting similar results for your life. The daily practices I've suggested above—focusing attention on a pleasant activity, part of your

---

* Threw that one in to see if you were paying attention.

morning routine, and a life-enhancing but tedious chore—are a good start. In addition, why not practice "noticing the environment" regularly throughout the day? The aim is to progressively extend these practices to more and more areas of your life, until you reach a point where you no longer think of them as "practices," "exercises," or "experiments"; you're just naturally being present.

Over time, this leads to a truly profound change in the way you live: rather than missing out on life, you start making the most of it.

[17]

Reinhabiting Your Body

The more disconnected we are from our body, the less we feel. This is because sensations in our body (from all the physiological changes taking place inside it) form the core of any emotion. So if you experience emotions and urges mainly in your head, that suggests significant cutting off from your body; you're tapping into the cognitive elements of the emotion, but you're not tuning in to the sensations. And if all you feel is numb, empty, or dead inside (as is common with trauma or major depression) that indicates extreme disconnection.

Around 10 percent of the population finds it hard to access their emotions. (Often this goes hand in hand with difficulty naming emotions. So if you find it hard to name what you are feeling, please follow the advice in *The Happiness Trap: Extra Bits*, chapter 14.) However, the good news is, you can get much better at accessing your emotions if you practice tuning in to your body—and the benefits for doing this are huge. They include the following:

- **Vitality.** You will gain a sense of vitality, of "coming back to life," "feeling fully human."
- **Joy and pleasure.** Cutting off from your body helps you to avoid painful feelings but also cuts you off from pleasurable emotions and feelings, like joy and happiness. So connecting with your body gives you access to the full range of emotions and feelings—both painful (e.g., sadness, anger, and anxiety) and pleasant (e.g., love, contentment, and joy).
- **Control over your actions.** The less aware you are of your emotions, the less control you have over your actions. When we bring

175

awareness to our feelings, they lose much of their ability to hook us and jerk us around.

- **Wise choices, good decisions.** A wealth of research shows that the better we can access our emotions, the more effective our decision-making, and the more likely we are to make wise choices in life.

- **Intuition, trust, safety.** Feelings in our body often alert us to threats and dangers that our conscious mind is not picking up. Without access to this information—often called "intuition" or "gut feelings"—we may unwittingly put ourselves at risk or allow ourselves to be taken advantage of.

- **Safety in your own body.** Do you feel unsafe in your own body? If you wish to feel safer in your body, your best option is to start progressively exploring it and practice better ways to handle the difficult feelings you'll encounter. If you don't do this work, your body will remain like a dark cave full of monsters that you want to avoid at all costs.

- **Success in life.** There is a direct correlation between success in life and what psychologists call "emotional intelligence": handling your emotions effectively and making good use of them for motivation, communication, and illumination (see chapter 12). Learning to tune in to your body and access your emotions plays a big part in increasing emotional intelligence.

- **Building better relationships.** One of the most important factors in building a meaningful and rewarding life is the cultivation of strong, healthy relationships. And no matter who those relationships are with—a partner, friends, children, family, work colleagues, or members of our community—we will be at a huge disadvantage if we don't have ready access to our full range of emotions. Why? Building good relationships requires emotional intelligence, not just in terms of handling our own feelings but also being able to tune in to and handle the feelings of others.

Have you ever watched part of a movie on TV without any sound? It's not very satisfying. The images may be great, but without music, dialogue, or sound effects, you lose a lot of the experience. If you watch carefully, you can still keep track of what's happening to some extent, but it's easy to misread what's going on.

And that's what it's like when we interact with others while we're cut off from our own feelings. It leads to conflict, tension, and difficult interactions with others, because we easily misread what they want or don't want—their intentions, their feelings—or we fail to see how our own behavior is affecting them.

Many of the exercises in this book help you tune in to your body: the Connect with your body component of dropping anchor (chapter 5); focusing on stretching (chapter 9); TAME your feelings (chapter 14); and kind hands exercises (chapter 15). However, if you find it hard to access your emotions, then it's helpful to practice regular . . .

Body Scans

Body scans involve scanning the body (or part of it), tuning in to the sensations, noticing them with curiosity, and allowing them to be there. Body scans can vary enormously in duration, from thirty seconds to thirty minutes. Usually, you start with shorter exercises of three to four minutes and build up the duration over time, and the more often you do these the better. Once a day is ideal, but once a week is better than nothing.

And if you're avoiding certain areas or zones of your body, set yourself a challenge: Gradually, over time, bring your awareness to those areas. Each day (or each week) pick an area you normally avoid and give it your full attention for a specified amount of time. For example, you might focus on this area for just two seconds the first time, then increase to four seconds the next time, and six seconds the third time. Once you can hold your focus there for ten to fifteen seconds, choose another difficult area to work on. Gradually "extend the territory" until you can scan your body from head to toe without avoiding any areas. (And of course, if this triggers difficult thoughts and feelings, make good use of your unhooking skills.)

If an area seems to have no feeling at all, then create some—either by moving it (e.g., wiggling your toes), massaging it firmly with your hand, or tensing up a muscle in that area.

Below is a brief body scan to experiment with. The first time you do this, spend about fifteen seconds on each instruction, so the exercise lasts for around three minutes. Then gradually make the exercise longer by increasing to twenty-five, thirty-five, or forty-five seconds per instruction. (In chapter 17 of *The Happiness Trap: Extra Bits* there's a free audio MP3 to guide you.) Please read the instructions once so you know what's involved, then try it out.

A Brief Body Scan

Get yourself into a comfortable position and either close your eyes or gently fix them on a spot in front of you. The aim is to slowly scan your body, fully focusing your attention on the feelings you encounter—no matter how faint they may be. Observe each sensation as if you're a curious child who has never encountered anything like this before. Don't STRUGGLE with the sensations you notice; whether they are pleasant, neutral, or unpleasant, allow them to be there.

As you do this, let your mind chatter away like a radio playing in the background (but don't try to ignore it or silence it). Naturally, from time to time you'll get hooked and lose track of the exercise. The moment you realize this has happened, acknowledge what hooked you, then refocus on your body.

Take fifteen seconds to notice with curiosity the sensations you can feel in your . . .

- feet and toes,
- ankles,
- calves,
- thighs,
- buttocks and pelvis,
- abdomen (tummy),
- chest,
- hands and fingers,
- forearms,
- upper arms,
- shoulders,
- neck, and
- head.

So how'd you do with that exercise? Most people find it challenging at first; they complain that it's uncomfortable, boring, or hard to stay focused. However, with regular practice it will pay big dividends.

It's also a good exercise to practice in bed when you're tossing and turning, unable to sleep; so much better than lying there . . .

Worrying, Ruminating, Obsessing

"DON'T WORRY ABOUT IT!" How often have you heard that supposedly useful advice? Or the more sophisticated version: "If there's something you can do about it, do it; if not, there's no point worrying about it"? Or the less sophisticated version: "Cheer up, it may never happen"?

It's easy to say "Don't worry," but it's very hard to do. In fact, often the ways in which people try to stop worrying—such as many of those struggle strategies we explored in chapter 3—actually make it worse in the long run. Of particular note, methods such as pushing worries away, distracting yourself, telling yourself to "SNAP OUT OF IT!" or trying to not think about it are all likely to have a rebound effect: they may (if you're lucky) give you short-term relief, but in the long term those worries return with a vengeance.

The same holds true for ruminating and obsessing. These mental processes, which we all get entangled in at times, are not that easy to stop. It is possible to interrupt them, but it requires effort. However, before we get into that, we need to answer . . .

Why Do I Keep Doing This?

This question is one of the most common things people ruminate on. And it deserves a good answer. Ruminating, worrying, and obsessing are all essentially problem-solving processes. When we ruminate, we tend to fixate on problems in the past: *Why did this bad thing happen?* (Or *Why does it keep happening?*) When we worry, we're preoccupied with problems in the future: *What if this bad thing does happen?* When we obsess, it may be about the past, present, or future, or even an alternative reality: *How different our life would be if only XYZ.*

Our mind is basically a problem-solving machine, always focusing on two main problems: (a) how to get what we want, and (b) how to avoid what we don't want. When we ruminate, worry, or obsess, we can think of it as "problem-solving in overdrive"; our mind's going over and over the problem, full speed ahead, desperately trying to come up with a good solution. But it's like a car stuck in the sand: the engine's on full throttle, the wheels are spinning wildly—but the car is going nowhere.

In other words, ruminating, worrying, and obsessing are all forms of *ineffective* problem-solving. These cognitive processes eat up a huge amount of our time, energy, and attention and are usually incredibly slow to deliver a solution.

So why do we keep doing it? Well, these processes are always triggered by some sort of problem: difficult situation(s), difficult thought(s), difficult feeling(s), or any combination thereof. And in response to these triggers, we ruminate, worry, or obsess, attempting to solve the problem. And there are four major "payoffs" we get for doing this:

1. **We escape—temporarily—from unpleasant feelings.** When we're caught up in our thoughts, it diverts our attention from unpleasant sensations in our body.
2. **We get an answer to the problem.** It may take a long time, but eventually we do (usually) come up with an answer or solution. That's why many people say, "Worrying helps me prepare for the worst" or "Ruminating helps me to understand myself."
3. **It feels like we're working hard.** These cognitive processes take effort, so we feel like we're working hard on our problems, doing something productive, making progress.
4. **It helps us avoid the discomfort of taking action.** When we're caught up in these cognitive processes, we often avoid taking action that's difficult or risky: we stay away from challenging situations, avoid making tough decisions, and procrastinate on things we're anxious about doing. (In the business world, they call this "analysis paralysis.") This gives us short-term relief from all those

difficult thoughts and feelings—especially anxiety, self-doubt, and fear of failure—that are guaranteed to show up when we *do* eventually take action or make that decision.

We might not get *all* of these payoffs, but we will usually get some of them. (There are usually other payoffs too, such as getting sympathy, support, or understanding from others.) And of course, we don't deliberately choose to worry, obsess, or ruminate in order to get these payoffs. The fact is most of us aren't even *aware* of these payoffs (until some all-knowing self-help guru kindly points them out). But nonetheless, those payoffs occur. (Psychologists call them "reinforcing consequences": consequences or outcomes of our behavior that reinforce or strengthen it over time.) And those payoffs are enough to keep us doing these things, even when logically and rationally we know they aren't taking us toward the life we want.

The payoffs we get for ruminating, worrying, and obsessing often become apparent only when we start to break these habits—especially payoffs number 1 (escaping from our feelings) and number 4 (avoiding the discomfort of taking action). As we interrupt and cut short these mental processes, there's often a short-term *increase* in emotional discomfort: we get to experience all those uncomfortable feelings that we were, in the short term, avoiding, especially anxiety and fear. And when those feelings surface, our automatic reaction is to immediately go back into worrying, ruminating, and obsessing. (Again, this is largely automatic: we don't deliberately choose to do this; we're usually not even conscious of it.)

So now you know why you keep doing these things, and why it's so hard to break the habit. The next question is . . .

Are You Willing to Do What It Takes?

If you wish to do less of these mental processes (no one ever totally stops them), that will require

- willingness to practice new skills to disrupt them and
- willingness to make room for the short-term increase in emotional discomfort—especially anxiety—that often occurs. (In the long term,

of course, your emotional discomfort will lessen. It's a trade-off: short-term pain for long-term gain.)

So take a moment to consider: What matters enough that you'd be willing to do these things? For example, if you were doing less worrying, ruminating, or obsessing . . .

- How would that help your closest relationships?
- How would that affect your health and well-being?
- How would that affect your performance at work?
- With whom would you be more present?
- On what would you be more focused?
- What would you do with the extra time and energy it would free up?

Please spend at least a couple of minutes reflecting on these questions and coming up with answers; then ask yourself, "In order to get these benefits, am I willing to do what it takes, to practice new skills and make room for a short-term increase in discomfort?"

If the answer is no, please be kind to yourself. Beating yourself up won't help. So practice self-compassion. Unhook from any self-judgment, make room for feelings such as sadness, disappointment, or frustration, and say something kind to yourself. Remind yourself, sometimes we're willing to do the hard things in life, and sometimes we're not—and that's okay. That's the human condition. Nobody's perfect. You might not be willing to do this right now, but hopefully you will be later.

If, however, the answer is yes, then please experiment as much as you possibly can with the strategies that follow.

Noticing and Naming, Being Present, Focusing and Refocusing

If your mind is not too revved up, a bit of noticing and naming is enough to disrupt that activity: "Here's worrying," "Obsessing about my health," "Thanks, Mind. I know you're trying to help, but I'm going to handle this in a better way."

In combination with this, we focus and refocus repeatedly on the activity we're doing, giving it our full attention.

Dropping Anchor

If your mind is spinning around at maximum speed, your best bet is to drop anchor:

Acknowledge your thoughts and feelings: "Here's my mind racing," "Here's tightness in my chest"; open up and allow them to be there.

Connect with your body: slowly stretch, straighten up, move, or breathe.

Engage in what you're doing: refocus your attention on the activity at hand.

Repeat this cycle at least three or four times.

Making Room and Self-Compassion

If uncomfortable feelings arise (as they probably will) make room for them, using whatever works best from chapters 14 and 15, such as noticing and naming them, observing them with curiosity, breathing into them, imagining them as an object, expanding around them, or laying a kind hand on top of them. And treat yourself kindly: acknowledge your suffering and respond with kind words and actions. This could include reminding yourself this short-term discomfort is in the service of long-term positive life changes.

Noticing, Naming, and Allowing "Intrusive" Thoughts, Feelings, and Memories

Sometimes the trigger for these cognitive processes is an "intrusive" thought, feeling, or memory (i.e., a recurring thought, feeling, or memory that is involuntary, unwanted, and disturbing or upsetting). If we push away, suppress, or distract ourselves from these "intrusions," we set up a vicious cycle: they go away in the short term, but there's a "rebound effect," and they return with even greater frequency or intensity. So when they occur, we notice and name them, open up, and allow them and, if necessary, combine this with dropping anchor. In this way, we disrupt the vicious cycle.

Use Often, Apply Widely

You can apply the strategies above to any cognitive process you find problematic, including things like daydreaming and fantasizing. And they're also a great help with difficult recurring memories. When memories hook us, we either OBEY (give them all our attention, so we miss out on life) or we STRUGGLE (using all the usual methods, with all the usual consequences). Everything we've covered above can help with memories: noticing and naming them, dropping anchor, making room for the feelings that go with them, practicing self-compassion, and repeatedly focusing/refocusing on what we're doing. There's no "delete button" in the brain, no way to eliminate painful memories, but over time, as you treat yourself kindly and allow your memories to be present without a struggle, you're likely to notice two things: they'll appear less often, and they'll steadily lose their impact.

We can also use these strategies to interrupt . . .

Ruminating on Our Emotions

When we ruminate, worry, or obsess about our emotions, we usually end up feeling even worse. To start this process off, our mind says things like the following:

- "Why am I feeling like this?" This question sets you up to run through all your problems one by one, seeing if you can pinpoint what caused your feelings. Naturally, this just makes you feel worse because it creates the illusion that your life is nothing but problems.
- "What have I done to deserve this?" This question sets you up for self-blame. You rehash all the "bad" things you've done, so you can figure out why the universe decided to punish you. As a result, you end up feeling worthless, useless, "bad," or inadequate.
- "Why am I like this?" This question leads you to search through your entire life history looking for the reasons why you are the way you are. Frequently this leads to feelings of anger, resentment, and hopelessness. And it very often ends in blaming your parents, genes, or brain biochemistry.

- "I can't handle it!" Variations on this theme include "I can't stand it," "I can't cope," "I'm going to have a nervous breakdown," and so on. Your mind is basically feeding you the story that you're too weak to handle this, and something bad is going to happen if you keep feeling this way.
- "I shouldn't feel like this." This is a classic! Here your mind picks an argument with reality. The reality is this: the way you are feeling right now is the way you are feeling. But your mind says, "Reality is wrong! It's not supposed to be this way! Stop it! Give me the reality I want!" This can keep us ruminating for hours on how our lives would be so much better if only we felt differently.

So What's the Alternative?

The alternative to ruminating, worrying, or obsessing about your emotions is to notice and name and allow them, to make room for them, and treat yourself kindly. And if you can spare a minute, ask yourself, "What does this emotion tell me really matters? What does it suggest I need to attend to?" As I said in chapter 14, often (not always) you'll find this emotion is pointing to something very important: a problem you need tackle, a fear you need to face, a behavior you need to change, a relationship that deeply matters, or a loss you need to come to terms with.

Dipping In and Out of the Stream

All the methods outlined above can help you cut down significantly on ruminating, worrying, and obsessing. However, the results will be even better if you practice dipping in and out of the stream. Inspired by the work of psychologist Adrian Wells, this exercise takes less than ten minutes. (And, like everything in this book, the more you do it, the better the results. Once a day is ideal, but even once a week is better than nothing.)

When we ruminate, worry, obsess, daydream, or fantasize, we get carried away by the stream of our thoughts. In this exercise, we repeatedly dip in and out of that thought stream. We recognize when the stream has carried us away, and we pull ourselves out of it. Part A—dipping in and out of pleasant thoughts—is easier. Part B—dipping in and out of uncomfortable thoughts—is more challenging but absolutely essential; you need to learn how to do this with any stream of thoughts, whether pleasant or painful.

First read through all the instructions so you know what's involved; then go back and do it for real. You'll need a timer, like your watch or a phone app, to do this. (Alternatively, download the audio from *The Happiness Trap: Extra Bits*.)

Part A: Dipping In and Out of a Pleasant Stream

Step 1: Set your timer for sixty seconds. Then start it and immediately begin daydreaming or fantasizing about something pleasant. Get as absorbed in the daydream or fantasy as possible.

Step 2: As soon as the bell rings (after sixty seconds) drop anchor for about fifteen to thirty seconds. (You don't need to time this step; just guess.) While dropping anchor, make sure you acknowledge the thoughts and feelings that are present (remember, this *isn't* distraction). For example, you might silently say to yourself, "Here are some pleasant thoughts." Then, once you're anchored, acknowledge you have a choice: you can go back into the stream, or you can focus your attention on whatever you're doing.

Then, set the timer again for sixty seconds.

Step 3: Now once again, enter that stream of pleasant thoughts, and lose yourself in it for one minute.

Step 4: When the timer rings, drop anchor for fifteen to thirty seconds. Then notice you have a choice: go back into the stream or engage in your life.

Step 5: For one last time, set the timer, dive back into your stream of pleasant thoughts, and stay there for one minute.

Step 6: When the bell goes off, again drop anchor for fifteen to thirty seconds.

Part B: Dipping In and Out of an Unpleasant Stream

Part B is more challenging, but don't skip it if you want results. It's exactly the same as part A, except now, instead of pleasantly daydreaming or fantasizing, you start worrying, ruminating, obsessing.

Step 1: Bring to mind something you worry, ruminate, or obsess about, and again, set the timer for sixty seconds. Then get as hooked as possible: for one whole minute, worry, ruminate, or obsess as much as you can.

Step 2: When the bell rings, drop anchor for about fifteen to thirty seconds. And again, make sure you acknowledge any difficult thoughts and feelings present (to prevent this from turning into distraction). For example, you may silently say to yourself, "Here's anxiety" or "Here are some scary thoughts." Once anchored, acknowledge you have a choice: you can go back into that stream, or you can focus your attention on the world around you or the activity you're doing.

Next, set the timer again for sixty seconds.

Step 3: Now lose yourself in the stream for another minute; make sure to worry, obsess, or ruminate vigorously.

Step 4: When the alarm goes off, drop anchor for fifteen to thirty seconds. And then notice your options: to dive back into the stream or be present in your life.

Step 5: For one last time, set the timer, plunge back into that stream of difficult thoughts, and let it sweep you away for one full minute.

Step 6: When the bell rings, again drop anchor for fifteen to thirty seconds.

Now that you know what's involved, please go back and do the exercise before reading on.

So how did you do? If you're like most people, there were times you found it hard to leave the stream and times you didn't even want to leave it! And isn't that what it's like when we go through the day, worrying, ruminating, and obsessing? Even though we know it's not helpful, we feel the pull to keep doing it. Hopefully, however, you found that by the end of the exercise it was a bit easier to unhook and refocus. If not, try it again, and this time really work hard at dropping anchor when the timer goes off; be sure to notice and name the difficult thoughts and feelings present (you're not trying to distract yourself from them) while also moving your body and refocusing your attention on the world around you.

The idea is to apply this skill repeatedly throughout the day: as soon as you realize you're lost in the stream of your thoughts, drop anchor for fifteen to thirty seconds; then acknowledge your choice: to go back into the stream and let it carry you away or to be fully present in whatever activity you're doing.

Does this mean we just ignore our problems? NOOOO! In chapter 23 you'll learn how to effectively address your problems, guided by your values, and create an action plan to deal with them. If you like, you can skip ahead to that now. But if you can hold off a little longer, then let's take a look at . . .

[19]

The Documentary of You

What do you most dislike about yourself? I've asked this question of thousands of people, either individually or in groups, and here are some common responses:

- I'm too shy/fearful/anxious/needy/fragile/passive.
- I'm stupid/silly/disorganized.
- I'm fat/ugly/unfit/lazy.
- I'm selfish/critical/arrogant/vain.
- I'm judgmental/angry/greedy/aggressive/obnoxious.
- I'm an underachiever/failure/loser.
- I'm boring/dull/predictable/too serious.

And that is just a *small* selection of the responses, which all point to the same basic theme: "I'm not good enough." It's a message our mind sends us again and again. Remember the two coaches we talked about in chapter 11: the harsh, critical one and the kind, encouraging one? This is our mind using the methods of the harsh, critical coach: a misguided attempt to help us "improve," "shape up," "be better," "fit in," or "achieve more"—by highlighting and exaggerating our flaws and failings. And this constant barrage of self-judgment makes us feel inadequate, unworthy, or unlovable.

So what are we to do about it? We've already looked at common strategies people use to STRUGGLE against negative thoughts: challenging them; pushing them away; distracting themselves; avoiding the people, places, and activities that tend to trigger them; using drugs, alcohol, food, or other substances to get some relief; people-pleasing, trying to be perfect; and so on. And we've discussed how although these methods often give short-term relief, they don't permanently eliminate these thoughts (no delete button in the brain); plus, when used excessively or inappropriately, they have significant costs. However, we haven't yet touched on one of the most popular self-help concepts in Western culture.

THE POWER OF SELF-ESTEEM!

Teachers, parents, coaches, therapists, friends, and family: they all tell us how important it is to have high self-esteem; and most of us have said the same thing to others. (And I certainly used to, before I discovered ACT.) Why is this idea so popular? Well, obviously, when we get hooked by the "not good enough" story, that's not helpful. So the commonsense solution is to replace the negative story with a positive one: focus on your strengths, your successes, and your good points. Build up a positive self-image and hold on to it tightly to keep that old "not good enough" story away.

But does this approach really work? Haven't you already tried it? If so, you'll know there are four big problems with this approach:

1. **You can't convince your mind.** You try hard to convince your mind you're a "good person." You put forward the argument: "I'm doing well at my job; I'm exercising regularly; I'm eating healthily; I help people out; so basically, that means I'm a good person." And if you can really manage to believe that you're a good person, then in that moment you have high self-esteem. But that moment

rarely lasts for long. Your mind soon says, "Yes, but really, you're just kidding yourself. Deep down, you know the truth: *you're not good enough.*"

2. **It's exhausting.** If you go down this path, you will constantly have to prove to your mind that you *really are* a good person. You have to gather up as many positive thoughts as you can to continually disprove those "not good enough" stories. And there's a whole army of self-judgments just waiting for the opportunity to advance! The moment you slip up—the moment you stop doing any of those things that justify "I'm a good person"—the self-judgment army attacks. You stop exercising for a few days and you get, "See? You knew it couldn't last!" You lose your temper with a friend, and you get, "What sort of lousy friend are you?" You make a mistake at work, and you get, "Jeez, what a loser!"

3. **The "big guns" just prolong the battle.** At this point in the battle with their thoughts, many people bring out the "big guns": they start using positive affirmations. This incredibly popular self-help technique involves repeating positive things to yourself like, "I deserve the best," "Every day, in every way, I am getting better and better," "I love who I am," "I am full of strength and courage," "I am in charge of how I feel and today I choose happiness." One huge problem with this method is that most people don't really believe what they are saying. It's a bit like saying, "I am Superman" or "I am Wonder Woman." No matter how often you said that to yourself, you wouldn't really believe it, would you?

4. **Positives attract negatives.** Another problem is that any positive self-judgment we use, even if it's "true," naturally tends to attract a negative response. If we say, "I'm a good person," our mind tends to reply "No you're not! What about the time you did XYZ!" Even if we say, "I accept myself," our mind typically replies, "No you don't! What about your thighs/wrinkles/stretchmarks/teeth/beer belly? What about all those bad habits?"

So is this really how you want to spend your days: fighting your own thoughts? Trying to prove to your mind that you're a good person? Continually having to justify or earn your worthiness? If you go down this path, you may well develop fragile self-esteem. This is extremely common among perfectionists and compulsive high achievers, whose self-esteem is largely dependent upon excelling at work. When they perform well, they feel great, but as soon as their performance drops (as it always will, sooner or later), their self-esteem comes crashing down. This leads them into a vicious cycle, putting increasing pressure on themselves to perform ever better—leading to high stress, fatigue, burnout, and even depression.

The reality is, no matter how hard you struggle against it, the "not good enough" story will always return in one form or another. So do you want to spend the rest of your life battling it? Wouldn't you prefer to have a fulfilling life without all that effort? If we wish to build a richer, more meaningful life, there's something much better than high self-esteem. But before we get to that, let's watch . . .

A Documentary on Africa

Have you ever watched a documentary on Africa? What did you see? Crocodiles, lions, antelopes, gorillas, and giraffes? Tribal dances? Warfare? Nelson Mandela? Colorful marketplaces? Amazing mountains? Beautiful villages in the countryside? Poverty-stricken shantytowns? Starving children? You can learn a lot from watching a documentary, but one thing is for sure: a documentary *about* Africa is not the same thing as Africa itself.

A documentary can give you *impressions* of Africa—video images and audio recordings that *represent* it. But a documentary can't give you the *real-life experience* of Africa: the taste and smell of the food; the feeling of the sunlight on your face; the humidity of the jungle; the dryness of the desert; the touch of an elephant's hide; the joy of directly speaking with the people. No matter how brilliantly filmed that documentary is, even if it's a thousand hours long, it can't come close to the experience of *actually being there*. Why not? Because a documentary *about* Africa is not the same thing as Africa *itself!*

Similarly, a documentary about you would not be the same thing as you yourself. Even if that documentary lasted for ten thousand hours and included all sorts of relevant scenes from your life, all sorts of interviews with people who know you, and all sorts of fascinating details about your innermost secrets—even then the documentary would not be you.

To really clarify this, think of the person you love most on this planet. Now, which would you prefer to spend time with: the actual living person or a documentary about them?

There's a massive difference between who we are and any documentary that anyone could ever make about us—no matter how "truthful" that documentary may be. And I've put "truthful" in quotation marks because all documentaries are hopelessly biased; they only ever show you one tiny part of the big picture. Since the advent of digital video, the typical hour-long television documentary shows the "best" of literally dozens, if not hundreds of hours of footage—highly edited for maximum dramatic effect and reflecting the viewpoint of the filmmakers. So inevitably it's going to be biased!

Now the human mind is like the world's greatest documentary maker. It's always filming: 24 hours a day, 168 hours a week, almost 9,000 hours a year. So by the time you get to age thirty, your mind's been filming for over a quarter of a million hours.

And what percentage of that film gets stored in your long-term memory? Five percent? One percent? Not even close! It's a zillionth of one percent. (How much do you remember of yesterday? Or last week? Or last month? How much do you remember of all the books you've read, movies you've watched, conversations you've had, meals you've eaten?)

So your mind makes this incredibly biased documentary about who you are—cutting out over 99.99 percent of everything you've done in your life—and then it says, "This is you. This is who you are." And the subtitle of that documentary is "I'm not good enough." And the problem is, we believe we *are* that documentary!

But if a documentary about Africa is not Africa, and a documentary about your loved one is not your loved one . . . then a documentary about you is not you. And no matter what shows up in that documentary, whether it's false or true, positive or negative, ancient or recent, facts or opinions, memories or predictions . . . the documentary will *never* be you. That documentary is nothing more or less than an elaborate construction of thoughts, images, and memories (and all the feelings that go with them).

I often refer to this documentary as "The Big Story" because it includes all the beliefs and ideas and judgments about who I am, why I'm like this, what I can and can't do, how I got this way, what's good/positive about me, what's bad/negative about me, what my strengths and weaknesses are, and so on. Technically, we call it our "self-concept."

And a self-concept is a good thing to have, because it enables us to reflect on ourselves, which is essential for personal growth. But we want to hold our self-concept lightly rather than let it hook us. Remember the two modes of getting hooked: OBEY and STRUGGLE? In OBEY mode, we give this self-concept all our attention, treat it as the absolute truth, and do whatever it tells us. And in STRUGGLE mode, we try hard to get rid of it. But neither response is helpful in the long term.

A healthier response is to unhook from "The Big Story" using any method we prefer. We can notice and name it: "Here's the 'not good enough' story." We can drop anchor. We can make room for all those painful feelings the story tends to trigger while supporting ourselves with kind words and actions. And we can focus and refocus attention on what we're doing: being fully present while our self-concept "hovers" in the background.

We can also stop trying to convince ourselves "I'm a good person," or to prove or justify our self-worth. Whatever judgments our mind may make about us—whether negative *or* positive—we can see them for what they are (words and pictures inside our head) and let them come and go like passing cars. Instead, we can hold "The Big Story" lightly, no matter how negative it might be: "Thanks, Mind. I know you're just trying to help by being hard on me."

The same goes even when the story is positive. By all means, let's acknowledge and appreciate our good points and strengths and successes—but if our mind turns that into a story like "I'm wonderful," "I'm brilliant," "I'm the greatest," "I know best," "I'm better than them," this easily pulls us into arrogance, narcissism, righteousness, overconfidence, or a false sense of superiority. So if your mind starts saying you are wonderful, hold it lightly: "Thanks, Mind. I know you're trying to help by being nice to me."

In other words, don't get too attached to either positive or negative self-stories. Hold them all lightly. Whether it's a small story (like a self-judgment) or "The Big Story" (your self-concept), remember when it appears: *there is so much more to you than this.* This story is a mental construction, a tangle of words and pictures inside your head, bundled up with sensations in your body, and it can't even begin to encapsulate the richness, fullness, and complexity of the whole human being you are. A documentary of Africa is not Africa; and the documentary of you is not you.

In *The Happiness Trap: Extra Bits* chapter 19, you'll find two free audio recordings of exercises to develop your ability to unhook from self-stories. One involves "watching" your thoughts float on by like leaves on a stream, and the other involves "listening in" to your thoughts, as if they are voices on the radio.

Of course, your thinking self will likely disagree with everything in this chapter. It will insist, "This *is* you! This *is* who you are!" But with your noticing self, you can step back and see the true nature of these stories: they are words and pictures and sensations, coming and staying and going on that ever-changing stage show of life. And you don't need to OBEY or STRUGGLE with these stories. Instead, you can practice . . .

Self-Acceptance and Self-Compassion

Self-acceptance involves a realistic self-appraisal—acknowledging our "good points" *and* our "bad points," our strengths *and* our weaknesses, our successes *and* our failures—while unhooking from our self-judgments; accepting we are human and therefore imperfect.

But to do this isn't easy. It hurts to acknowledge negative things about ourselves; it triggers many painful thoughts and feelings. So we also need self-compassion: acknowledging how hard and painful it is to be human; naming those harsh self-judgments and "thanking our mind"; speaking to ourselves with words of genuine kindness; and making room for painful feelings while holding ourselves kindly.

And at the same time, we take action in line with our values, enhancing our life by doing what matters. And we give our full attention to what we do, so we can do it well and make the most of it.

If we do this over and over (and over again), we will gradually develop a deep sense of self-worth that's far superior to anything we might achieve by challenging negative thoughts or practicing positive affirmations. However, we might need to spend some time on . . .

[20]

Healing the Past

I'm nine years old, standing outside the headmaster's office, trembling as I hear him shouting down the phone at my mother. "It's a disgrace!" he shouts. "Your son comes to school unwashed, with smelly hair and dirty clothes, often smelling of urine. I've worked in schools in the poorest parts of the city, and I've never seen kids this badly neglected. I'm sending him home to you now. I've informed the social workers and they're going to come later today."

The walk home from school only takes five minutes but seems like hours. My mother, still in her dressing gown (which she wears all day long), opens the front door and drags me in by my hair. She slaps me, punches me, pulls my hair over and over again, shouting things like "How could you do this to me? How could you embarrass me like this? Look at you! You're filthy! You're disgusting. Why don't you wash yourself? You're nine years old, not a baby! How dare you go to school smelly and dirty?"

After the beating ends, she makes me clean up the revolting pigsty of our house, so it will look reasonably respectable for the social workers. Then she tells me to go take a bath and wash my hair.

To be fair to her, my mother was suffering. She herself had a terribly abusive childhood at the hands of my violent grandfather, and had also, during World War II, spent two traumatic years in a Japanese POW (prisoner of war) camp. And about a year before the incident above, my father left home and moved to another country, whereupon my mother became deeply depressed. She spent most of her days zoned out on prescription medication: highly addictive sedative drugs, called barbiturates (which are nowadays rarely used). She was struggling so much she was oblivious to my needs.

Meanwhile, I was deeply distressed and wetting the bed every single night. Then in the morning, without washing, I would get myself dressed, make my breakfast, and head off to school—all while my mother was still fast asleep. So the headmaster wasn't exaggerating when he talked about "smelling of urine."

All in all, I had a pretty shitty childhood: lots of neglect, abandonment by my father, abuse from two close relatives. And I know many readers have had tough childhoods too—some of them far worse than mine. One extremely common result of such an upbringing is that the "documentary of you" is extremely negative, and you develop a strong habit of harsh self-judgment. (However, this is also common even when you have a good childhood, for reasons discussed earlier.)

When we've got a longstanding habit of harsh self-judgment and a tendency to cling tightly to that negative documentary of who we are, it makes self-kindness so much harder: we find the prospect of being kind to ourselves odd, unfamiliar, uncomfortable, and even anxiety provoking. So if you've been resisting the self-compassion exercises, rest assured you're not alone. Many people do. Personally, I struggled with self-compassion for years, until I came across the exercise below, which offers us a way to bypass our resistance. (And if you *have* been practicing self-compassion, this exercise will help you to take it further.)

Giving Support Exercises

Many of us find it hard—at least initially—to be compassionate to ourselves as adults; to acknowledge our pain and respond with kindness. But *in our imagination*, we can travel back in time and "find" the little child we used to be, acknowledge their struggles and their suffering, and reach out to them and offer support. So in this giving support exercise, you imagine yourself traveling back in time to your childhood or teenage years; back to a time when you were hurting, suffering, or struggling in some way, but the adults around you were not offering the kindness, care, and support you really needed. You then imagine the "you of today" giving the "younger you" the support they didn't have at that time.

Note: *Do not go directly back in time to some awful, traumatic event.* It's often overwhelming to do that kind of work alone, and it might backfire;

if you're having flashbacks or distressing traumatic memories, find a therapist with specialized training in trauma to help you. In a giving support exercise, instead of going back to the traumatic event, you go back to sometime *after it occurred*—hours, days, or even weeks afterward.

Once you've traveled back in time and found the younger you, you give them support in any way they want. Most people use compassionate words and gestures, but it's your imagination, so you can do whatever you like—as long as it's kind and supportive.

I'm going to take you through a giving support exercise now. (If you want my voice to guide you, use the free audio from chapter 20 of *The Happiness Trap: Extra Bits*.) The exercise begins with dropping anchor. And if something overwhelming happens (I'm not expecting it—just being cautious), please stop the exercise and drop anchor.

Giving Support to the Younger You

You are about to do an exercise in imagination. Some people imagine with vivid, colorful pictures; others imagine with vague, fuzzy, unclear pictures; and still others imagine without any pictures at all, instead using words, ideas, and concepts. However you imagine is just fine.

You're going to imagine traveling back in time to visit a younger version of yourself, at some point in your life when you were struggling, and the people around you were unable to give you the care and support you needed. This could be when you were a child, a teenager, or a young adult.

Find a comfortable position and spend a few moments dropping anchor: acknowledging what's going on in your inner world; connecting with your body through moving, stretching, or breathing; and engaging in the world around you: noticing what you can see, hear, and touch.

Once you're anchored, either close your eyes or fix your gaze on a spot and allow yourself to imagine.

Imagine getting into a time machine or portal of some sort or stepping into some magical glowing light. And imagine this takes you back in time to visit the younger you, at a time when they are lonely, sad, scared, or suffering in some other way.

Step out of the time machine (or magical light) and make contact with the younger you. Take a good look at this person and get a sense of what they are going through. Are they crying? Are they angry or frightened? Do they feel guilty or ashamed? What does this young person really need? Love, kindness, support, understanding, forgiveness, acceptance?

In a kind, calm, and gentle voice, tell this younger you that you know what has happened, that you know what they've been through, that you know how much they are hurting.

Tell this younger you that they don't need anyone else to validate that experience because you know.

Tell this younger you that they got through this difficult patch in their life, and it is now a distant memory.

Tell this younger you that you are here, that you know how much this truly hurts, and you want to help in any way you can.

Ask this young person if there's anything they need or want from you—and whatever they ask for, give it to them. If they ask you to take them somewhere special, go ahead and do it. Offer a hug, a kiss, kind words, or a gift of some sort. This is an exercise in imagination, so you can give them anything they want. If this younger you doesn't know what they want or doesn't trust you, then let them know that's fine; they don't need to say or do anything.

Tell this young person anything you think they need to hear to help them understand what has happened and (if this has been happening) to help them stop blaming themselves.

Tell them that you are here for them, that you care, and you'll do whatever you can to help them get through this.

Continue to radiate caring and kindness toward this young person in any way you can think of: through words, gestures, deeds—or, if you prefer, through magic or telepathy.

Once you have a sense that this younger you has accepted your caring and kindness, it's time to bid farewell. Give them a gift of some sort to symbolize the connection between you. This could be a toy or teddy bear for a younger child; for someone older, perhaps it's an item of clothing, a book, a high-tech gadget, a magical object, or anything else that springs to mind.

Say goodbye and let them know that you'll come back to visit again. Then get in your time machine (or step into the light) and come back to the present.

Now drop anchor for a minute or so. Acknowledge what's showing up inside you. Connect with your body—have a good long stretch. Engage with the world around you: use your eyes and ears and notice where you are and what you're doing.

I hope you found that exercise helpful; that it helped you tap into a sense of self-compassion. It's often helpful to do this regularly; indeed, on each occasion you do it, you might choose to visit a different point in time.

After completing the exercise, ask yourself, "How can I treat myself the way I treated that young child? What are small words or actions of kindness, caring, and support that I can offer myself as I go about my day?"

Echoes of the Past

We can't alter what has happened in the past, but we don't have to let it dictate who we are. Our past history has influenced the way we think, feel, and act—but no matter what eventuated and how it impacted us, we can at any point learn new ways of being in the world and making the most of life here and now.

Echoes of the past will continue to arise in the present. Old patterns of thinking will reactivate; old patterns of behavior will reassert themselves; and old patterns of feeling will reoccur within the body, especially when "old wounds" open up. We can't eliminate them, but we can get better and better at consciously noticing these old patterns and responding effectively when they occur. In the Acknowledge phase of dropping anchor, we might say, "Here's some old programming showing up" or "Here's that old pattern again." When noticing and naming thoughts, we might say "Here's an old voice from the past." When making room, we might say, "Here's pain from an old wound."

And if old memories are haunting you, then as well as using all the strategies above, you can pause for a moment and consider the following:

- Does this memory have something useful to offer?
- What does it tell you that you care about?
- What values does it remind you of?
- What does it suggest you could do in the world today to help make it better or prevent things like this from happening again?

These difficult memories are yet another example of your mind being an overly helpful friend, trying way too hard to help you learn or grow from your past experiences. So see if you can find something of use within them. You won't *always* succeed, but often you will.

Then once you've finished with those memories, bring your attention back to the present. Notice where you are, and what you're doing—right here, right now. Because every time you do this, you're helping yourself to develop . . .

[21]

The Art of Appreciation

Have you ever gazed in wonder at a brilliant sunset or an impossibly large full moon or the ocean waves crashing on a rocky shore? Ever looked adoringly into the eyes of your child or your partner? Reveled in the aroma of baking pies or the fragrant scent of jasmine or roses? Listened in delight to a singing bird, a purring cat, or the laughter of a small child?

Every day offers a wealth of opportunities to appreciate the world we live in. Practicing your focusing and savoring skills will help you make the most of your life right now, even as you're taking action to change it for the better. Popular expressions like "Count your blessings" and "Stop and smell the roses" point to the abundance in our lives. We are surrounded by wonderful things but, sadly, we usually take them for granted. So here are a few suggestions for waking up and experiencing the richness of the world around you:

- When you eat something, take the opportunity to savor it, to fully taste it. Let your thoughts come and go and focus on the sensations in your mouth. Most of the time when we eat and drink, we're scarcely aware of what we're doing. Given that eating is a pleasurable activity, why not take the time to appreciate it fully? Instead of wolfing your food down, eat it slowly—actually chew it. (After all, you wouldn't watch a video on fast-forward, so why eat your food that way?)
- Next time it's raining, pay attention to the sound of it—the rhythm, the pitch, the ebb and flow of the volume. And notice the intricate patterns of the raindrops on the windows. And when it stops, go for a walk and notice the freshness of the air and the way the footpaths glisten as if they'd been polished.

- Next time it's sunny, take a few moments to appreciate the warmth and the light. Notice how everything brightens—houses, flowers, trees, the sky, people. Go for a walk, listen to the birds, and notice how the sun feels against your skin.
- When you hug or kiss someone—or even shake hands—fully engage in it. Notice what you can feel. Let your warmth and openness flow through that contact.
- Look with new eyes at the people you care about, as if you'd never seen them before. Do this with your spouse or partner, friends, family, children, coworkers, colleagues. Notice how they walk, talk, eat and drink, and gesture with their faces, bodies, and hands. Notice their facial expressions. Notice the lines of their faces and the color of their eyes.
- Before you get out of bed in the morning, take a few slow, gentle breaths in and out, and focus on the movement of your lungs. Cultivate a sense of wonder that you are alive, that your lungs have provided you with oxygen all night long, even while you were fast asleep.
- In *The Happiness Trap: Extra Bits*, chapter 21, do the audio exercise "Appreciating Your Hand." You won't believe this until you try it, but you will appreciate your hand in a whole new way. You'll be amazed at how you normally just take it for granted.

Enjoy, but Don't Cling

So far in this book, we've spent a lot of time on uncomfortable thoughts and feelings but precious little on appreciating the pleasant ones. This is deliberate. As we explored earlier, the more importance we place on having pleasant feelings, the more we'll struggle against the uncomfortable ones, creating and intensifying the whole vicious cycle of struggle and suffering. Pleasant feelings will come and go, just like every other feeling. So let's enjoy them and appreciate them when they visit, but let's not cling to them!

In other words, next time you're feeling happy or calm, joyful or content, or some other pleasant emotion, take the opportunity to fully notice what that feels like. Notice what you feel in your body. Notice how you're breathing, talking, or gesturing. Notice any urges, thoughts, memories, sensations, and images. Take a few moments to appreciate this emotion; to enjoy it. But don't try to hold on to it. Treat pleasant feelings the same way as your difficult ones: acknowledge them, allow them, and let them freely come and stay and go in their own good time.

Making the Most of It

As you open your eyes and notice the things you've previously taken for granted, you'll notice more opportunities, you'll be more stimulated and interested, you'll find more contentment, and your relationships will improve. I like to put it like this: *Life gives most to those who make the most of what life gives.*

Be Present, Open Up, Do What Matters

This brings us to the end of part 2 of this book. So far we've focused mainly on your abilities to be present (focus your attention on what's important, notice and engage in what you're doing) and open up (unhook from thoughts and feelings and allow them to freely come and stay and go). In part 3, we're going to develop your ability to do what matters: to get in touch with your values and translate them into effective, life-enhancing actions.

These three short phrases—*be present, open up, do what matters*—pretty much summarize the whole ACT model. The greater our ability to *be present* and *open up*, the easier it is to unhook from difficult thoughts and feelings and interrupt our away moves. And the more we *do what matters*, the better life gets. The diagram below maps this out.

The technical term for our ability to be present, open up, and do what matters is *psychological flexibility*. And the research is crystal clear: the greater our psychological flexibility, the greater our health, well-being, and happiness.

Of course, as we take action to create the life we want, we will face many fears, obstacles, and challenges—so uncomfortable thoughts and feelings are inevitable. But more and more, through being present and opening up (dropping anchor, noticing and naming, making room, self-compassion, focusing and refocusing, savoring and appreciating, etc.) we can overcome such barriers and do what it takes to build a better life.

Away

Toward

Hooked

Unhooked

← Do What Matters
Act effectively, guided by your values.

← Be Present, Open Up
Use your unhooking skills

Difficult
situations,
thoughts & feelings

PART THREE

HOW TO MAKE
LIFE MEANINGFUL

[22]

A Life Worth Living

A few years back, my good friend Fred started up a business venture that went horribly wrong. As a result, he and his wife lost almost everything they owned, including their house. In dire financial straits, they decided to move from the city out to the country, so they could live somewhere decent with affordable rent. There Fred found a job at a local boarding school that catered to foreign students, mainly teenagers from China and Korea.

This job was totally unrelated to Fred's previous business experience. His duties involved maintaining order and security in the boarding school, ensuring that the kids did their homework, and making sure they went to bed at the right time. He would also sleep in the boarding school overnight and help the children get organized for school the next morning.

Many people in Fred's shoes would have been deeply depressed. After all, he'd lost his business, his house, his savings, and now he was stuck in a low-paying job that kept him away from his wife five nights a week! But Fred realized he had two choices: he could dwell on his losses, beat himself up, and make himself miserable—or he could make the most of it.

Fortunately, he chose the latter.

Fred tapped into his core values: being helpful, supportive, caring, and encouraging. In line with these values, he began to teach the children useful skills, such as how to iron their clothes and cook simple meals. He also organized the school's first-ever talent contest and helped the kids film a humorous documentary about student life. On top of this, he became the students' unofficial counselor. Many of them came to him for help and advice in dealing with their various troubles: relationship difficulties, family issues, problems with studies, and so on. None of these things were part of Fred's job description, and he didn't get any extra pay for doing them; he did them purely and simply because he was acting on his values of giving and caring. And as a result, a job that could have been tedious and unfulfilling became meaningful and satisfying.

Did Fred have lots of painful thoughts and feelings? You betcha! He was hurting badly—as would anyone facing a big reality gap with no chance of closing it any time soon. When Fred chose to live by his values, that didn't magically sort out all his problems and make him live happily ever after. But it did improve his quality of life, making it more meaningful and fulfilling. Imagine if he'd gone through each day at work hooked by thoughts like "Life sucks!" "I hate this job," "I've ruined everything," "I'm a hopeless loser." How much would he have missed out on had he spent his days lost in his thoughts and struggling with his feelings instead of living by his values and being present?

Values and Goals

In chapter 10, I described values as our heart's deepest desires for how we want to behave; how we want to treat ourselves, others, and the world around us. I'll explain this in more detail shortly, but first let's consider five benefits of knowing and using our values:

1. They help us make wiser choices, so we can do things that tend to work better.
2. They're like an inner compass that can guide us, help us find our way, and give us a sense of purpose.
3. They provide motivation, giving us the strength to do what really matters.
4. When life is dull and gray, they add some color.
5. When you act on them, they give you a sense of fulfillment—a sense of being true to yourself, living life your way, behaving like the sort of person you really want to be.

It's important to know the difference between values and goals. A value is a quality we desire to bring to our behavior; a quality that guides the words we use and how we say them, and the actions we take and how we do them. In contrast, a goal describes what we want to have, get, achieve, or complete. So if you want to have a great job, that's a goal; but if you want to be responsible and reliable, those are values. Here are some more examples:

- To find a partner: goal. To be loving (whether or not you have a partner): value
- To buy a house for your family to live in: goal. To be supportive and caring toward your family (whether or not you buy a house): values
- To go traveling overseas: goal. To be curious, open, and appreciative while you are traveling (even if you're just on your way to work): values
- To have a child: goal. To be loving and nurturing (whether or not you have a child): values
- To have lots of friends, make people like you, or be popular: goals. To be warm, open, and understanding (whether or not you have lots of friends): values
- To recover from this physical illness or heal an injury: goals. To be self-caring, self-supportive, self-compassionate (no matter what state your physical health is in): values

Notice in each example above, you can live by the values whether or not you achieve the goal in question. So if you want to obtain a degree, become rich or famous or powerful, own a house or a car, have a good body, get other people to treat you well, or recover from an illness . . . those are all goals. Values are how you want to treat yourself, others, and the world around you—both now and in the future—while you are pursuing your goals, when you achieve your goals, and when you *don't* achieve your goals.

Think of values as what you want to bring to life's table. On the vast table of life, there are many dishes. Some of these dishes we love, like our favorite food or music, or a warm and caring connection with a close companion. Some of these dishes we hate, like a terrible illness or the death of a loved one. And the rest of the dishes are somewhere in between.

From moment to moment, the dishes on life's table continually change. And we may rant about the dishes we want that are not there or rage against those we wish had *not* been served. But although these are normal reactions, they are not helpful. A more useful approach is to consider: *What do we want to bring to life's table?* No matter how that table is set, there is always much we can bring to it: love, kindness, caring, curiosity, openness, courage, wisdom, self-compassion, or any other values we choose. We can consciously bring these qualities into being through our words, our deeds, and our actions. And this is what we mean when we talk of living by our values.

In chapter 10 we discussed people living in refugee camps in conditions of scarcity and adversity that most of us can barely imagine, where all sorts of privileges that we take for granted—like freedom, food, water, housing, medical care, and electricity—are completely out of their reach. Yet they are still able to live by their values in little ways, every day; and the more they do so, the better their quality of life within the camp. This is such an important insight, especially if you are in a situation that deprives you of what you want most or stops you from doing many of the things you want to do (e.g., if you're in a prison or hospital, stuck in an awful job, or suffering from a chronic illness or injury).

However, living by our values doesn't mean we give up on all our goals. Let's go back to Fred. He stayed in that job because he needed to earn money to live; and every day at work, he continued to live his values. However, he didn't give up on his goal of finding work he genuinely wanted. He'd always been an excellent organizer and administrator, with a particular interest in theatrical and musical events, and this was the area he most wanted to work in. Eventually, after many months of unsuccessfully applying for all sorts of jobs, Fred found one as the organizer of a local arts festival. It was a job that fulfilled him, paid him well, and allowed him to spend a lot more time with his wife.

Fred's story serves as a great example of how we can live by our values even as we continue to pursue our goals. It's also a good example of how we can improve any job—even if it's one we don't want—by bringing our values to the table. That way, even while we search or train for a better job, we can get more satisfaction from the one we have. In chapter 23 we're going to look at how to set realistic goals and maximize your chances of achieving them—but for now we're going to keep the focus on values. Why? Because a life that's heavily goal-focused is a life of chronic discontentment. To understand why, let's consider. . .

Two Kids in the Back of a Car

There are two kids in the back of a car, and Mom's taking them to Disney-land, a three-hour drive away. One kid is totally fixated on the goal: *Get to Disneyland!* He's sitting on the edge of his seat, impatient, frustrated. Every few minutes he's whining, "Are we there, yet?" "I'm bored," "How much longer?" (Does this sound familiar?)

The second kid has exactly the same goal—*get to Disneyland!*—but he's also in touch with his values of playfulness and curiosity, so he's playing games like "I spy with my little eye" and looking out of the window, no-ticing the cows and sheep in the fields, admiring the giant trucks zooming past, waving at friendly pedestrians. He's living in the moment, appreci-ating where he is rather than fixating on where he's not.

When they reach Disneyland, both kids will be happy because they achieved their goal—but only one of them enjoyed the trip. Then on the way home, the first kid is whining, "Are we there yet?" while the other is again making the most of the journey.

Now suppose a different scenario: the car breaks down *on the way* to Disneyland, so the kids never get there; both are disappointed, but which one has had the most rewarding journey?

When we go through life like the first kid, it's exhausting: continually chasing goal after goal after goal. The mind hooks us with this story: "I'll be happy *after* I get this job, lose weight, find a partner, get a promotion, have a child, buy a car, finish this project . . ." And if we let this story run our life, we will experience loooong periods of dissatisfaction and frus-tration while we frantically pursue those goals, punctuated by brief mo-ments of happiness *if* we achieve them. (And even those pleasant feelings quickly evaporate as soon as the next goal looms.) The values-focused life will always be more fulfilling than the goal-focused life because we get to appreciate every step of the journey as we move toward our goals (even if we don't achieve them).

A Life Worth Living

Many of my clients ask questions like, "What's the point of life?" "Is this all there is?," "Why don't I feel excited about anything?," "Why is my life so dull/empty/boring?" Others say things like, "Life sucks!" "Maybe the world would be better off without me," "I have nothing to offer," "Sometimes I wish I could go to bed and never wake up again." Such thoughts are commonplace not just among the 10 percent of adults who suffer from depression at any given time but also among the rest of the population. And values provide a powerful antidote: a way to give your life purpose and meaning.

Any activity we do will be more meaningful and fulfilling if it's motivated primarily by our values. We can go to work in OBEY mode, hooked by rules like "I have to do this job to pay the bills." And we can go to work in STRUGGLE mode, trying to avoid difficult thoughts and feelings: "Working helps me escape feeling like a loser." Alternatively, we can go to work motivated by our values: "I'm living my values, being supportive and caring for my family."

Likewise, when we're at work we can go through the day hooked by "This job sucks," or we can treat each day as an opportunity to live by our values, such as being helpful, honest, and cooperative. This won't turn a dull job into a dream job, but it will make it more meaningful and fulfilling. And the same holds true for everything we ever do, especially all those dull, tedious, or stressful things we need to do to make our life better.

But hey, that's enough of the theory. Let's do something more practical.

Connect and Reflect

The connect and reflect exercise involves thinking about someone you care about and reflecting on what you like to do together. (If you can't visualize it, that's not a problem; just get a sense of it.)

Part A

Think of someone you care about who is active in your life today—someone who treats you well, who you like to spend time with. And remember a time, recent or distant, when you were together, doing an activity you like. This needn't be anything dramatic; it could just be hanging out together, having a drink or a meal, playing a game, going for a walk, swimming at the beach, having a chat, going for a drive, hugging and kissing, kicking a ball around, playing with the kids . . . any activity you enjoy.

Once you've picked a memory, make it as vivid as possible. Relive it as if it is happening here and now. Sense it, feel it, recreate it. Where are you? What are you doing? What can you see, hear, touch, taste, or smell?

Notice the other person in this memory—what do they look like? How are they dressed? What are they saying or doing? What's their tone of voice, the expression on their face, their body posture?

Make the most of this memory. Let yourself *feel* it. What does it feel like to be doing something you enjoy with someone who treats you well? Appreciate it. Lap it up. Savor it.

Please do this for at least a minute, before moving on.

Part B

Now step back and look at the memory as if you're watching it on a TV screen (or get a sense of studying/examining the memory).

Now focus on yourself as you are *inside* that memory. What are you saying and doing? How are you interacting with the other person?

In particular, how are you treating the other person? How are you responding to them? For example, are you being open, loving, kind, fun-loving, playful, lighthearted, connected, engaged, interested, appreciative, honest, real, curious, courageous, intimate, sensual, creative, or enthusiastic?

Really think about this for a minute. What qualities are you bringing to the table?

Now consider this: What does this remind you about the way you want to treat other people? And the sort of relationships you want to build?

Please think about this carefully for a minute or two.

Now please do this experiment again, but this time choose another pleasant memory that involves a different person.

Again: What does this tell you about the way you want to treat others and the sort of relationships you want to build?

Now please do this one last time, but this time choose a memory of doing something enjoyable, meaningful, or satisfying *by yourself*.

Then consider this: What does this remind you about the way you want to treat yourself? And the sort of relationship you want to build with yourself?

How did you do? For some people these experiments give rise to "warm and fuzzy" feelings. For others, they trigger painful thoughts and feelings. And both types of reaction are completely normal.

But the point of these exercises isn't to trigger any particular feelings; it's to help you connect with some values. Were you able to do so? Did you get a sense of who you want to be in the relationship you picked? A sense of how you want to treat the other person and/or yourself? See if you can come up with at least three or four values you connected with. (And if difficult thoughts and feelings are showing up, use your unhooking skills: thank your mind, make room, and treat yourself kindly.)

Now before the next experiment, let's quickly touch on two important points about values . . .

Values Are Not Rules

Rules are basically commands, orders, and laws imposed by your mind. Like a tyrant, your mind tells you, "You must OBEY these rules. And if you don't, something very bad will happen!" So if you're feeling heavy, burdened, or trapped, you are probably hooked by rules rather than connecting with your values. Here are some examples to illustrate the difference:

- Being loving: value. I MUST always be loving, no matter what!: rule
- Being kind: value. I SHOULD be kind at all times, even when people are abusive: rule
- Being efficient: value. I HAVE TO ALWAYS be efficient, and MUST NEVER make any mistakes: rule

Basically, rules are strict instructions your mind says you have to obey. They usually contain words like *have to, must, ought, should, right, wrong, always, never, do this, don't do that, can't until, won't unless, can't because,* and so on. There are always many ways to act upon our values, even in the most difficult situations. Rules, in contrast, massively narrow our options: the more strictly we OBEY them, the less choice we have.

Of course, rules are often useful; it's good to know which side of the road we have to drive on. But many of our self-imposed rules keep us stuck: "I must do it perfectly—and if I can't, there's no point in doing it,"

"I have to drink to cope," "I shouldn't let people get close because they'll hurt me," "I have to always put others first; their needs are more important than mine." The more hooked we are by our rules, the stronger the compulsion to follow them—and the greater the anxiety that shows up when we bend or disobey them.

In addition, when rules hook us, they suck all the life out of our values. When we live by our values flexibly, we have a sense of meaning, purpose, empowerment, or vitality; but when we get hooked by rules, we experience pressure, obligation, heaviness, shame, guilt, anxiety, or a sense of being trapped.

Naturally, then, we want to unhook from rules while digging out the values buried beneath them. All the usual unhooking methods can help. For example, we can notice and name: "I'm noticing the rule that I have to XYZ," or "Aha! Here's that rule again." Or we can thank our mind: "Thanks, Mind. I know you're trying to help by giving me strong guidelines on how to live. And I'm going to take a different approach and see how that works." Or if the compulsion to obey the rule is very strong, we can drop anchor.

Values Continually "Move"

Our values are like the continents on a globe of the world. No matter how fast you spin that globe, you can never see all the continents at the same time; some are moving to the back, others coming to the front. So throughout the day, the positions of your values change: as you change roles and move into different situations, some values come to the foreground while others recede into the background.

This means we often need to prioritize which values we act on in a given situation. For example, when it comes to close relationships, we might have values such as being loving and caring. But if we have a parent who is continually hostile and abusive to us, we might cut off all contact with that person because our values around self-protection and self-respect take priority. However, our values around being loving and caring haven't disappeared; we've just moved them to the "back of the globe" in that specific relationship. Meanwhile, in our good, healthy relationships, loving and caring remain "at the front of the globe."

The Values Checklist: Revisited

In chapter 10 I asked you to read through a values checklist and assess which ones seem important to you and which ones don't. Given all the extra skills and knowledge you have now, I encourage you to go back and do it again. You might find the experiment gives you different results this time around. Or you might not. Either way, it's worth doing again, if only to give you more clarity about what your values are. So please do this now, before reading on.

Did you do it? Was it easy or difficult? Did uncomfortable thoughts and feelings show up? Was it the same or different from last time? People have vastly different experiences doing any sort of work with values; a few find it easy, most find it challenging, and some find it incredibly painful or anxiety provoking. So if painful thoughts and feelings do show up, please don't give up; use all those unhooking skills and treat yourself kindly.

Barriers

Our mind can throw up all sorts of barriers to hold us back from our values. After doing this exercise, Karl said sadly, "I'll be honest with you, Russ. I want to say 'loving' and 'kind,' but when I look at what I've been doing—how bitchy and mean and selfish I've been—it's pretty obvious those aren't my values." This is a common misunderstanding. Many people assume that our problematic, destructive, or self-defeating behaviors reflect our core values. But research shows us the very opposite; such behaviors rarely if ever reflect our values. The reason we do these things is because we get hooked by our thoughts and feelings and pulled *away from* our values.

So I reminded Karl that values are *desired* qualities of behavior. I told him, "Values describe how we *want* to behave, in a world where we can choose. So if there's any value you'd *like* to have, *want* to have, *aspire* to have—then by definition, it's *already* your value; it's a quality of behavior you *desire*. If you'd like to be loving, then 'being loving' is one of your values. If you want to be kind, then 'kindness' is one of your values."

"But I'm not doing anything kind or loving," said Karl.

"So you've highlighted something important," I replied. "You've hit on the very important difference between values and actions. For any given value, you can either act on it, or not. If you want to act on the values of kindness and being loving, then even if you've never done so in your life, you can start today."

"But how do I know if these are my *real* values?" asked Karl. This is a common question, and I usually answer it with an old English saying . . .

"The Proof of the Pudding Is in the Eating"

Suppose there's a delicious pudding (or some other dessert if you're not keen on puddings . . . or a pizza, if you don't like desserts . . . or a fruit salad if you don't like pizza) and it's there, freshly made, on the table in front of you. It looks and smells delicious—but is it? You can analyze it, ponder it, question it, contemplate it, philosophize about it for hours on end . . . but no matter how much you think about it, you still won't know how good or bad it tastes. The only way to know is to eat some.

It's the same with your values. If you don't know whether they're "really yours," you won't resolve that issue by ruminating or philosophizing about it. The only way to know is to act on those values; to experiment with bringing them into your life and notice what happens as you do. If you find that when you act on them, you get a sense of being more like the person you want to be, then you know you're on the right track; if you don't get that sense, then you can experiment with some different values.

Flavoring and Savoring

People often get overwhelmed because they try to change their whole lives overnight. That's a recipe for stress and failure. The trick is to think small; take baby steps. Look for little ways to get better at living by your values. Over time, these small steps have large effects. With that in mind, I'm going to suggest another practice, called "flavoring and savoring."

Each morning, choose one or two values you want to bring into play. So, for example, you might pick the values of being helpful and being open or the values of being kind and being courageous. This is an ongoing experiment, so you can change the values you're playing with daily or weekly, as desired.

(If you can't decide which values to pick, then work your way alphabetically down through the list. Experiment with them and notice what happens. Try them on for size, like a new suit. If it's a good fit, well and good. But if not, try on some others.)

As you go through your day, look out for opportunities to "sprinkle" those values into your activities—especially into your relationships with other people. In other words, whatever you're saying or doing, by yourself or with others, see if you can give it the flavor of those values (as long as that seems appropriate for the situation).

And as you flavor it, savor it! Notice what you're doing, give it your full attention, be fully present, and actively appreciate the experience—just like savoring your favorite food or music.

[23]

One Step at a Time

Have you ever sculpted a beautiful statue from a rough block of marble? No, nor have I. But I've seen sculptors in movies, and one thing's for sure: They don't chip away at the marble in ten different places simultaneously. They make *one chip at a time*. And bit by bit, one small chip at a time, that rough block of stone becomes something wondrous.

The same principle applies to building a better life. If you try to work on too many areas simultaneously, you'll end up highly stressed, increasingly anxious, or get overwhelmed and give up. The trick is to think small: focus on making small changes in one aspect of life at a time. Over time, those small changes have large effects. (And if your mind starts protesting, "No! That's not good enough. I need to sort my whole life out *now!*" . . . well, you know the drill.)

Sometimes people say to me, "Yeah, that sounds good in theory, but that won't work in *my situation*. When you're up against what I have to deal with, there's nothing you can do." I never try to debate this issue with them; instead, I introduce them to . . .

The Challenge Formula

No matter how difficult our situation, we always have choices. Whatever sort of challenge we face, our three options are as follows:

1. Leave.
2. Stay and live by your values: do whatever you can to improve the situation, make room for the pain that goes with it, and treat yourself kindly.

3. Stay—but do things that either make no difference or make it worse.

Now of course, option 1—leave—isn't always possible. For example, if you're in prison, you can't just leave. But if leaving the situation *is* an option, seriously consider it. If you're in a high-conflict relationship, a meaningless job, or an undesirable neighborhood, is your life likely to be better if you leave rather than stay?

If you can't leave, won't leave, or don't see it as the best option available, then you are down to options 2 and 3. And unfortunately, option 3 comes naturally to all of us; in challenging situations, we easily get hooked by difficult thoughts and feelings and pulled into self-defeating patterns of behavior that either keep us stuck or make things worse.

So if option 1 isn't on the table, the path to a better life lies in option 2: do whatever you can to improve the situation. Very importantly, this includes reaching out to others who can help and support you. And it might also involve joining groups or movements that actively work toward making positive changes in your culture, society, or community.

Of course, you can't expect to feel happy when you're in a difficult situation; you will inevitably have lots of painful thoughts and feelings. So the second half of option 2—make room for your pain and treat yourself kindly—is essential.

In chapter 10 I mentioned an ACT program used by the WHO in refugee camps around the world. The challenge formula is a central pillar of that program. Obviously, refugees can't just leave their camp, stop the war, or end the persecution they've fled from, so option 1 isn't available. But option 2 is. Within the camp, the many little values-based actions someone makes throughout each day—such as being friendly and supportive to other people, practicing self-compassion, or actively savoring a meal—have a significant impact on their life. And the same is true for all of us. So let's now look at how we can practically do this.

Four Domains of Life

To ensure you don't get overwhelmed by trying to work on too many things simultaneously, let's divide life into four main domains: work, love, play, health. The aim is to work on *just one domain* at a time. We're using these terms very broadly, as follows:

1. *Work* is an umbrella term for paid work, volunteer work, or domestic/caregiver work. It also includes training and education, both formal (like a course or apprenticeship) or informal (e.g., from reading books, watching documentaries, or having a friend teach you how to do something).
2. *Love* is a catch-all phrase for relationships with people you consider important in your life. This could include your partner, parents, friends or relatives, or even work colleagues; anyone with whom you have (or wish to build) a strong bond.
3. *Play* encapsulates everything you do for rest and recreation: your sports, hobbies, or creative outlets; the things you do for fun, relaxation, or to explore the world around you.
4. *Health* refers to all the things you do to look after your physical well-being, psychological well-being, and (if relevant) your spiritual/religious well-being. This can include exercising, healthy cooking and eating, getting into nature, reading books like this one, seeing a coach or therapist, practicing your unhooking skills, self-compassion, prayer, meditation, yoga, community work, and so on.

These four domains all overlap, which is good because it facilitates the "domino effect": small changes in one area of life have positive effects on others.

In the table below there are four squares, one for each life domain. (You can print a copy from chapter 23 of *The Happiness Trap: Extra Bits*.) Please feel free to subdivide squares if you wish. For example, some people split the love box into friends/partner/children, or the health box into physical/psychological, or the work box into paid/volunteer.

Please write down between one and three values inside each square (or subdivision). Choose the values that seem most important to you; values you want to start or keep putting into play, within that domain. (You may find that some values appear in several squares, or subdivisions, whereas others appear in only one.)

After you've done that, score *on average* how well you've lived by these values (i.e., how much they've influenced your words and actions) over the past week: 10 = very well, and 0 = not at all. (And if you have subdivided a box, give a score for each subdivision.) I emphasize "on average" because from moment to moment, how well we live our values varies massively. One moment, we're being who we want to be; the next, we get hooked by our thoughts and feelings and pulled into away moves, saying and doing things that are far removed from the person we want to be.

The Values Square

WORK	LOVE
Values I want to start or keep putting into play:	Values I want to start or keep putting into play:
How I've lived by these values, on average, over the past week: 0 = not at all; 10 = very well	How I've lived by these values, on average, over the past week: 0 = not at all; 10 = very well
My score:	My score:
PLAY	**HEALTH**
Values I want to start or keep putting into play:	Values I want to start or keep putting into play :
How I've lived by these values, on average, over the past week: 0 = not at all; 10 = very well	How I've lived by these values, on average, over the past week: 0 = not at all; 10 = very well
My score:	My score:

Please do this before reading on.

How did you do? Did some difficult thoughts and feelings show up as you did that? If so, that's completely normal; almost everyone finds their scores are lower than they'd like, and our mind is quick to judge us, so guilt, shame, or anxiety often arises. And you know the routine: allow those thoughts and feelings to be there, thank your mind for its input, be kind to yourself, and focus on what you're doing. The next step is to set . . .

A Short-Term Goal in Just One Domain

Pick one of those four domains (or one subdivision of a domain) to work on for the week ahead. That's right, *just one* domain; and only for the week ahead. It's important to start small, because if we try to make too many changes at once, we'll get overwhelmed and give up.

Over time, the idea is to work on all domains of our life and set medium-term and long-term goals too (we'll get to that in later chapters). But if we want to be successful in that endeavor, we need to go slow. Remember that ancient Chinese proverb: "A journey of a thousand miles begins with one step." And Aesop's famous fable: "Little by little does the trick." And the old proverb: "Mighty oaks from tiny acorns grow." And the well-known saying . . . oh, enough already; I'm sure you get the point.

So your aim now it to set a short-term goal for your chosen domain—something you can do in the next few hours or days, in line with the values you've chosen. But first, a few important tips on goal setting . . .

NOT TOO EASY, NOT TOO HARD: If your goal's too easy, that's not personal growth. It should stretch you a little, pull you out of your comfort zone. But if it's too hard, you'll either give up or try and fail. So find the middle ground.

NO EMOTIONAL GOALS: Don't set emotional goals that describe how you want to feel. They will only pull you back into self-defeating struggle strategies.

NO "DEAD PERSON'S GOALS": A "dead person's goal" is one that a corpse can do better than you. For example, if you want to stop smoking—that's something a dead body can do better than you because, no matter what, they'll definitely never smoke again. (Unless you cremate them.)*

Any goal that is about *not* doing something is a dead person's goal; corpses are truly brilliant at *not* doing things. So to convert it to a "live person's goal" (i.e., something that a live person can do better than a dead one), you need to ask yourself, "If I *don't* do this activity, what *will* I do instead?" For example: "Instead of smoking a cigarette, I'll drop anchor, surf the urge to smoke, and do some stretching or go for a walk or mindfully drink a glass of water." (That is definitely something you can do better than a corpse.)

MAKE IT SPECIFIC: It's important to be specific about the actions you will take. For instance, "I'll go swimming for thirty minutes, twice a week" or "I'll go for a ten-minute walk every lunchtime," as opposed to making vague statements like "I'll do more exercise."

Also, specify when and where you'll do it. For example, "I'll go for a run in the park right after work on Wednesday."

MAKE IT REALISTIC: Ensure the goal is realistic, given your current resources. Your resources include time, money, energy, physical health, skills, knowledge, and the help and support of others. So, for example, if your physical health is impaired, going for a run or working out at the gym might be unrealistic, but it might be realistic to go for a walk. And remember, this is a *short-term* goal: you need to be able to realistically do this within the next week.

ANTICIPATE DIFFICULT THOUGHTS AND FEELINGS: When you leave the comfort zone, what shows up? Yup, that's right: discomfort. So expect that reason-giving machine in your head to come up with all sorts of reasons not to do this. And likewise, expect uncomfortable feelings—especially anxiety—to show up in your body. What thoughts and feelings do you think are likely to show up for you? (Often, they show up even as you're doing this exercise.) Are you willing to make room for these difficult thoughts and feelings in order to move toward the life you want? (If

* Sorry. Bad taste. I couldn't resist it.

the answer is no, you'll need to go back and change your goal: reduce the difficulty; make it smaller, simpler, easier.)

So, are you ready to go ahead? Research shows you're far likelier to take action if you write down your goals than if you just think about them. So please, for the sake of a better life, go get a pen—and write in the book or copy the diagram below onto some paper or download the worksheet from *The Happiness Trap: Extra Bits*—and take a few minutes to fill it in.

Life domain:

Values:

Goal:

When and where will I do this, and what specific actions will I take?

What difficult thoughts and feelings are likely to show up?

Am I willing to use my unhooking skills with these difficult thoughts and feelings and do what matters to build the life I want—yes or no? (If no, change the goal: smaller, simpler, easier.)

On a scale of 0–10, how realistic is it that I will do this? (If less than 7, change the goal: smaller, simpler, easier.)

Please do this now, before reading on.

Putting Your Values into Play

Did you do the previous exercise? Sometimes people try to skip this bit. If that's you, gotcha! You will be tracked down, captured, and tickled mercilessly until you repent for your sin. Seriously, though, please don't skip it. This may seem like a lot of hard work right now, but after some practice it will start to come naturally, without the need for all this planning.

Earlier, we talked about effective goal setting and action planning as an alternative to worrying. This is what I meant. It may seem like a hassle, but you'll find it's a lot less time-consuming than worrying. And a lot more productive. And like any skill, it gets easier with practice. Over time, you'll be able to go straight from values to actions in three quick steps:

1. First you ask yourself, as you deal with this aspect of your life, "Who do I want to be?" or "What do I want to stand for?"
2. Then once you've tapped into a couple of values, you ask yourself, "How am I going to put these values into play? What can I say or do?"
3. Finally, you ask yourself, "Am I willing to make room for the discomfort this will involve?"

Does this all sound a bit contrived—too orderly, detailed, structured? Wondering what happened to good old spontaneity, to taking life as it comes? Rest assured, there will be plenty of room for spontaneity once you're moving in the right direction. But first, you've got to get moving!

A Few Examples

Remember Soula? She had just turned thirty-three and was feeling sad and lonely because she was still single while all her friends were in long-term relationships. In the domain of love, Soula's values were being loving, caring, open, sensual, and fun-loving. She was able to live these values in her closest relationships with friends, family, and herself. However, she also wanted to live them with a partner—which she didn't currently have. So her major long-term goal was: find a partner. So I asked her to come up with a short-term goal that she could do in the next week; something that would move her a step closer to the long-term goal. She decided to join an online dating service, create her profile, and spend at least one hour looking through potential candidates.

As she started on the task, she was surprised at how much anxiety showed up. Her reason-giving machine told her that it would be a total waste of time and money, and all the guys would be losers, con men, or psychopaths. But she thanked her mind for trying to keep her safe, made room for her anxiety, and went ahead.

Now let's return to Donna. After she had come to terms with the deaths of her loved ones and given up drinking alcohol, Donna faced the daunting task of rebuilding her life, piece by piece. She had lost a lot of weight, and her body was in terrible condition, so now, on top of everything else, she was continually worrying about her health and the damage she'd done to her liver. Because of this, she chose to focus on the domain of health. Her main values here were self-caring and self-encouragement. Her short-term goals were: eat a healthy lunch; follow it with a fifteen-minute walk; and go to bed at 11:00 p.m. (instead of 2:00 a.m.). Now I'm sure you noticed that's actually three goals, not one. It's fine to set more than one goal if you prefer, as long as they seem realistic and not overwhelming.

In her first week, Donna managed to eat the healthy lunch, do the walk on five out of seven days, and get to bed by 11:00 p.m. on four nights. She was very pleased with that. No, it wasn't perfect, but so what? It was a significant improvement in terms of looking after her physical health. And trying to be perfect is a recipe for misery.

So back to you: Have you completed the exercise above yet? If not, please do it now. And here's a tip for you: research shows you're far more likely to follow through on a goal if you make a commitment to another person (who is supportive and trustworthy). So is there someone you could call, text, email, Zoom, or talk to in person and tell them what you're going to do? (If not, fair enough; but if yes, I encourage you to do so, even if it's uncomfortable.)

My Guarantee to You

Soula and Donna were able to follow through on their goals because they did the necessary work: learning how to unhook, getting in touch with their values, setting realistic goals. And here's my guarantee to you:

I guarantee that if you do everything we've covered in this chapter . . .

Then when it comes to achieving your goal . . .

I absolutely 100 percent guarantee . . .

That either . . .

You *will* achieve it . . .

Or you won't!

ONE HUNDRED PERCENT GUARANTEED, OR YOUR MONEY BACK!

Now there's a humorous side to that comment, but also a serious side. At times, you will use the strategies I've suggested, and you'll follow through, and things will go well. But at other times, that *won't* happen. Why? Because you're human. And fallible. And wonderfully imperfect, like the rest of us. You're not some fictional superhero who always follows through on their goals, always does "the right thing" in the face of all obstacles. You're a human being. And that means that just like all the rest of us, at times you'll follow through on your goals—and at other times, you won't.

So, if you do follow through on this goal, well done. Notice what it's like to act on your values, moving toward the life you want to build; be fully present and savor the experience.

And if you don't follow through? Well, let's call your original goal "plan A." Now if plan A falls through, for whatever reason, then plan B is *find another way to act on those values.*

After all, life is complex, and plans change. And our aim isn't to achieve every single goal we ever set; that would be ridiculous. Our aim is to get better at living by our values. So if plan A is off the table, shift to plan B—and as you act on those values, notice what it's like; appreciate the experience of moving in a meaningful direction.

Now if you don't manage to do either of the above, (a) be kind to yourself; remember you're human and imperfect and all of us do similar things at times, and (b) notice what gets in your way; especially what thoughts and feelings hook you. This will be golden information for the next chapter, which is all about overcoming our barriers to change.

Okay, enough said. Off you go, and good luck!

[24]

The HARD Barriers

Ask any therapist, coach, or counselor, and they'll tell you this happens *all the time*. In session, a client gets all fired up, brimming with enthusiasm, excitedly saying, "I'm going to do this, and that, and the other." Then they come back to the next session, feeling guilty or embarrassed because they haven't done any of it. So when my clients do this, do you know what I tell them?

I say, "You are so like me!" (You should see the look of shock upon their faces.) "Yes," I continue, "do you know how often I say I'm going to do something, but I don't actually do it?"

"You?" they exclaim in astonishment. "But, but, but . . . you're a doctor . . . you're an author . . . you . . . bear a striking resemblance to Chris Hemsworth!" (Okay, they don't say that last bit.)

"We're all in the same boat," I tell them. "This is the human condition. We get excited, and we say we're going to do these things . . . and sometimes we do . . . and sometimes we don't." Then I help them to unhook from their harsh self-criticism and practice self-compassion. *And then* we look at what got in the way.

So back to you. If you *did* follow through on plan A or plan B, well done. But if you didn't, then rest assured, you've got plenty of company. We all fail to follow through at times. And beating ourselves up about it doesn't help. So unhook from "not good enough," hold yourself kindly, and let's explore . . .

What Gets in the Way?

Again and again, as we move toward a more meaningful life, we will push up against the HARD barriers:

H: Hooked
A: Avoiding discomfort
R: Remoteness from values
D: Doubtful goals

Let's take a look at each one.

Hooked

That reason-giving machine inside our head is so incredibly inventive; it has so many ways to talk us out of taking action: "I don't deserve a better life," "I'll fail," "I'll screw it up," "Something bad will happen," "I don't have what it takes," "I'm too busy/tired/depressed/anxious," "I'll do it later," and so on and so on.

And none of that is a problem . . . unless we get hooked. If these thoughts hook us, then for sure they'll pull us off track. But they won't if we unhook. So the antidote is to make good use of your unhooking skills: notice and name those thoughts or thank your mind or, if majorly hooked, drop anchor.

Avoiding Discomfort

Personal growth and meaningful change necessitate leaving your comfort zone. This inevitably brings up discomfort in the form of difficult thoughts, sensations, emotions, memories, and urges. If we aren't willing to open up and make room for these experiences, then we won't do the challenging things that matter to us.

The antidote? Yup, more unhooking skills. TAME those difficult feelings: allow them, breathe into them, make room for them, and hold yourself kindly. Get into the habit of asking yourself, "Am I willing to make room for this discomfort in order to do what matters?"

Remoteness from Values

There's not much point in doing this challenging stuff if it's not important or meaningful. So if we're ignoring, neglecting, or forgetting our values, we'll lack motivation. The antidote is to truly connect with our values; they are always there deep inside us, no matter how remote from them we are. (A value is like your body: even if you've totally neglected it for years, it's still there, and it's never too late to make use of it.) Recognize that with each and every step you take, no matter how small it may be, you are living your values. And that's what truly matters.

Doubtful Goals

Is your goal genuinely realistic? Are you trying to do too much or do it too quickly? Trying to do it perfectly? Trying to do things for which you lack the necessary resources (e.g., time, money, energy, health, social support) or necessary skills?

If your goals are excessive, you'll feel overwhelmed and will probably give up; or you'll try and fail. The solution is to break your goals down; make them smaller, simpler, easier, so they're realistic for your current level of resources. Ask yourself, "What's the smallest, easiest step I could take that would bring me even a tiny bit closer to achieving this goal?" Then go ahead and do it.

Then once you've taken that step, ask the question again: "What's the next small, easy step that would bring me a little bit closer to my goal?" (It's like that old joke: How do you eat an elephant? One mouthful at a time!)

And if you lack the necessary skills to achieve your goals? Then your new goal is to learn them. (You can't expect to cycle the Tour de France if you haven't first learned to ride a bike.)

And if you lack other resources you need (like time, money, health, energy, social support, or equipment) and there is no way to currently find them? Then you'll need to drop that goal (at least for now; you can always come back to it later) and set a different one that's realistic.

The Reason-Giving Machine Will Never Stay Silent for Long

Don't expect your mind to become a cheerleader: "Ra! Ra! You can do it! Ra! Ra! Just get to it!" That's sooooo unlikely to happen. For sure, it *does* occasionally happen, like when you set a goal that's a long way off: "I'll do it next year!" ("*Yes!*" says your mind.) Or when you set a goal that's easy-peasy, lemon-squeezy, no discomfort involved. But when it's a short-term goal and it pulls you out of your comfort zone, the reason-giving machine will have its say. The following are a few of its classics.

"I'll Screw It Up"

"I'll get it wrong," "I'll make mistakes." Again, this is our mind being an overly helpful friend. What it's trying to say is: (a) pay attention to what you're doing, and (b) it's important to practice.

The reality is, we will all often make mistakes; that's a fundamental part of being human. Almost every activity you take for granted today—reading, talking, walking, riding a bicycle—was once hard to do. (Think how many times a baby falls on its bottom while learning to walk.) But the point is, you learned by making mistakes. You learned what not to do, and you learned how to do it differently, so you became more effective. Making mistakes is an essential part of learning, so embrace it. Thank your mind and let go of aiming for perfection—it's much more satisfying and fulfilling to be human.

"I Don't Know If I Can Do It"

To quote the author Henry James, "Until you try, you don't know what you can't do." In setting goals for ourselves, we're talking about what is possible, not what is certain. There's very little certainty in this world. We can't even be certain we'll still be alive tomorrow. So none of us can ever be certain that we'll achieve our goals. But what we can be certain of is this: if we don't even attempt to achieve them, there's no possibility of success. To quote the legendary hockey player Wayne Gretzky, "You miss 100 percent of the shots you don't take."

"But What If . . .?"

The reason-giving machine loves "what if?" stories. "What if I try and I fail?" "What if I invest all that time and energy and money and it all amounts to nothing?" "What if I make a fool of myself?" If you let yourself get hooked in by these stories, you can easily waste endless hours debating with yourself instead of taking action. So notice and name the story, step out of the stream, and put your values into play.

I'm sure your mind can come up with many more reasons than these. And they can be very persuasive. But you don't have to OBEY them. For example, how often have you had thoughts such as "I can't do this!"—and then gone ahead and done it? How often have you thought about taking hurtful, harmful, or self-defeating actions—but *not* actually done so? (It's just as well that we don't always OBEY all our thoughts, otherwise most of us would be in prison or the hospital.)

To prove that you don't have to OBEY your thoughts, here are two brief experiments:

1. Silently say to yourself, "I can't scratch my head! I can't scratch my head!"—and as you do, lift your arm and scratch your head.
2. Silently say to yourself, "I have to close this book! I have to close this book!"—and as you do, keep the book open.

How'd you do? No doubt you found that you didn't actually have to OBEY those thoughts; you had some choice over what you did. And the better your unhooking skills, the more choice you have.

Earlier, I mentioned a young man called Marco who was overweight and unfit and wanted to get back into shape. Marco chose health as a domain and self-care as a value. His first short-term goal was: *Get up half an hour early tomorrow morning and go for a run.* Instantly, the reason-giving machine fired up: "But I like sleeping in, it will be too cold, I'm too unfit, it will hurt my knees, I don't know where my runners are, I look funny in my sports gear."

I said to him, "Those are all perfectly valid reasons *not* to go for a run. Now . . . suppose the person you love most in the world was kidnapped.

And the kidnappers say they will never release this person unless you follow through with this goal. Would you do it?"

"Yes, of course," he said.

"What, you mean you'd get up early and go for a run, even though you've got all of these perfectly valid reasons not to do it?"

Marco got the point that we don't have to wait until the reason-giving machine goes silent (or turns into a cheerleader) before we take action. We can have ten, twenty, or thirty perfectly valid reasons *not* to do something—*and* we can still go ahead and do it. We can notice and name those reasons and let our mind chatter away like a radio playing in the background while we get in touch with our values, start taking action, and focus on what we're doing.

Sometimes people protest when I ask them the kidnap question above. "But that's silly!" they say. "The person I love has *not* been kidnapped!!"

And I reply, "You're right. But the point is, an important part of your life has been 'kidnapped.' It's been taken away from you. So do you want to get it back? And if so, are you willing to *do what matters*, even though the reason-giving machine will try hard to talk you out of it?"

The HARD Barriers

So, now you know the four HARD barriers: Hooked, Avoiding discomfort, Remoteness from values, and Doubtful goals. (And if by chance you haven't encountered them yet, don't worry—you soon will.) So what next?

Well, if you *did* follow through on plan A or B from the previous chapter, then set yourself *another* short-term goal (or even two or three—as long as that's realistic and not overwhelming). This may be in the same domain (or subdivision) or a different one, whichever you prefer. And the aim is to use all the same steps as before. And if the HARD barriers show up, you know what to do.

On the other hand, if you *didn't* follow through last time, then figure out which of the HARD barriers stopped you (sometimes it's all of them) and apply the recommended antidotes. Then, either have another attempt at your previous goal or set yourself a new one.

And again, if plan A falls through, switch to plan B. Find another way—no matter how small it may be—to live those values.

[25]

Difficult Decisions

Rebecca thinks she has a values conflict. But does she?

She's a forty-year-old single mom who works as a real estate agent. The job is very demanding, but she enjoys it and wants to excel. She has two young kids to look after—Sammie, age seven, and Nina, age nine—and she finds it hard to balance the demands of work and family.

So does Rebecca have a values conflict?

Absolutely not. What she has is a time-management conflict: how much time does she invest in her family, and how much time does she invest in her career?

Her top values as a mother are being loving, caring, and playful. These values will not change if she spends ten hours a week with her family, twenty hours, or fifty hours. Her top values at work are being friendly, efficient, and responsible. These values will not change whether she spends ten hours a week at work, twenty hours, or fifty hours.

No matter how much time she invests in her family or her career, her values will remain the same. It's not a values conflict but a time-management conflict: how to divide her time between two important life domains. And no matter how clear she is about her values, this will not resolve the issue. Rebecca has to choose how much time to spend in each domain of life—and there won't be a perfect answer. She will need to experiment, find out what works best for her. And whatever she chooses, her mind will likely criticize her for not spending enough time in one area or the other (or maybe even both).

However, no matter how she divides her time between work and family, Rebecca can have the satisfaction of living her values fully. When she's with her kids she can be loving, caring, and playful. And when she's at work she can be friendly, efficient, and responsible. And when her mind beats her up for spending too much time in one area, or not enough in the other, she can unhook from the "not good enough" story, make room for her guilt or anxiety, and treat herself kindly, recognizing there is no perfect answer for this complex situation.

Tough Decisions and Difficult Dilemmas

We've all, at times, had to grapple with a difficult dilemma or tough decision. "Do I stay in this relationship or leave?" "Do I quit this job, or do I stay?" "Do I enroll in that course or the other one?" "Do I start the medical treatment or not?" "Do we try to have children or not?" "Do I tell them the truth/reveal my secret or hide it?"

When we're in these situations, our mind easily goes into overdrive, desperately trying to figure out what to do; to make the right decision. The problem is, it can take days, weeks, months—or even years in some cases, such as unhappy marriages or unfulfilling jobs—before we finally choose one option over the other. And, in the meantime, we can easily spend our days wandering around in a thick psychological smog—endlessly pondering "Do I or don't I?"—and, in the process, we make ourselves anxious or stressed, and we miss out on life, here and now.

So, how can ACT help us?

Step 1: Acknowledge You've Got a Dilemma

If you are facing a major dilemma or a really tough decision, it's highly unlikely you will resolve it in the next few hours. Can you make room for this reality? Struggling against it will only make it worse.

Step 2: Commonsense Steps—
Costs, Benefits, and More Information

Sometimes a dilemma can be resolved by the age-old "commonsense" method of doing a "cost-benefit analysis." In other words, write down a list of all the benefits and all the costs for each option. If you've already done this and it hasn't helped, fair enough—at least you tried. But if you haven't yet done this, or if you've done it half-heartedly, or you've done it in your head but not on paper, then it's worth a try.

When you write it all down in black and white, that's a radically different experience from thinking it through inside your head or talking it through with a friend—and it could help you finalize your decision or resolve your dilemma.

Also, keep in mind that sometimes the issue can be resolved by finding out more information from a reliable source (a book, a person, a website, an organization, etc.) So make sure you have gathered enough information to make an informed decision. If you are lucky, this new information will make the costs and benefits of each option clearer and help you decide what to do.

However, the inconvenient truth is this: the greater the dilemma, the tougher the decision and the less likely these "commonsense" methods are to be helpful. Why? Because if one option was obviously far better than the other, you wouldn't have a dilemma in the first place!

Step 3: No Perfect Solution

Next, recognize there is no perfect solution. So whichever choice you make, you are likely to feel anxious about it, and your mind is likely to tell you "That's the wrong decision" then point out all the reasons why you shouldn't do it. If you're waiting until the day there are no feelings of anxiety and no thoughts about making the wrong decision, you'll probably be waiting forever.

Step 4: There's No Way Not to Choose

Recognize that whatever your dilemma is, you're already making a choice. Each day you don't quit your job, you are choosing to stay. (Until the day you hand in your resignation, you are staying in that job.) Each day that you don't leave your marriage, you are choosing to stay. (Until the day you pack your bags and move out of the house, you are staying in that marriage.) Each day that you don't sign the consent form for the operation, you are choosing not to have surgery. Each day you stay silent about the secret you are keeping, you are choosing not to reveal it.

Step 5: Acknowledge Today's Choice

Following on from the above, kick off each day by acknowledging the choice you are making for this day. For example, say to yourself, "Okay, for the next twenty-four hours, I choose to stay in the marriage" or "For the next twenty-four hours, I choose to keep this secret." If twenty-four hours seems too long, then make a choice for the next twelve hours or six hours (or even for the next sixty minutes). At the end of that time period, reassess and then make another choice for the next twenty-four (or twelve or six) hours.

Step 6: Take a Stand

Given your choice in step 5 above, what do you want to stand for in the next twenty-four (or twelve or six) hours? What values do you want to live by in this domain of life? If you're staying in the marriage for another day (or another hour), what sort of partner do you want to be for that one day (or hour)? If you're staying in your job for another day (or another hour), what sort of employee do you want to be for that one day (or hour)?

No matter what situation you're in, you can always find ways to act on your values. For example, suppose you choose to stay silent about the secret you're hiding, but the value of being honest is very important. If so, there are zillions of other ways to live the value of honesty in everyday life. For example, you could practice self-compassion, which involves being honest with yourself about how much you're hurting. Or you could write honestly about your feelings in a journal. Or you could honestly confide in someone how difficult it is to keep this secret.

Step 7: Make Time to Reflect

Put aside time on a regular basis to mindfully reflect on the situation. The best way to do this is as in step 2: using a diary or a computer, write down the costs and benefits of each option and see if anything has changed since last time you did this. You could also try to imagine what life might be like—both the positives and the negatives—(a) if you went down one path, and (b) if you went down the other path.

For most people, ten to fifteen minutes three or four times a week is more than enough reflection time—but you can put aside as little or as much as you like. The key thing is, make it focused; in other words, don't try to do it at the same time as watching TV, doing housework, driving home, going to the gym, or cooking dinner; just sit quietly with your pen and paper or a computer and do nothing else but reflect, as above, for the allotted time.

Step 8: Name the Story

Throughout the day, your mind will try to pull you back into the dilemma, over and over again. But if this was truly helpful, you'd already have resolved your dilemma, wouldn't you? So practice naming the story. For example, try saying to yourself, "Aha! Here it is again. The 'stay or leave' story. Thanks, Mind. I know you're trying to help, and it's okay—I've got this covered." Then focus your attention on doing some meaningful, values-guided activity. You will probably find it helpful to remind yourself, "I'll think about this later, in my reflection time."

Step 9: Open Up and Make Room

Feelings of anxiety will almost certainly arise—again and again and again—whichever option you choose. So practice opening up and making room for those feelings. Acknowledge to yourself, "Here's anxiety." Remind yourself, "This is normal. It's what everybody feels in a challenging situation with an uncertain outcome."

Step 10: Self-Compassion

Last, but not least, be compassionate with yourself. Treat yourself gently. Talk to yourself kindly. Unhook yourself from all that unhelpful, self-judgmental mind chatter, using whatever techniques you find best.

Remind yourself that you're a human being with emotions; you're not some high-tech computer that can coldly analyze the probabilities and spit out an answer. Remind yourself that this is a *bloody hard* decision—if it were easy, you wouldn't have a dilemma in the first place!

Acknowledge that you're in pain, you're hurting. And do plenty of kind, caring, nurturing, considerate things for yourself; things that soothe, nurture, or support you in this time of hardship. This could include anything from spending quality time with close friends, taking care of your body, treating yourself to a favorite leisure activity, making time for yourself to pursue a sport or creative outlet, cooking a healthy dinner, or doing the kind hands exercise from chapter 15.

Recycle through these steps every day (or several times a day, if necessary), and one of three things will happen:

1. Over time, one option will become obviously more attractive than the other.
2. Over time, one option will disappear; it's no longer available.
3. Over time, your dilemma will remain unsolved.

If either 1 or 2 happens, the decision is made; the dilemma is resolved. If 3 happens, then at least you get to go through each day mindfully living by your values and treating yourself kindly, instead of being lost in a smog of anxious indecision.

[26]

Breaking Bad Habits

We've all got them. And plenty of them. Bad habits (things we do repeatedly that take us away from the life we want) come naturally to us all and are rarely easy to change. To quote the famous author Mark Twain, "Habit is habit and not to be flung out of the window by any man, but coaxed downstairs a step at a time." (Twain also said, "Giving up smoking is easy . . . I've done it hundreds of times.")

So it's somewhat misleading to talk about "breaking" a habit—as if we can just snap it in half, throw it in the bin, and it's done with. Remember, the brain works by addition, not subtraction; we can't simply delete those old neural pathways that underpin our bad habits. Those pathways will remain and give rise to impulses and urges to keep doing whatever that away move happens to be. But we can lay down new neural pathways on top of the old ones. We can develop new, more effective patterns of behavior and consciously choose to do these new toward moves instead of the old away moves.

And if we practice, practice, practice these new behaviors repeatedly, then eventually, over time, with lots and lots of repetition, we will reach a point where we start to do them automatically, naturally, readily—at which point we could say that we have developed a new habit. However, it takes a looooong time for a new behavior to become habitual. Don't believe all those bloggers, self-help books, and motivational speakers who claim it takes twenty-one (or twenty-eight or thirty-five) days to form a new habit. Those numbers sound good, but there's no scientific validity to them. Someone literally just made them up because they *do* sound good—and now everyone repeats them as if they're facts. But you only need to look closely at your own experience to realize it usually takes many months, if not years, of repeated practice, before a new pattern of behavior becomes habitual. So until we eventually reach that point where our new behavior is automatic, we will need to make a conscious effort to repeatedly "catch ourselves in the act": to notice that we are about to start (or already have started) doing this away move and to interrupt it and choose a toward move instead.

The good news is, when we apply the skills we've covered in this book, we can interrupt pretty much any bad habit and choose a more effective one instead (as illustrated below).

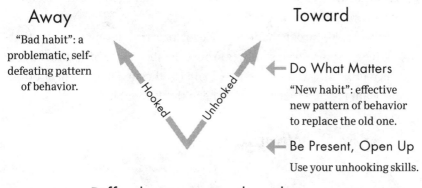

Away

"Bad habit": a problematic, self-defeating pattern of behavior.

Toward

← Do What Matters

"New habit": effective new pattern of behavior to replace the old one.

← Be Present, Open Up

Use your unhooking skills.

Difficult situations, thoughts & feelings that trigger the "bad habit."

A good way to kick off this process is to run through these five questions:

1. What are the triggers?
2. What are the payoffs and costs?
3. What's a good alternative behavior, and why?
4. What unhooking skills are needed?
5. What or who can help?

Let's work through this now. Choose a bad habit you'd like to work on (any ineffective, problematic, or self-defeating pattern of behavior you do repeatedly) and write down your answers to each question. (There's a worksheet for this in *The Happiness Trap: Extra Bits*.) To help you out, I'll provide you with examples for one extremely common problematic behavior: procrastination.

Ready to roll? Got your pen and paper? Okay, first write down the behavior you want to reduce, and then consider . . .

Question 1: What Are the Triggers?

What situations, thoughts, and feelings typically trigger this behavior? Any particular people, places, events, thoughts, memories, urges, emotions? (If you're not sure what triggers it, for now, just write down "not sure." Then over the next few days, use your being present skills to carefully notice when and where you do it, and what thoughts and feelings show up immediately beforehand.)

Example: My problematic behavior is procrastinating on important tasks. The triggers are usually (a) thinking about a boring, difficult, or anxiety-provoking task I need to do, and (b) the anxiety, dread, or other unpleasant feelings that show up when I think about it.

Question 2: What Are the Payoffs and Costs?

Any type of behavior has both payoffs and costs. (By "payoffs," I mean benefits or gains.) And if we ever want to know *why* we keep doing some problematic behavior, we first notice the triggers, and then we identify the payoffs. Basically, the payoffs of any behavior (whether it's a toward or an away move) boil down to the following:

- You avoid or escape something you don't want (inside you, outside you, or both).
- You get something you *do* want (inside you, outside you, or both).

Below are some extremely common payoffs. The behavior helps us to

- escape or avoid challenging people, places, situations, or activities;
- escape or avoid unwanted thoughts, emotions, memories, urges, or sensations;
- get our needs met;
- gain attention or approval;

- get others to do what we want;
- "look good" to or "fit in" with others;
- feel better (e.g., relaxed, relieved, calm, happy, safe);
- feel righteous (we are "in the right" and others are "wrong"); or
- feel like we are working hard on our problems.

There are many possible payoffs for any behavior but most of them will fit under one or more of the broad categories above (usually several). Occasionally, despite our best efforts, we just can't figure out the payoffs—and that's okay. We don't *have* to know. It's much more important to get clear on the costs.

Of course, when we contemplate changing our behavior, we are already aware of some of the costs—otherwise, why would we bother changing? However, we want to reflect more deeply and truly connect with what this behavior is costing us; otherwise, we might not be bothered enough to do the hard work required. So we want to ask ourselves the following questions, honestly:

- Are there any costs or drawbacks to this behavior? Any unintended negative consequences?
- Is there anything important we lose or miss out on when we do this?
- Does it hold us back from anyone or anything important?
- Does it have any negative impact on our health, well-being, work, relationships, or life satisfaction?

Example: My Payoffs for Procrastinating
- I avoid tasks that are boring, challenging, or anxiety-provoking.
- I avoid anxiety, dread, and other unpleasant feelings.
- I get to do other things instead that are more interesting, easier, or more fun.
- Each time I decide to put it off a bit longer, I get a feeling of relief.

Example: The Costs for Procrastinating
- Important tasks that could improve my life are not getting done.
- I'm missing out on the benefits I'd get from doing those tasks, such as A, B, and C (e.g., feeling of satisfaction or achievement, being

true to myself, improvements in my health or relationships, moving closer toward an important long-term goal).
- In the long term, putting it off is increasing my anxiety, reducing my sense of well-being, and putting a strain on X, Y, and Z (e.g., my health, my finances, my relationships).
- I'm wasting precious time and energy distracting myself with other activities.

After doing this, ask yourself, "Do the costs outweigh the payoffs?"

If the answer is no (and you're genuinely being honest with yourself), then clearly you don't see this behavior as a significant problem, so pick a different one to work on.

If the answer is yes, then consider . . .

Question 3: What's a Good Alternative Behavior, and Why?

Once you're clear the habit is costing you more than it's giving you, the next step is to consider what new, effective behavior you will do instead. Here are a few examples:

- If you don't yell at your kids or partner when you're frustrated, annoyed, or angered by their behavior—what will you do instead?
- If you don't drink or take drugs, overeat or smoke when you're feeling miserable, stressed, anxious, bored, and so on—what will you do instead?
- If you want to spend less time watching TV, playing computer games, hanging out on social media, or sleeping in—what will you do instead?

This brings us back to goal-setting skills: in this case, choosing new, effective behaviors guided by values. Here are some examples regarding the bullet points above:

- Instead of yelling, we might calmly and patiently request them to change what they're doing; or we might accept what's happened and make a joke out of it; or we might talk calmly and honestly about how we feel when they do that.

- Instead of turning to drink, drugs, food, or tobacco, we might first TAME our difficult feelings, then follow this by doing any activity we find meaningful and fulfilling, whether that's playing with the dog or cat, reading a book, watching a movie while working out, planning a holiday, doing something creative, poring through old photographs, spending quality time with friends or family, and so on. (It's important to run through TAME first—to open up and make room for the feeling—otherwise all these activities will function as distraction.)
- Instead of spending so much time doing these activities, we can schedule in other things we find more meaningful, such as the examples in the previous bullet, above. (And if you're stuck for ideas about how to spend your time meaningfully, have a look at the list of three hundred activities in *The Happiness Trap: Extra Bits*, chapter 26.)

We also want to be clear on *why* this is a good alternative. In other words, what are the payoffs for doing this? How could this help our health, well-being, relationships, or work? Is this taking our life in the direction we want? What values will we be living? What long-term goals does this move us toward?

Example: Instead of procrastinating on this task, I will make a start on it.

On (specify day, date, time) _____ I will spend (specify duration) _____ minutes working on it.

I will begin with (specify first step) _____

_____.

On a scale of 0–10, how realistic is this? _____

The payoffs are: I'm living my values; an important task is getting done; and I'll get benefits such as A, B, and C (e.g., feeling of satisfaction or achievement; improvements in my health, well-being, or relationships; taking my life forward in a meaningful direction; moving closer toward an important long-term goal).

Question 4: What Unhooking Skills Are Needed?

Because this new behavior pulls us out of our comfort zone, difficult thoughts and feelings are guaranteed to arise. So it's wise to plan ahead; as the saying goes, "Forewarned is forearmed."

- What unhelpful thoughts (e.g., reasons not to do it, rigid rules, harsh self-judgments) will arise?
- What unpleasant feelings (e.g., anxiety, anger, shame) will show up?
- What unhooking skills (e.g., thanking your mind, naming the story, dropping anchor, urge surfing, kind hands) will we need to apply?

It goes without saying, if our unhooking skills are weak, we'll need to practice them. And the cool thing is, the more we practice the entire range of unhooking skills, the less discomfort we actually have to deal with. If we see the thought "You'll fail" as only words, it's a lot less bothersome than when we respond in OBEY mode. And when we turn off that struggle switch, our feelings are a lot easier to live with, because they don't get amplified.

Example: When I'm about to start on this task, unhelpful thoughts will show up such as "Leave it until later." "It can wait." "I don't have the energy." "I'm not in the mood." "I hate doing this." "It's so boring." "Putting it off for another day won't matter." And difficult feelings will show up such as anxiety, knots in my stomach, and urges to do other things instead (like eat a snack, make a cup of coffee, surf the net, or check my emails).

I will unhook from these thoughts and feelings through dropping anchor and making room.

Question 5: What or Who Can Help?

Many things can help us develop new patterns of behavior: getting support and encouragement from other people, setting up reward systems, restructuring the physical environment, and so on. We'll explore these strategies and more in the next chapter. Here I want to mention just two strategies that are incredibly useful: starting small and kind self-talk. Let's briefly look at each.

Starting Small

When you first join a gym, you don't go straight for the heaviest weights in the room; you start with light weights and gradually build up your muscles. And the same principle applies for developing any new behavior. Start with smaller, less-challenging goals and gradually up the ante, over time. So consider: What's a not-too-challenging way to start off? What's something that's doable, realistic, and not too great a leap out of your comfort zone?

As it happens, this principle is the ALL-TIME-BEST-EVER-GOLD-STANDARD-KNOCK-YOUR-SOCKS-OFF strategy for procrastination. Don't try to complete the whole task or project in one go: nibble away at it, one small piece at a time. Set a goal of working on the task only for a brief amount of time—after which you can stop. (Or carry on if you wish to.)

Example: I will work on this task for just twenty minutes. At the end of that time, I can stop. (Or carry on, if I wish to).

Kind Self-Talk

A bit of kind, encouraging self-talk can often do wonders for our motivation.

Example: I can do this. It's just twenty minutes of my time. At the end of that time, I can stop—or I can carry on if I feel like it. I know that often once I make a start on something, I gather momentum and keep going. But if that doesn't happen, then at least I've done twenty minutes, and that's a start. I can build up from there. I'm willing to make room for my discomfort in order to do what matters.

Action Time

If you've run through the steps above, it's time for action. (And if HARD barriers get in your way, you know what to do; see chapter 24 if you've forgotten.) However, please do remember: You don't *have to* do this; it's a personal choice. A choice to live by your values, to behave more like the sort of person you want to be. So as you do it, engage in it; focus your full attention on the task at hand. And make room for all the thoughts and feelings that arise.

In other words: *be present, open up, and do what matters.*

Staying the Distance

The philosopher Alfred Souza wrote: "For a long time it had seemed to me that life was about to begin—real life. But there was always some obstacle in the way, something to be gotten through first, some unfinished business, time still to be served, a debt to be paid. Then life would begin. At last, it dawned on me that these obstacles were my life."

He was on to something. Life is full of obstacles, and whenever we meet them, we can either say yes—make room for our thoughts and feelings, and do what matters—or we can say no, and retreat. If we repeatedly say no, our life stagnates or shrinks. If we repeatedly say yes, our life gets bigger. Fortunately, even when we don't *want* to say yes, we can still *choose* to. And each time we make that choice, we grow as a person.

Over time, saying yes to our obstacles will gradually become easier, more habitual. And the experience we gain from doing this gives us a deep reservoir of strength, which we can draw from when the going gets tough. What we're talking about here is a quality I've been referring to as "willingness." To get a better sense of this concept, consider . . .

The Lost City of Oompa-Loompa

You're an intrepid explorer, hacking your way through the jungle in search of the ancient city of Oompa-Loompa. And suddenly you come across this huge, smelly swamp full of leeches. And the only way you can reach those ancient ruins is to wade through all that mosquito-infested muck. It's either that or go back, no third option. So which do you choose?

If you choose to keep going, it's not because you enjoy wading waist-deep through cold, smelly swamp water, getting eaten alive by leeches and mosquitoes—it's because exploring those ancient ruins truly *matters* to you. You're willing to have that discomfort not because you *like* it, *want* it, or *enjoy* it but because it enables you to do something important and meaningful.

Soula got the point of this story. To pursue her goal of finding a partner, she started going on dates with guys she met through the online dating agency. She was willing to make room for feelings of vulnerability, insecurity, and anxiety and for thoughts like "I'm wasting my time," "I'll only meet weirdos and losers," and "If I do meet anyone nice, they won't like me." Her willingness to have that discomfort enabled her to go on some dates and meet some nice guys.

Likewise, to spend more quality time with her family, Michelle was willing to make room for the anxiety of assertively saying no instead of always people-pleasing. Similarly, to reclaim her life and put her alcoholism behind her, Donna was willing to open up and make room for her sadness and practice self-compassion instead of trying to drink her pain away.

Then there was Kirk, a wealthy commercial lawyer. When Kirk truly connected with his values, his work was no longer meaningful. He had become a lawyer primarily for status and money and to win the approval of his parents (who were both successful lawyers). What he really wanted to do, though, was to support and care for people, especially to help them grow, learn, and develop. Ultimately, he decided to retrain as a psychologist. To do this, he was willing to make room for a lot of discomfort: loss of income, many years of extra study, parental disapproval, anxiety over whether he was doing the right thing, thoughts about "all those years wasted," and so on. The last time I saw Kirk, he'd graduated as a psychologist and loved the profession. But he'd never have gotten there without willingness to make room for all that discomfort.

Personal Growth

If we wish to keep growing as a person, we need to keep opening up and doing what matters. So far, we've been setting short-term goals in just one life domain, because that's the best way to get moving. However, as time goes on, we also want to set medium- and long-term goals, in all the life domains we consider important. So let's make a start, right now.

Medium-Term Goals

Choose a life domain, connect with two or three values you want to put into play, and ask yourself, "What larger challenges (in line with these values) can I set for the next few weeks and months?"

As usual, be specific. For example, if the domain is health and the value self-caring, a medium-range goal might be, "Three nights a week, I will cook dinner using recipes from a healthy cookbook" or "I will go for a twenty-minute walk every lunchtime."

Long-Term Goals

For the same domain and values as above, ask yourself, "What major challenges can I set for the next few years?" This is where you dare to think big. What would you like to achieve in the next one, two, three, four, or five years from now? Long-term goals could include anything from changing careers, finding a partner, or having kids to buying a house, learning an instrument, or traveling the world. Allow yourself to dream.

And if you draw a blank here—if your mind says, "I have no idea!"—rest assured, that's extremely common and not a problem. Just stick to short-term and medium-term goals. Over time, you will grow, and your life will expand, and sooner or later those long-term goals will come to you. Or they won't. And whether they do or whether they don't, it actually doesn't matter; because in the meantime, you're living your values and being who you want to be and making the most of life as it is in this moment.

Other Life Domains

Once we've made some progress in a given life domain, it's usually a good idea to switch to another. And after we've made some progress in that one, switch to yet another.

There's no right or wrong way to do this; no formula to follow. We each need to experiment and find what works best for us. Some people swap domains weekly; others monthly; others only after they achieve a particular goal. And some people find they can work on several domains simultaneously, but most of us find it overwhelming to focus on more than one or two at a time.

So it's important to keep checking in with yourself. Are you feeling overwhelmed, burdened, trapped, overstretched? If so, you're exceeding your resources, trying to do too much, too soon (or too perfectly). So cut back; make your goals both realistic *and* life-enhancing. If they're sucking the life out of you, you've fallen back into the trap of the goal-focused life (see chapter 22).

Also watch out for this common mind trap: "What should I do with my life?" Ever been hooked by that one? I certainly have, and I can tell you, it's a recipe for misery. The more it hooks you, the more dissatisfied you become with the life you have. The problem is, this question is sooooo big, almost nobody can answer it (except for the tiny number of people who have some sort of grand calling for their whole life—usually to do with religion, politics, or saving the world).

For most of us, this is not a useful question to ask; it's just too big, too overwhelming. Far more useful questions are these: In this *one* domain of my life, what do I want to do for . . .

   . . . the next few hours?
   . . . the next few days?
   . . . the next few weeks?
   . . . the next few months?

Once you've answered that, pick another domain and ask the same questions. And so on and so on. I'm confident you'll find this is a much more fulfilling way to live than trying to figure out "What should I do with my life?"

Now for the second half of this chapter, let's look at another very important topic: how to sustain a new behavior . . .

How to Keep New Behavior Going

There are hundreds, if not thousands of tools out there to help us with the difficult challenge of sustaining our new patterns of behavior—but we can pretty much bundle them all into what I call "the seven Rs": Reminders, Records, Rewards, Routines, Relationships, Reflecting, and Restructuring the environment. Let's take a look at each.

Reminders

We can create all sorts of simple tools to help remind us of the new behavior we wish to persist with. For example, we might create a pop-up or a screensaver on our computer or smartphone with an important word, phrase, or symbol that reminds us to act mindfully or to use a particular value.

We might use the old favorite of writing a message on a card and sticking it on the fridge, propping it against the bathroom mirror, or taping it to the car dashboard.

Or we might write something in a diary or calendar or in the "notes" app of our smartphone. We might write just one or two words, like "drop anchor" or "be kind"; or an acronym like ACE; or a phrase like "be present, open up, do what matters."

Alternatively, we might put a brightly colored sticker on the strap of our wristwatch, the back of our smartphone, or the keyboard of our computer, so that every time we use these devices, the sticker reminds us to do the new behavior.

Records

We can keep a record of our behavior throughout the day, noting down when and where we do the new behavior and what the benefits are and also when and where we do the old behavior and what the costs are. Any diary or notebook—on paper or on a computer screen—can serve this purpose. (There's a worksheet for this in *The Happiness Trap: Extra Bits*.)

Rewards

When we do some form of new behavior that involves acting on our values, hopefully this will be rewarding in its own right. However, we can help to strengthen the new behavior with additional rewards.

One form of reward is kind, encouraging self-talk (e.g., saying to yourself: "Well done. You did it!"). Another form of reward is sharing your success and progress with a loved one who you know will respond positively.

On the other hand, you might prefer more material rewards. For example, if you sustain this new behavior for a whole week, you buy or do something that you really like (e.g., get a massage or buy a book).

Routines

If you get up every morning at the same time to go for a run, do some yoga, or meditate, over time this new pattern of behavior will start to come more naturally; you won't have to think so hard about doing it, it will require less willpower, and it will become a part of your regular routine. So experiment: whatever your new behavior may be, see if you can build it into a regular routine so it becomes a normal part of daily life. For example, if you drive home from work, then every night, just before you get out of your car, you might do two minutes of dropping anchor and reflect on what values you want to put into play when you walk in through the front door.

Relationships

It's easier to study if you have a "study buddy"; easier to exercise if you have an "exercise buddy." In AA programs, they team you up with a sponsor who is there to help you stay sober when the going gets tough.

So can you find a kind, caring, encouraging person who can help support you with your new behavior? (This could be a therapist, counselor, or coach.) Maybe you can check in with this person on a regular basis and tell them how well you are doing, as mentioned in "Rewards."

Or maybe you can email your support person the records you've been keeping. Or maybe you can use the other person as a reminder; ask them to remind you to do the new behavior, if and when that would be useful. For example, you might say to your partner, "When you see me worrying, can you please remind me to drop anchor?"

Reflecting

Regularly take time to reflect on how you are behaving and what effect it is having on your life. You can do this via writing it down (records) or in discussion with another person (relationships).

Or you can do this as a mental exercise throughout the day or just before you go to bed or just as you're waking up in the morning. You simply take a few moments to reflect on questions such as the following:

"How am I doing?"

"What am I doing that's working?"

"What am I doing that's not working?"

"What can I do more of, less of, or differently?"

Make sure you also reflect on the times when you fall back into your old behavior. Notice what triggers those relapses and setbacks and notice what it costs you (i.e., how do you suffer?) when that happens. This doesn't mean beat yourself up! This means *compassionately* reflect on the genuine costs to your health and well-being of falling back into old habits and use your awareness of the suffering this causes you to help motivate yourself to get back on track.

Restructuring the Environment

We can often restructure our environment to make our new behavior easier and therefore more likely to sustain. For example, if the new behavior is "healthy eating," we can restructure the kitchen to make that easier: get rid of or hide away the junk food and stock the fridge and pantry with the healthy stuff.

If we want to go to the gym in the morning, we could pack up our sports gear in our gym bag and place it by the side of the bed or somewhere else obvious and convenient, so it's all ready to go as soon as we get up. (And of course, when we see our gym kit lying there, it acts as a reminder.)

So there you have it: the seven Rs—Reminders, Records, Rewards, Routines, Relationships, Reflection, and Restructuring the environment. Now be creative; mix and match these methods to your heart's content to create your own set of tools for lasting change. Good luck with it!

[28]

Breaking the Rules

At times our mind can be a bit of a tyrant. It lays down strict rules and tells us, "You have to OBEY! And if you *don't*, the consequences will be *dire!*" We all follow these rigid rules to some extent—and often we aren't consciously aware of them. They can usually be identified by words like *should, have to, must, ought, can't unless, won't until, shouldn't because, always, never, do it this way, don't do it that way*, and so on.

Here are some common examples:

- I have to do things perfectly; I mustn't make mistakes.
- I have to keep others happy; my needs don't matter.
- I have to keep checking up on others; I can't trust them.

When rigid rules hook us, life constricts. For example, the first rule above pulls us into the stress of unhealthy perfectionism; the second one into the strain of excessive people-pleasing; and the third one into bad habits of continually checking up on others—like an overcontrolling parent or a workplace "micromanager."

Back in the 1940s, psychologist Karen Horney referred to these kinds of issues as "the tyranny of the shoulds"; and in the 1960s, psychologist Albert Ellis called them "*must*urbation." Let's take a look at how to break free from this tyranny.

Payoffs and Costs

In chapter 26 we explored the art of breaking bad habits, and all the same principles apply here. So first we look at the payoffs and costs of responding to a rule in OBEY mode.

The Payoffs

When Michelle OBEYED her people-pleasing rules, it motivated her to look after and take care of others; protected her from rejection or hostility; gained her approval, affection, or gratitude; helped her avoid conflict; boosted her self-image as caring, kind, helpful, a "giver"; and helped her briefly escape the "I'm unlovable" story.

You can take almost any rigid rule—whether it's based on the demands of your parents, your religion, your culture, your workplace, or your own self-imposed demands to be perfect—and find similar payoffs. When we OBEY rigid rules, it helps us to *temporarily* avoid or escape unwanted thoughts and feelings, especially fear, anxiety, guilt, shame, and "not good enough" stories; it also helps us get or achieve things we want.

The Costs

There are usually many long-term costs for OBEYING rigid rules, including chronic stress, exhaustion, burnout, lack of fulfillment, tension and conflict in close relationships, a sense of missing out in life, feelings of heaviness or being trapped, or a life that's largely drained of joy and contentment. Michelle experienced all of the above. In addition, the more her life revolved around pleasing others, the more it strengthened her belief, "I'm not important; my needs don't matter." And over time, her fear of disapproval actually increased. Why? Because as long as we avoid what we're scared of, we never have a chance to learn that we can handle it. Eleanor Roosevelt summarized this brilliantly: "You gain strength, courage, and confidence by every experience in which you really stop to look fear in the face. You are able to say to yourself, 'I have lived through this horror. I can take the next thing that comes along.' You must do the thing you think you cannot do."

Obviously if OBEYING your rule *doesn't* have significant costs, there's no problem. But if it *is* taking a toll on your health, well-being, and happiness, then please take a minute to deeply connect with the costs before reading on.

A Freer, Fuller Life

The alternative to living bound by rigid rules is a freer, more fulfilling life. You see, underneath rigid rules there are always important values. And we can put those values into play in ways that give us a lot more freedom.

For example, buried underneath perfectionism we usually find values such as being efficient, reliable, competent, and responsible. And underneath people-pleasing we tend to find values such as self-protection, giving, caring, and helping. We can learn how to live by these values *without* turning them into life-draining rules; we can learn to act on them flexibly, in ways that enhance our well-being and improve our quality of life in the long term.

When we do this, we'll still get many of the benefits of OBEYING rigid rules but without all the costs. Yes, we will lose some of the payoffs—especially that temporary avoidance of anxiety and other uncomfortable feelings—but that's the trade-off for a freer, more satisfying life.

Now pause for a moment and notice what thoughts and feelings are showing up. Anxious? Skeptical? Is your mind protesting? Is the reason-giving machine activated? Or are you excited, curious, open to something new? Whatever your reaction is, notice it, name it, allow it, and read on.

The good news is, we can all bend or disobey rigid rules and live better, freer, more enjoyable lives—*provided* we're willing to make room for the uncomfortable thoughts and feelings that will inevitably arise like fear, anxiety, guilt, self-judgment, reason-giving, and so on. In other words, we'll need to use *all* our unhooking skills!

Choosing Toward Moves

If we wish to disobey these rigid rules, we need to consider this: What toward moves will we do instead? How will we put those values (the ones that were buried underneath the rules) into play, in ways that free us up and enhance our health and well-being? This is illustrated below.

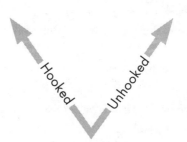

Away		Toward
Away		**Toward**
Problematic, life-draining patterns of behavior based on OBEYING rules.		Freely and flexibly living by your values in life-enhancing ways.

Hooked *Unhooked*

Rigid Rules
Difficult situations,
thoughts & feelings

For example, perfectionistic rules pull you into setting unrealistic goals: trying to achieve too much, too soon, too perfectly. So a good alternative toward move is to set realistic, values-guided goals, like those in chapter 22. And this will require your unhooking skills. Before you set any new goal, you'll need to switch off "autopilot" and get present. (When we're on autopilot, we automatically OBEY our rigid rules without even realizing it.) You'll then want to pause for a few seconds while you drop anchor or take a slow, gentle breath and, if necessary, TAME your anxiety or surf the urge to set a perfectionistic goal. After unhooking, you then set a realistic, flexible, life-enhancing goal.

And, as always, start small; begin with less difficult challenges before building up to more demanding ones. For example, one of Karl's perfectionistic behaviors was to rewrite his emails at least four or five times until satisfied; what should have been a simple five-minute task became a half-hour ordeal. Now the thing is, Karl was excellent at writing emails. And sometimes he absolutely had to send them off quickly; due to a crazy deadline, there was just no time to rewrite them. But whenever he did this . . . *nothing bad happened.* His emails were always to the point, practical, and well received. All that rewriting reduced Karl's anxiety but served no other purpose. Knowing this, Karl's first goal was "I will only allow myself to rewrite my emails once."

Karl also started to set time limits on his tasks. If he knew he could complete a task "reasonably well" within thirty minutes (but his away move was to go over and over and over it, trying to make it perfect, thereby stretching it out to two hours), then he would set the goal "I will allow myself only thirty minutes to do this." At other times, his goal was "I will only do this to 80 percent of my best possible effort."

(Obviously, if you decide to use such strategies yourself, you need to be sensible about it. A perfectionistic brain surgeon wouldn't operate to 80 percent of their best ability. However, they might apply this strategy to writing an email to the hospital administration.)

Every time Karl completed his tasks "less than perfectly," he was flooded with anxiety. But he made room for his discomfort in order to do what matters. He knew he couldn't get rid of "must do it perfectly" (no delete button in the brain). But he learned how to notice it and name it and thank his mind and let it play on like a radio in the background. And he spoke kind words to himself: "Good enough is good enough," "I don't have to do it perfectly," "Everyone makes mistakes. I'm only human."

Over time, he learned that nothing terrible happened when his work was less than perfect. On the contrary, he became more efficient and productive: less procrastination, more tasks completed. And he found his work far more enjoyable when he wasn't continually fixating on the need for a perfect result.

Learning New Skills

Sometimes, in order to break free from rigid rules, we'll need to learn new skills. Michelle provides a good example. She wanted to free up time to do things for herself, instead of always rushing around helping out others. This meant she would need to start declining other people's requests and demands—and start respecting her own needs and rights. In other words, she would need to learn assertiveness skills.

Assertiveness means standing up for our own rights, wants, and needs in a way that is firm but also fair, calm, and respectful. We all have the right to decline unreasonable requests from others, and we all have the right to ask for what we want, but the manner in which we do so is very important. The fair, calm, and respectful way we behave when being "assertive" is radically different from that of "aggressive" behavior, which involves demanding what you want (or refusing what you don't want) in a way that dismisses or tramples on the rights of others. When we're aggressive, we're like a battering ram, smashing down the door to get what we want; there's none of the calmness, fairness, and respect for others that assertiveness involves.

Being assertive is also radically different from being "passive." When we're passive, we are like the proverbial doormat, letting everyone else walk all over us. Our rights, wants, and needs don't matter; everyone else's are more important. "Passive" was Michelle's default setting. So she started working on how to say no, *assertively*. To do this, she used three useful strategies for bringing any new pattern of behavior into your life: *practice*, *pause*, and *start small*.

Practice

Any new skill requires practice. So in private, in front of her bedroom mirror, Michelle practiced assertively declining requests, using statements like "I'm going to say no, because I have something else very important going on," "Thanks for the offer, but I'll give it a pass this time," "I'm flattered you want my help, but I need to decline because I've got way too much on my plate," "I'd like to help out but unfortunately it conflicts with other priorities."

And specifically for requests by her manager at work, Michelle practiced this one: "I would like to help, but I already have so many priorities; could we please discuss which one is the most important at present, and which ones you'd like me to put on hold?" (Note: Part of rehearsal includes planning when and where you will apply your new skills and strategies. For example, it wouldn't have gone down well if Michelle had said that to her manager as a passing comment at the water cooler; she organized a time for the discussion.)

Michelle also practiced saying, "Let me get back to you." This is an especially useful assertive phrase for buying yourself time. You can follow this statement by saying that you "need to check with someone else," "see what's in the calendar," or you're "juggling a lot of balls" so you "need to check the diary and see what's doable." You can then take the time you need to make the choice that's right for you. And if you *do* then choose to say no, it's often easier to send a text or email, or make a phone call, than to do so in person.

Pause

When you feel the urge to OBEY your rigid rule, a brief pause can work wonders. Do a five-second anchor drop: take a slow, gentle breath or push your feet down and straighten your back. The few seconds this buys you is enough to disrupt your default setting.

When people asked her to do something, Michelle would take a slow, gentle breath and wait three or four seconds before replying. That brief pause gave her enough time to remember the assertive statements she'd been practicing.

Start Small

When experimenting with new skills, we want to start small and build up our abilities over time. So Michelle began by declining requests assertively in situations that weren't too difficult: when someone called her on the phone and asked her to complete a survey; when a shopkeeper said, "If you buy two, you get a third one for free"; and when her daughter said, just before dinner, "Can I have some chocolate, please?" Then gradually, over time, she worked up to declining requests in higher-stakes situations.

Over several months, Michelle gradually developed her assertiveness muscles—declining requests (and demands) from many people who had taken her help for granted. And each time she did so, it triggered high anxiety. But she told herself kindly, "I have the right to say no." And she made room for her anxiety in order to do what matters.

Some people were fine when Michelle said no. But others gave her a hard time. They became snappy or said how "disappointed" they were or tried various ways to manipulate her into changing her mind. And sometimes she caved in and said yes when she didn't really want to. But mostly she persisted with her assertive nos—and each time she did, she felt a sense of triumph.

Bit by bit, Michelle reduced her obligations and freed up her time so she could do more of the things she genuinely wanted. Along the way, she broke off relationships with two "toxic" friends who wouldn't take no for an answer. This was very anxiety provoking in the short term, but in the long term she realized she was much better off without them.

Of course, there's a lot more to assertiveness than declining unreasonable requests; it also involves making requests and asking for what you want—calmly, fairly, and respectfully. For Michelle, this was even harder than saying no; even the thought of it triggered the tyrant within: "Your needs don't matter." So Michelle's next goal was to sign up for an online course in assertiveness skills. (If you'd like to know more about assertiveness and other skills for building healthier relationships, you may want to check out my book on relationship issues, *ACT with Love*.)

Over time, Michelle shaped her life in meaningful ways. She was still helpful, loving, and supportive to others—but now she did this on her own terms (instead of always OBEYING her rigid rule). And as she started living life her way and unhooking from her rules and self-judgments, making room for her anxiety and practicing self-compassion, her life got a whole lot better. Her anxiety lessened, her depression disappeared, her stress levels were lower, and her life became far more fulfilling.

Imposing Your Rules on Others

Above we've focus on self-imposed rules ("I should . . . XYZ"). But equally problematic are the rules we impose on others ("He/she/they/you/we should . . . XYZ"). When we get hooked by rules about what others should or shouldn't be doing, it's a recipe for conflict and tension in those relationships. Why? Because we get angry, hurt, anxious, or disappointed when others do not OBEY our rules. So if you're getting into conflict and tension with your loved ones or people at work, ask yourself, "What rules am I imposing on them? If I hold these rules tightly, does that help me to build the relationships I want?"

Then come back to your values. Who do you want to be in this relationship? How do you want to treat the other party? How can you be assertive rather than passive or aggressive—say no to what you don't want and ask for what you do want, in a way that's calm, fair, and respectful?

Any given value is a two-way street: it describes how we want to treat ourselves *and* others. So if you've been focusing too much on yourself, reflect on how you want to treat others. And if you've been focusing too much on others, look at how you want to treat yourself. There's no simple formula for doing this; you really need to experiment and notice what works. But it's worth making the time to do this, because all relationships inevitably have . . .

[29]

Ups and Downs

No matter how well you learn to walk, sooner or later you will stumble. Sometimes you'll catch yourself in time and sometimes you'll fall over. Sometimes you may even hurt yourself. The fact is, from the day you took your very first step, you have fallen down many hundreds of times—and yet at no point did you ever give up walking! You always picked yourself up, learned from the experience, and carried on. It is this sort of attitude that we are referring to when we use the word *commitment* in ACT.

Commitment doesn't mean being perfect, always following through, never giving up or going astray. *Commitment* means that when we do inevitably stumble or go off track, we pick ourselves up, find our bearings, and carry on in the direction we want to go.

This is well exemplified in the legend of the great Scottish hero Robert the Bruce. It's a true story that happened seven hundred years ago, in a period of history when the king of England ruled over Scotland. The English king was violent and cruel, and he brutally oppressed the Scots for many years. But in the year 1306, Robert the Bruce was crowned king of Scotland, and he made it his number one priority to liberate his country. Soon after he took the throne, he raised an army and led it into war against the English, on the blood-soaked battlefield of Strathfillan. Unfortunately, the English army had greater numbers and superior weapons, and the Scots were savagely defeated.

Robert the Bruce escaped and went into hiding in a cave. Cold, wet, exhausted, and bleeding from his wounds, he felt utterly hopeless. So great was his shame, so crushing his despair, he thought about leaving the country and never returning.

But as he lay there, he looked up and noticed a spider, which was trying to spin a web across a gap in the wall of the cave. This was no easy task. The spider would spin a strand and string it from one side of the gap to the other. Then it would spin another and another, weaving back and forth to build the web. Yet every few minutes a strong gust of wind would blow through the gap, breaking the web and sending the spider tumbling.

But the spider didn't give up. The moment the wind died down, it would crawl back up to the edge of the gap and start spinning again from scratch.

Again and again, the wind blew the web apart, and again and again the spider started rebuilding. Eventually, the wind died down long enough for the spider to spin a truly firm foundation, so that the next time the wind kicked up, the web was strong enough to withstand it, and the spider was finally able to finish the job.

Robert the Bruce was amazed by this spider's persistence. He thought, "If that tiny creature can persist despite all those setbacks, then so can I!" The spider became his personal symbol of inspiration, and he coined the famous motto: "If at first you don't succeed, try, try again." After his wounds had healed he raised another army and continued to battle against the English for the next eight years, finally defeating them in 1314 at the Battle of Bannockburn—a battle in which his own men were outnumbered ten to one!

Of course, Robert the Bruce didn't know he would succeed at his goal. He only knew that freedom truly mattered. And as long as he pursued that freedom, he was living a life he valued. (And he was therefore *willing* to make room for all the hardship that went with it.)

Such is the nature of commitment: you can never know in advance whether you will achieve your goals; all you can do is keep moving forward in a meaningful direction. The future is not in your control. What is in your control is your ability to continue your journey, step-by-step, learning and growing as you progress—and getting back on track whenever you wander.

Redefining Success

There's a potential danger in inspirational stories such as that of Robert the Bruce. The danger is in the way we define success. Whether we're talking of artists, doctors, athletes, businesspeople, rock stars, politicians, or police officers, "successful people" are typically defined in terms of the goals they've achieved. If they've achieved a particularly impressive goal, we say they are "successful." But if we buy into this woefully limited definition, then we condemn ourselves to the goal-focused life: long stretches of frustration punctuated by fleeting moments of gratification if and when we do achieve our goals.

So I invite you now to consider a new definition: *Success in life means living by your values.*

Adopting this definition means you can be successful right now, whether or not you've achieved your major goals. Fulfillment is here, in this moment—any time you act in line with your values. And you are free from the need for other people's approval. You don't need someone to tell you that you've made it. You don't need someone to confirm that you're doing the right thing. You know when you're acting on your values, and that's enough.

Soula, Donna, and the other people we've met in this book weren't heroes of the sort we find in movies. They didn't accomplish awe-inspiring feats or triumph against overwhelming odds. But they were all successful in connecting with their hearts and making meaningful changes in their lives. (Of course, as I've said before, living by your values doesn't mean giving up on your goals; it merely means shifting the emphasis, so life becomes about appreciating what you have now rather than always focusing on what you don't have.)

It's also worth mentioning that every one of the clients I've written about did, on many occasions, go off track. They all lost touch with their values at times, got caught up in unhelpful thoughts, struggled with painful feelings, and acted out in self-defeating ways. But sooner or later they always got back on track again.

Take Donna, for example. It took her the best part of a year to recover completely from her alcoholism. There were plenty of times where she stayed off the drink for a few weeks, but then something would trigger another binge: the anniversary of the car crash; the anniversary of the funeral; the first Christmas Day since her husband and daughter had died. Occasions such as these brought up many painful feelings and memories for Donna, and with them came strong urges to drink. At times she "forgot" all the skills she'd learned in therapy and turned to alcohol to try to escape her pain.

But as time went on, Donna got better and better at catching herself. Her first relapse came on the day of her daughter's birthday. This triggered an entire week of heavy drinking. Her second relapse involved only three days of drinking and her third lasted for just one day.

Donna learned quickly that there's no point in beating yourself up when you screw up or fail to follow through. Guilt trips and self-criticism don't motivate you to make meaningful changes; they just keep you stuck, dwelling on the past. So after each relapse, Donna came back to the basic ACT formula:

Be present.
Open up.
Do what matters.

What does this mean in practice? Well, the first step, once we've gone off track, is to consciously acknowledge it, to be fully present with what's happening. At the same time, we need to acknowledge that once this has happened, we can't change it; there is no way we can possibly alter the past. And while it might be valuable to reflect on the past and think about what we might do differently next time around, there's no point in dwelling on it and crucifying ourselves for being imperfect. So we acknowledge that we went off track, and we hold ourselves kindly. We unhook from "not good enough." We open up and make room for the painful thoughts and feelings that inevitably arise when we fall back into our away moves. We practice kind hands or kind words. We remind ourselves, with great kindness and understanding, "What's happened has happened. It's in the past and is now unchangeable. Like everyone else on the planet, I'm an imperfect human being and at times I screw up."

The second step is to consider: "What do I want to do now? Rather than dwelling on the past or beating myself up, what can I do in the present that's important or meaningful?"

Then the third step is, of course, to take action in line with that value.

Try, Try Again?

Robert the Bruce's motto "If at first you don't succeed, try, try again" is certainly powerful—but it's only half the story. The other half of the story is that we must assess whether what we're doing is effective. A better motto might be "If at first you don't succeed, try, try again; and if it still isn't working, try something different."

But there's a fine line to tread here, too. When we face a significant challenge, the "It's too hard!" story often shows up. "You can't do it! Give up!" our mind will tell us. And the reason-giving machine prints out a list of twenty good reasons to quit. Naturally, then, our temptation is to give up and try something else. However, often persistence is precisely what is required.

This is where our focusing-and-refocusing and being-present skills come in handy. By paying full attention to what we are doing and noticing the impact it is having, we're in the best position to answer this question, "In order to achieve my goals, do I need to persist with what I'm doing—or change it?" Then, depending on our answer, we commit to either changing or persisting.

An Attitude of Optimism

As we saw in the last chapter, Soula joined a dating agency and started going out with a variety of different men. At first this was an awkward, embarrassing, and nerve-racking process for her. Her mind repeatedly told her she was a "loser" and that she would only ever meet "other losers." But despite these unhelpful stories, Soula persisted and over time she gradually became more comfortable with the process.

Some of her dates were disastrous: the men were boring, arrogant, sexist, egotistical, or just generally obnoxious. On the other hand, some of her dates were a lot of fun: the men were witty, charming, intelligent, open-minded, and attractive. It was always hit-and-miss. At one point she dated a guy for seven weeks, fell madly in love with him, and then found out he'd been cheating on her the whole time. Naturally, she was devastated and, being human, she went off track for a while. For over a month she fell back into her old habits: staying home alone, cutting herself off from friends, dwelling obsessively on her loneliness, and eating ice cream by the bucket to cheer herself up. Still, eventually Soula realized what she was doing, and she applied the basic ACT formula: *be present, open up, do what matters.*

She made room for her sadness and her loneliness, and she treated herself kindly. She focused again on life here and now and reconnected with her values of loving and caring. She realized that although she hadn't yet achieved her long-term goal (of cultivating a loving, meaningful relationship with an intimate partner), she could live her values of loving and caring *right now*, in a thousand little ways, in her relationships with her friends and family (and with herself). So she resumed spending quality time with her loved ones, and she also continued the dating process.

A little while later Soula fell in love with another man, whom she dated for over seven months. Unfortunately, it didn't work out; they split up because Soula wanted to get engaged but he wasn't ready to settle down. And I hate to disappoint you, but there's no fairy-tale ending to Soula's story. The last time I saw her, she was still dating. However, she was also investing in meaningful, loving relationships with her friends and family and herself—and although this didn't get rid of her desire for a partner, it certainly gave her a lot of satisfaction and fulfillment.

What's more, she had developed a sense of humor about the dating game. She had learned to see it as an opportunity to meet new people, discover new social venues, and learn more about men! She also used dates as opportunities to try new activities, from playing miniature golf to riding horses. In other words, the process of dating became a values-guided activity: a means for personal growth rather than a painful ordeal driven by loneliness.

As we go through life, we encounter all sorts of obstacles, difficulties, and challenges, and each time this happens we have a choice: we can embrace the situation as an opportunity to grow, learn, and develop, or we can fight, struggle, and try whatever we can to avoid it. A stressful job, a physical illness, a failed relationship—all these are opportunities to grow as a person, to develop new and better skills for dealing with life's problems.

ACT is an inherently optimistic approach. It doesn't teach you to identify and challenge pessimistic thoughts and replace them with optimistic ones, but it does have an optimistic stance toward life. ACT assumes that no matter what problems you encounter, you can learn and grow from them; no matter how dire your circumstances, you can find at least some measure of fulfillment in living by your values; and no matter how many times you wander off the path, you can always get back on track and start again.

Choose to Grow

A core theme in this book is that life involves pain. Sooner or later we all experience it—physically, emotionally, and psychologically. But in every painful life circumstance there is an opportunity for us to grow. Earlier in the book we encountered Roxy, a thirty-two-year-old lawyer who had been diagnosed with MS. Before her illness, Roxy's life had been totally focused on work. Success in her career meant everything, and she had done very well for herself, getting promoted to junior partner and earning a huge salary. But she was working an average of eighty hours a week, lived on take-out food, rarely exercised, and was always "too tired" to spend time with friends and family. Her relationships with men were typically short-lived because she never had the time or energy to invest in them. And she rarely found time to chill out and have fun.

Facing the possibility of severe disability or premature death awoke Roxy to the fact that there's more to life than work and money. She realized that our time on this planet is limited, and she connected with what was most important, deep in her heart. She cut back on her work hours, spent more time with the people she cared about, and began to look after her health through swimming, yoga, and sensible eating.

She also changed the way she related to people at work. She had always been so driven to excel, she'd paid little attention to social niceties in the workplace and, as a result, appeared to her colleagues as closed off and cold. Now she started treating her colleagues differently: showing an interest in their lives outside work and opening up, letting them know more about her own life. As she warmed to her colleagues, they in turn warmed to her, and she started to make some genuine workplace friendships.

By embracing the opportunity in her difficulty, Roxy made her life far richer and more meaningful. Of course, she would rather not have had the illness in the first place, but since that was not in her control, she chose to go down the path of personal growth.

Stories like this are commonplace. I have seen many people face a serious diagnosis—cancer, heart disease, a stroke—and completely reevaluate their lives as a result. But we don't have to wait until death is staring us in the face; we can make meaningful changes whenever we wish. So when difficulties show up in your life (as they often will), develop the habit of asking yourself, "How can I think about this in a way that enables me to live by my values?" or "How can I look at this in a way that helps me to act more effectively?" The more often we do this, the more our life becomes . . .

[30]

A Daring Adventure

You may know the story of Helen Keller. Born in Alabama in the United States in 1880, she was struck by a terrible illness (probably meningitis) when she was only nineteen months old. This left her deaf and blind. Yet against all the odds, she eventually learned how to read and write, and she went on to become a prolific author and powerful mover for social change. And she famously said, "Life is a daring adventure, or nothing."

So which are you going to choose? If we want to turn our life into a daring adventure—to step out of our comfort zone and let our values guide us into uncharted territory, not knowing what will happen and with no guarantees it will turn out the way we wish—then we'll need to make room for all the discomfort that's guaranteed to show up along the way. So, given this is the final chapter, let's recap some useful things that can help us on our big adventure.

Being Present, Opening Up, Doing What Matters

One more time, for good luck: the three overarching principles of ACT are as follows:

1. **Be present.** Focus your attention on what's important and engage in what you do.
2. **Open up.** Unhook from your thoughts and feelings; allow them to be as they are and let them freely flow through you.
3. **Do what matters.** Act effectively, guided by your values.

The technical term for our ability to be present, open up, and do what matters is "psychological flexibility." Earlier I mentioned the impressive fact that there are more than three thousand published studies on ACT, and they all show the same thing: the higher your level of psychological flexibility, the better your quality of life. But don't believe this just because of the research. Try it out and trust your own experience. If ACT's principles work for you, if they give you a rich, full life, then it makes sense to embrace them as fully as possible.

At the same time, see this as a personal choice. You don't *have to* live by these principles. There's no obligation, no right or wrong, good or bad. If you embrace these principles, it won't make you a good person or superior to others in any way. And if you ignore them, it won't make you bad or inferior. If you go around thinking you *have to* live by these principles, that's just OBEYING yet another rigid rule; it creates a sense of coercion, as if you were being forced to do something you don't really want to do—which is sure to drain your life rather than enhance it.

The way you live your life is a personal choice. And while most people find these principles transform their lives in many positive ways, it's important to remember they aren't the Ten Commandments! Apply them if and when you choose to, in the interests of making life better. But don't make them into rules you must OBEY!

I'm quite sure there will be plenty of times when you "forget" what you've learned in this book. You'll get caught up in unhelpful thoughts, struggle uselessly with your feelings, and act in self-defeating ways. But the instant you recognize what you're doing, you can choose to do something about it—if you want to, that is. Again, this is a personal choice. You don't *have to* do anything. In fact, I'm sure there will be times that you deliberately choose *not* to use the principles in this book. And that's okay. Just aim to be more aware of the choices you make and the effects they have on your life, especially when it comes to choice points such as those we're about to discuss.

Choice Point: Stay Stuck or Get Unstuck?

It may be that you've reached this point in the book and still haven't made many (or any) significant changes. If that's what's happening, you've probably come up against one or more of the HARD barriers:

H: Hooked

A: Avoiding discomfort

R: Remoteness from values

D: Doubtful goals

So if you're feeling stuck, or you're putting off taking action, take a few moments to identify barriers in your way and apply the "antidotes" as discussed in chapter 24.

Choice point: OBEY, STRUGGLE or Unhook?

Our default settings when difficult thoughts and feelings arise are OBEY or STRUGGLE. In OBEY mode, we give them all our attention, allow them to dictate our actions. In STRUGGLE mode, we fight or flee them. And although these modes of responding aren't always problematic, they do often pull us into away moves.

Unhooking skills give us many other ways of responding to difficult thoughts and feelings. We can notice them with curiosity and openness and see their true nature: words and pictures in our head and physical sensations in our body. We can name them nonjudgmentally and allow them to freely come and stay and go as they please. We can acknowledge our pain and treat ourselves kindly while focusing and refocusing our attention on what truly matters.

Choice Point: Get Swept Away or Drop Anchor?

Dropping anchor is by far the most widely applicable unhooking skill in this book. You can do it any time, any place, with any activity, whether your emotional weather is pleasant or unpleasant, mild or extreme. You can use it to unhook, make room, wake up, refocus your attention, engage in what you're doing, regain control over your actions, or hold yourself steady to "weather the storm." You can do a ten-second or a ten-minute version or anything in between, depending on the demands of the situation. So if you've skipped it, or only dabbled in it, or tried it once and didn't like it, I encourage you to revisit chapter 5 and really give it a good workout.

Choice Point: Rise to the Challenge or Not?

When times are tough, remember the challenge formula. No matter what sort of problematic situation you encounter in life, you always have choices. Your options are:

1. Leave.
2. Stay and live by your values: do whatever you can to improve the situation, make room for the pain that goes with it, and treat yourself kindly.
3. Stay—but do things that either make no difference or make it worse.

At times the best way to improve a challenging situation is to leave it. But if you can't or won't leave it, option 2 will be much more rewarding than option 3.

Choice Point: Instant Success or Long-Term Frustration?

If you like the idea of instant success (and who doesn't?) then you'll surely want to embrace the values-focused life. When we live such a life, we still set goals and pursue them—but they aren't the be-all and end-all. Instead, we define success as living by your values. And because there's always some small way to do this in any moment of life, instant success is possible whenever we wish.

Choice Point: A Pleasant Feeling or a Meaningful Life?

In chapter 1 we looked at two different meanings of happiness: (a) a transient feeling of pleasure and contentment, and (b) a rich and meaningful life, in which we feel the whole range of human emotions, both pleasant and painful. When we stop pursuing the former and start building the latter, we escape from "the happiness trap." (And when we do the reverse, we fall back into it.)

Choice Point: Missing Out or Making the Most?

When we're hooked by thoughts and feelings—in STRUGGLE or OBEY mode—we're missing out on life. Unhooking skills, especially being present, focusing, and savoring, enable us to appreciate what we have in our life right now. This is important, because now is the only time we ever have. The past doesn't exist; it's nothing more than memories in the present. And the future doesn't exist; it's nothing more than thoughts and images in the present. The only time you ever have is this moment: *now.* So make the most of it. Appreciate it in its fullness. And remember: *Life gives most to those who make the most of what life gives.*

Choice Point: Self-Kindness or Self-Judgment?

I've said it before, and I'll say it again: you're human. So just like me and everyone else on this planet, you're going to screw up, make mistakes, go off track. There'll be times you forget everything in this book. You'll get hooked by your thoughts and feelings, pulled away from your values, and you'll act in ways that are far removed from the person you want to be. And you will hurt and suffer as a result.

So can you be compassionate with yourself? Can you acknowledge how hard it is to be human and treat yourself kindly? Can you recognize your suffering as something you share with all other humans on the planet? We get to improve our behavior, but we don't get to be perfect. We all go off track; we all make mistakes; and we all suffer as a result. But being hard on ourselves doesn't help. It just gets us more stuck than before. So unhook from the "I'm not good enough" story and treat yourself like you'd treat a suffering friend: kind words, kind hands, kind deeds.

The Ultimate Choice

Auschwitz was the most notorious of the Nazi death camps. We can scarcely begin to imagine what took place there: the horrific abuse and torture; the extremes of human degradation; the countless deaths through disease, violence, starvation; and the infamous gas chambers. Viktor Frankl was a Jewish psychiatrist who survived the unspeakable horrors of Auschwitz and other camps, which he described in gruesome detail in his awe-inspiring book *Man's Search for Meaning*.

One of the most fascinating revelations in this book is that, contrary to what we would expect, the people who survived longest in the death camps were often *not* the physically fittest and strongest but rather those who were most connected to a sense of meaning and purpose in life. If prisoners could connect with their values, it gave them something to live for; something that kept them going, despite all their suffering. Those who could not do this soon lost the will to live—and thus, their lives.

For example, one of Frankl's core values was being helpful. So throughout his time in the camps, he consistently helped other prisoners to cope with their suffering. He listened compassionately to their woes, gave them words of kindness and inspiration, and tended to the sick and the dying. Most importantly, he helped people to connect with their own deepest values so they could find their own sense of purpose. This would then *literally* give them the strength to survive.

Another powerful insight from *Man's Search for Meaning* is that even in a Nazi concentration camp, people have choices. Frankl describes Nazis that at times chose to act with kindness toward Jewish prisoners. For example, he mentions a Nazi guard who, at great personal risk, secretly slipped Frankl a piece of bread. "It was far more than the small piece of bread which moved me to tears at the time. It was the human 'something' that this man gave to me—the word and look which accompanied the gift." In stark contrast, Frankl also describes Jewish prisoners who chose to act with appalling hostility and sadism toward their fellow Jews. The message is clear: even in the most extreme circumstances, choices are available.

Frankl writes, "We who lived in concentration camps can remember the men who walked through the huts comforting others, giving away their last piece of bread." He acknowledges that such people were few in number, but he points out they offer undeniable proof that "everything can be taken from a man but one thing: the last of the human freedoms—to choose one's attitude in any given set of circumstances, to choose one's own way."

Every time I read that quote, I get goose bumps. "To choose one's attitude in any given set of circumstances, to choose one's own way." How inspiring is that?

But . . . how do we *actually* do that? I mean, it's easy to choose our attitude when life's going well, giving us what we want, with no major reality gaps; when our health is good, we're on vacation, the weather is great, and we haven't a care in the world. But how do we choose our attitude when life is really difficult? When there are huge gaps between the reality we want and the reality we've got? Do we just "think positively"? Or read a Nike poster and "Just do it"?

If we want to choose our attitude when life is incredibly hard, we first need to drop anchor. We acknowledge the painful reality we are dealing with, make room for all those painful thoughts and feelings, and treat ourselves kindly. Then we get in touch with our values and choose what we will stand for in the face of this. In other words: *be present, open up, and do what matters.* The greater our ability to do this, the more freedom we have—no matter what obstacles life puts in our path.

And that brings us to the end of this book, but not to the end of your journey. Life goes on, minute by minute, hour by hour, and day by day. So make the most of it. Ask yourself often, every day, "Am I present? Am I open? Am I doing what matters?"

Keep going, keep living, keep loving. And I wish you all the best for your daring adventure.

Acknowledgments

Words cannot adequately express the enormous gratitude I feel toward Steven Hayes, the originator of Acceptance and Commitment Therapy (ACT). He has given a great gift to me, my family, my clients, and the world at large. I am also indebted to the wider ACT community for all the useful advice, experience, and information that is so freely shared among them at workshops, conferences, and via the internet. I am especially grateful to Kelly Wilson and Kirk Strosahl whose insights I have frequently drawn upon throughout these pages, and likewise to all those colleagues in the ACT community who gave me feedback and advice for the first edition: Jim Marchman, Joe Ciarrochi, Joe Parsons, Sonja Batten, Julian McNally, and Graham Taylor.

With regard to the first edition, I would particularly like to acknowledge my brother, Genghis, who was (as always) an inexhaustible source of advice, strength, and encouragement, especially during those dark times when I felt like giving up on it.

And regarding the second edition, I am incredibly grateful to my partner, Natasha, for all her love and support and encouragement. Not only did she give me truly invaluable feedback during the writing process (including numerous helpful suggestions for ways to improve the book), but also kept me supplied with Lindt chocolate, whenever my energy levels flagged.

I'd also like to thank all the friends and family who helped out with the first edition, by reading the book (or parts of it) and giving me feedback: Johnny Watson, Margaret Denman, Carmel Cammarano, Paul Dawson, Fred Wallace, and Kath Koning.

And I am especially grateful to all the good folks at Exisle Publishing, who have worked so hard to bring this book together: for the first edition, Benny St. John Thomas, Penny Capp, and Sandra Noakes; for both the first *and* second editions, Gareth Thomas and Anouska Jones; and for her stellar work on editing the second edition, Karen Gee. Last but not least, many thanks to my former agent, Sammie Justesen, for bringing myself and the Exisle team together.

Russ Harris
Melbourne, Australia, July 2021

Resources

Free Resources

In addition to *The Happiness Trap: Extra Bits*, there's a huge treasure trove of free materials—including audio recordings, eBooks, handouts and worksheets, YouTube videos, book chapters, articles, blogs, and published studies—available on the "Free Resources" page of www.The-HappinessTrap.com.

The Happiness Trap: Eight-Week Online Program

This is a personal-growth program for well-being and vitality, inspired by the book but going way beyond it. It's a beautifully filmed (and very entertaining) online course, suitable for pretty much anyone and everyone who wishes to build a richer, fuller life.

Other Books by Russ Harris

The Illustrated Happiness Trap by Russ Harris and Bev Aisbett

A fun, comic-book version of the original—especially for teenagers and adults who are not into reading. (It's alternatively titled *The Happiness Trap Pocketbook: How to Stop Struggling and Start Living* in Australia.)

The Reality Slap: How to Survive and Thrive When Life Hits Hard
(2nd edition)

An ACT-based self-help book for grief, loss, and crisis, with a major emphasis on self-compassion. (The second edition has more than 50 percent new material.)

When Life Hits Hard: How to Transcend Grief, Crisis, and Loss with
Acceptance and Commitment Therapy

This is the same book as *The Reality Slap* (2nd edition), mentioned above. Because it has over 50 percent new material, the US publishers decided to change the title and release it as a new book.

ACT with Love: Stop Struggling, Reconcile Differences, and Strengthen Your
Relationship with Acceptance and Commitment Therapy

A popular self-help book on the use of ACT for common relationship issues.

The Confidence Gap: From Fear to Freedom

A self-help book that looks at confidence, success, and performance from an ACT perspective; especially suitable for life coaching, executive coaching, and sports and business performance.

ACT Made Simple: An Easy-to-Read Primer on Acceptance and Commitment
Therapy (2nd edition)

The world's best-selling textbook on ACT, with over one hundred thousand copies sold and translations into twenty languages. A classic in the field of psychotherapy literature. (The second edition has over 50 percent new material.)

Trauma-Focused ACT: A Practitioner's Guide to Working with Mind, Body,
and Emotion Using Acceptance and Commitment Therapy

My most recent textbook for therapists, this covers in depth how to use ACT with all types of trauma-related issues.

Getting Unstuck in ACT: A Clinician's Guide to Overcoming Common
  Obstacles in Acceptance and Commitment Therapy

The first advanced-level textbook on ACT. This does not cover the basics; it assumes you know them. Instead, it focuses on common sticking points for both clients and therapists.

ACT Questions & Answers: A Practitioner's Guide to 150 Common Sticking
  Points in Acceptance and Commitment Therapy

Also known as "Everything you wanted to know about ACT but were afraid to ask!" This is another advanced-level textbook for therapists, in an easy-to-read Q&A format.

The Weight Escape: Stop Fad Dieting, Start Losing Weight, and Reshape
  Your Life Using Cutting-Edge Psychology by Joe Ciarrochi, Ann Bailey, and Russ Harris

A self-help book on the ACT approach to fitness, weight loss, and self-acceptance with any size body.

ACT Companion: The Happiness Trap App

Australian psychologist Anthony Berrick created this excellent smartphone app. It's loaded with cool ACT tools, including the choice point, and contains over two hours of audio recordings—some with my voice, some with Anthony's.

Online Training for Therapists, Counselors, and Coaches

I have created a range of online courses for professional training in ACT, from beginner to advanced level. They cover everything from trauma, depression, and anxiety disorders to adolescence, grief and loss, and brief interventions. They are available at www.ImLearningACT.com.

Values Cards

I've created a pack of full-color values cards containing simple descriptions of values accompanied by delightful cartoons. More specifically, they're "values, goals, and barriers" cards; there are extra cards for goal setting, action planning, and dealing with barriers such as values conflicts, fusion, and so on. In Australia, you can purchase these at www.act-mindfully.com.au. For orders outside Australia, go to www.edgarpsych.co.uk/shop.

Facebook Groups

The Happiness Trap Online Program Facebook group is a supportive and welcoming community of people who have either read the book or done the online program. It's a great place to discuss any difficulties—or successes—you have had with the ACT approach.

The ACT Made Simple Facebook group is for health professionals only—coaches, counselors, therapists, doctors, nurses, OTs, and others who use ACT with clients or patients as part of their work. It's a supportive online community (with, at the time of writing, over thirty-five thousand members) where practitioners, students, and researchers can share resources, ask questions, discuss struggles and successes, get the latest updates and free materials from me, and so much more.

Index

About the Author

Russ Harris is a world-renowned trainer of Acceptance and Commitment Therapy (ACT). Russ's background is in medicine. As a GP he became increasingly interested in the psychological aspects of health and well-being, and increasingly disenchanted with writing prescriptions. Ultimately this interest led to a total career change. He now works in two different, yet complementary roles—as a therapist and as a life coach.